MW00679305

12.00
WOL

ON INTERPRETATION

ON INTERPRETATION

*Meaning and Inference
in Law, Psychoanalysis,
and Literature*

PATRICK COLM HOGAN

**THE UNIVERSITY OF
GEORGIA PRESS**
Athens & London

© 1996 by the University of Georgia Press
Athens, Georgia 30602
All rights reserved
Designed by Walton Harris
Set in by 10/13 Galliard by Tseng Information Systems, Inc.
Printed and bound by Thomson-Shore, Inc.

The paper in this book meets the guidelines for permanence and
durability of the Committee on Production Guidelines for
Book Longevity of the Council on Library Resources.

Printed in the United States of America

00   99   98   97   96   C   5   4   3   2   1

Library of Congress Cataloging in Publication Data

Hogan, Patrick Colm.
On interpretation : meaning and inference in law, psychoanalysis,
and literature / Patrick Colm Hogan.
p.   cm.
Includes bibliographical references and index.
ISBN 0-8203-1724-1 (alk. paper)
1. Interpretation (Philosophy)   2. Meaning (Philosophy)
3. Inference.   4. Law—Philosophy.   5. Psychoanalysis.
6. Literature—Philosophy.   I. Title.
B824.17.H64   1996
121'.68—dc20   94–23970

British Library Cataloging in Publication Data available

In loving memory of my uncle,
Brother Paschal Scully, O. S. F.
(1922–1995)

CONTENTS

ACKNOWLEDGMENTS

It took roughly twelve years to complete this book (with interruptions for other projects). In the course of this time, I have been fortunate enough to receive considerable help from friends and colleagues in a range of disciplines. In legal study, I am particularly grateful to John Garvey—who first encouraged me to work on legal interpretation—and the dozen or so other participants in the University of Kentucky Law School Colloquium of 1986–87 who read and discussed with me an early version of chapter 3. Their response was invaluable.

The psychoanalytic ideas presented here have been aired at conferences in clinical psychoanalysis in Paris, New York, and Chicago. I am grateful to the many practicing analysts—including Merton Gill, Richard Chessick, and Roy Schafer—who have discussed clinical problems with me and sharpened my thinking on these issues. I should also mention that my understanding of the work of Jacques Lacan has benefited particularly from exegeses by and discussions with Jacques-Alain Miller and Stuart Schneiderman.

In a more general way, the following work was made possible by the stimulation provided by former teachers: in philosophy, Donald Davidson (in whose seminar on the philosophy of language I first began thinking about many of these issues) and Paul Ricoeur; in literary theory, Norman Holland (with whom I studied psychoanalysis and reader-response criticism, and who has since been a helpful friend and stimulating intellectual antagonist), Walter Ong, and Northrop Frye (who kindly read and commented on an early draft of my discussion of *King John* and *King Lear* in chapter 5). My friend and colleague Jack Davis read the entire manuscript with great care and attention and provided helpful comments throughout. I am extremely grateful to him for this and for his more general support and generosity.

Another colleague, Howard Lasnik, provided challenging criticisms of my discussion of linguistic theory. Along the same lines, I am grateful to Dick Reynolds for stylistic scrutiny of my discussion of legal interpretation.

Colleagues at other institutions have been helpful also. Of these, I should mention Ruth Marcus, who encouraged this project from early on (I hope she will not find the result too shocking), as well as Adolf Grunbaum, Mary Mothersill, and Elizabeth Anscombe, with whom I was fortunate enough to discuss some of the issues in the fourth and fifth chapters.

Students too have contributed to this work: James Andersen, through a thesis chapter on E. D. Hirsch; Tom Bauer, for personal support at a difficult time; Katherine Cole, for research assistance and for preparing the figures in chapter 3.

Karen Orchard (along with her staff at the University of Georgia Press) has been enormously helpful, again; I am happy to have had the opportunity of working with her a second time. And I am grateful to all three (anonymous) readers for their careful attention to the manuscript and for their valuable comments.

Finally, my greatest debt is to Noam Chomsky. Not only did he argue with me for years about grammatical analysis and the philosophy of language, he was constantly encouraging and truly helpful at a personal level. Moreover, his work provided much of the inspiration for this volume and for my more general approach to the theory of interpretation. In methodological rigor, conceptual clarity, precision, attentiveness to details of evidence, and other things, Noam provided me with an ideal that I could seek to emulate and to which I could aspire, my disagreements with his specific conclusions notwithstanding.

An earlier version of the discussion of *King John* and *King Lear* was presented at the annual convention of the Shakespeare Association of America at Montreal in 1986. Parts of the introduction and first chapter appeared in a different form in "The Limits of Semiotics," *diacritics,* 23, no. 4 (Winter 1993): 82–92.

ON INTERPRETATION

INTRODUCTION

Objects and Methods

Interpretation is not a new topic for theoretical inquiry. It has been scrutinized and theorized by some of the best minds—east and west, north and south—for millennia. And yet, as with many topics in the humanities, we still find ourselves debating the most basic issues. For example, in his recent volume, *The Limits of Interpretation,* Umberto Eco has sought to explore and define the possibility of principled interpretive dispute. Eco recognizes that interpretation can be very important; whether it is practiced by a justice of the Supreme Court or a literary critic, it has consequences. And, like many of us, Eco is uncomfortable with the idea that an activity so crucial to legal practice, mental health, diplomacy, literary study, and even the most personally significant acts of everyday life, might be simply arbitrary. Thus, he sets out to determine what must be the most fundamental issue in the theory of interpretation: what constrains the possible randomness of interpretation?

At one level, the answer to this question is self-evident: meaning and method, the object sought and the manner of seeking. But the problem is to explain these notions clearly and adequately. Unfortunately, Eco, like most of his predecessors, has relatively little to say about either topic, and what he does say is unclear, vacillating, and frequently self-contradictory. Most often, Eco follows common intuitions and appeals to "literal meaning" as the object that defines the limits of interpretation. But he is never really able to say what literal meaning is. Most often he refers us to dictionaries (see, for example, 1990, 5), but this only pushes the problem back one step. Having disparaged interpretation for intention (understood in the partially narrow, partially vague sense of conscious authorial something-or-other), he repeatedly anthropomorphizes language and texts in an effort to make some sense of their meaning. Thus he refers to "the text intention" (148), an opaque notion, and even attributes "rights" to "the text" (7). Though it might seem that only people make inferences,

1

Eco brands "every text" a "complex inferential mechanism," and though it may seem that only people have idiolects, Eco makes "the text" into "a kind of *idiolectal mechanism*" (260). In a similar vein, Eco stresses that "the interpreted text imposes some constraints" (6) and repeatedly emphasizes the "contextual pressure" (21) exerted on the interpreter by the text. He writes that "a text controls and selects its own interpretations but also . . . its own misinterpretations" (61), a control exercised by context. Of course, this presupposes that the meaning of the context is already fairly determinate, and this is owing to the purported existence of literal meaning or "zero-degree meaning," as he sometimes calls it (36)—but the nature and accessibility of this remain obscure.

As if an appeal to a vaguely autonomous "literal" meaning were not opaque enough, Eco is not even consistent in maintaining this sort of meaning as his standard. Thus, at certain points, he attributes meaning not to texts and dictionaries but to authors or to members of a linguistic community. For example, in judging Derrida's interpretation of Peirce, Eco establishes as a standard of judgment whether or not Peirce "would have been satisfied with Derrida's interpretation" (35), thereby clearly establishing conscious authorial truth-conditional meaning as the limiting object of interpretation. After a discussion of rhetorical techniques in a letter by Pliny the Younger, Eco wishes to have it both ways and makes the confusing statement that "Really Pliny the Younger (or his text) is *doing* things with words" (135). Later he indicates that, indeed, texts cannot do things, despite this parenthesis: "We must agree with Strawson . . . when he says that 'mentioning or referring is not something that an expression does; it is something that someone can use an expression to do'" (208).

Elsewhere, Eco sees meaning as defined by a reader's intuition (54), thus shifting from authorial to individual readerly intent (though at the same time he identifies this intuition with an autonomist or nonpsychological "English code"). At other times, he turns to larger communities, defining meaning by reference to "every member of a community of healthy native speakers" (36).

It seems, then, that Eco's discussion is not adequate to provide the necessary clarification and explanation of meaning and method. More important, this is not a failing peculiar to Eco. Readers familiar with the range of current writings in the theory of interpretation will recognize that Eco is not at all unique in his apparent inability to specify limits for interpretation. Indeed, Eco is one of the most rigorous and erudite literary theorists writing today. What, then, is the problem? As I shall argue, the difficulty that underlies Eco's vacillation and obscurity on the topic of meaning rests in the metaphysical and epistemological presuppositions that Eco shares with almost all recent literary theorists—and, in fact, almost all not so recent literary theorists as well. In the following pages, I shall seek to articulate and dispute some of these widespread and historically persistent presuppositions, propose alternatives, and explore some of the practical consequences of these alternatives.

As I have already indicated, any systematic theory of interpretation has two parts. The first concerns the object of interpretation—the meaning at which the interpretation aims. The second concerns the manner of interpretation—the method by which the interpretation might seek to attain its object. One concerns the *what* of interpretation; the other concerns the *how*. Cutting across this broad theoretical division are the various interpretive disciplines. My aim in the following pages is to examine object and method in interpretation, first of all in a general, theoretical framework and, second, in the context of the particular practices and goals that define three distinct interpretive disciplines—law, psychoanalysis, and literary criticism. In doing this, I hope to demonstrate that a great deal of the theoretical debate surrounding meaning and interpretation has been seriously misguided, for even the most seemingly divergent views typically share very dubious assumptions about being and about knowing.

Specifically, in chapter 1, I argue—contrary to prevailing views in literary study—that interpretive method is and should be a case of ordinary inferential reasoning and thus that there is no general methodological difference between interpretation in the humanities and theory construction in the physical sciences. In addition, I argue that the nature of interpretation does not entail cultural, historical, or other forms of relativism, as is commonly thought. Quite the contrary, in fact. A clear understanding of interpretive method indicates that intercultural, historical, and other 'hard cases' of interpretation differ from ordinary interpretation in degree only, and not in kind.

As to the object of interpretation, in this opening chapter, I set out and defend the view that it makes no sense to argue about what meaning 'really is'.[1] The question of the meaning of 'meaning' is merely a question of stipulation, in the sense that 'meaning' is simply what one stipulates it to be—authorial grammatical intent, readers' associative response, or whatever. In other words, there is, I argue, a fact of the matter as to whether or not a particular assertion, wish, attitude, and so forth, is part of authorial grammatical intent for a given work, part of such-and-such a reader's associative response to that work, and so on. But there is no fact of the matter as to whether or not that assertion or whatever is part of the 'true meaning' or 'meaning per se' of a given work. Indeed, it makes no sense to speak of 'the meaning' of a given work. Rather, it only makes sense to speak of some particular *sort* of meaning of that work—for example, conscious authorial moral aim. And this sort of meaning is not and cannot be *discovered* to be the true or proper object of interpretation *in general*. Rather, it is *chosen*, from a broad range of possible alternatives, as the specific object of our interpretive enquiry *on a particular occasion*.

Note that such a stipulative approach addresses Eco's problem of setting limits to interpretation, and it does so in a practical manner. It also goes some way toward ending an almost ubiquitous problem in the various interpretive disciplines, most obviously literary criticism, but also law and other areas—that is, the apparent inability of interpreters to stop debating at cross-purposes. Most often, when interpreting, we aim for the 'real' meaning of a work. First of all, such an entity does not exist. Second, we tend implicitly to conceive of this nonentity in vague but very diverse ways. For example, I might tacitly conceive of a work's meaning in terms of a sort of average reader's truth-conditional meaning at the time the work was produced; someone else might tacitly conceive of it as unconscious authorial associative meaning. Thus we are most often aiming at an object that not only does not exist but is not even conceptually coherent across speakers. Agreement is often unattainable in matters of interpretation even under the best conditions. But there is a significant difference between seeking, for example, conscious authorial moral aim (or any other explicitly stipulated variety of meaning) and seeking the obscure and nonexistent 'real' meaning of a work. There are possibilities for serious debate and rational evaluation of alternatives in the first case, but not in the second.

Unfortunately, even the general theoretical problems of interpretation do not end here, however, for stipulation is not entirely free. The range of real stipulative alternatives is broad, very broad, but it is not infinite. In the second chapter, then, I seek to examine and define, in general terms, the constraints upon stipulation—not in order to claim that one cannot stipulate certain things, that one should be forbidden to do so, but rather to point out that it simply makes no sense to stipulate some things, because they do not exist. In particular, I argue that though there are quite a large number and quite a variety of intents (intents of authors and of individual readers, conscious intents and unconscious intents), and thus quite a large number and quite a variety of intentional meanings, we have no reason to believe that there are such things as nonintentional meanings—Platonic, social, essential, or whatever. Thus, we cannot productively look for such nonintentional meanings in particular works, making them the objects of our interpretive inquiries. In this way, any particular discipline of interpretation can usefully concern itself only with varieties of intent, the relative importance of each variety, and the methods appropriate for inference to specific varieties in specific cases.

It is important to stress that, despite this limitation, the range of possible semantic objects remains huge. For example, we have the conscious, truth-conditional meaning of the author; the unconscious, associative meaning of the author; the moral aim of the author; the conscious, truth-conditional meaning of a given reader (usually in some vague way aimed to coincide with some sort of authorial intent); the unconscious, associative meaning of a given reader; the moral reaction of a given reader; the conscious truth-conditional meaning of (tacitly constructed or, alternatively, agreed upon by) a given group of critics; the meaning as determined by the most basic semantic rules common to the idiolects of the members of a given community (which may or may not coincide with their conscious constructions); the publisher's political aim—and so on and so on. Confining interpretation to such a range of possible objects obviously does not impose narrow limits on interpretive activity. On the contrary, it opens up a wide variety of real possibilities and makes them practical by articulating and clarifying them.

Of course, not all of these objects are relevant in all contexts. To say that all varieties of intent are possible objects of interpretation is not to say that all are equally important for any given purpose—which brings us to the issue of interpretation in the various disciplines, the topic of the third, fourth, and fifth chapters (on law, psychoanalysis, and literature, respectively). The principles laid out in the first and second chapters are, again, very broad and allow vast scope for interpretation. By these principles, interpretation cannot be considered a single, uniform activity but must be understood as comprising a highly differentiated set of distinct activities. It is these distinct activities (or clusters of such activities) that we must consider when examining interpretation in one or another discipline. Note that this view of interpretation as highly differentiated is not typical for theories of interpretation, which tend to presume that interpretation is uniform. Consider, for example, a theory such as that of E. D. Hirsch, which would focus interpretation on (an undifferentiated range of) authorial intents, or that of the various New Critics, which would direct our attentions to the putatively autonomous linguistic structure of the literary text, or that of later Stanley Fish, which is concerned with the tacit constructions of interpretive communities. These theories function to specify a single normatively appropriate or descriptively possible object of interpretation. If one begins with a general theory of this sort—and almost all general theories of interpretation are precisely of this sort—then one will end up with theories of disciplinary interpretation (theories of legal interpretation, literary interpretation, and so forth) that are variations of one another. One interprets for conscious authorial truth-conditional meaning or autonomous linguistic structure in literature, then in law, and so on, or one looks at interpretive communities in literature, then in law, then in psychoanalysis, and so on. In other words, in these cases, there is a sort of 'master' theory that is applicable directly and indifferently to literature, law, and so forth.

In contrast with this common approach, the broad theory of interpretation that I set out in the first and second chapters is not directly applicable to any particular discipline. It must, rather, be specified in each case. We must stipulate the relevant object or objects, and we must define our methodological principles in the context of the purpose and operation of whatever discipline we are considering. As a result, the theory of legal interpretation will turn out to be different from the theory of psychoanalytic interpretation, and both will turn out to be different from the theory of literary interpretation. These theories are, of course, deeply related in that their differences are merely the result of setting parameters differently within a common set of principles. But the differences are nonetheless very real and very significant. This will no doubt seem odd to readers who are accustomed to 'master' theories and the presupposition of cross-disciplinary identity in interpretive practices. But, though it is an unusual approach, I believe it is the right approach. The various interpretive disciplines are not all the same, despite important common principles; for example, we distort legal interpretation if we treat it as a form of literary interpretation. Consider, by way of analogy, two natural sciences: astronomy and biology. Both concern certain sorts of physical systems and both follow general principles of rational inference—thus both are appropriately considered under a general philosophy of science. But clearly that philosophy of science could not provide a master theory of 'science *as such*', a theory applicable directly and indifferently to all natural sciences.

This is because biology and astronomy, much like literature and law, have different concerns and goals and thus must be concerned with different objects and must differently specify the broad methodological principles that they hold in common.

In keeping with this, I develop substantially different specific theories of legal, psychoanalytic, and literary interpretation. In the case of law, my focus is on the *object* of interpretation; thus I seek to isolate and hierarchize varieties of intent germane to the legal system. Judges and lawyers make tacit appeal to very many sorts of 'meanings' in their actual legal practices—in arguments, in decisions, and so forth. However, attempts to isolate and debate the limits of legal interpretation have typically ended in the same sort of vagueness and self-contradiction that we saw above in Eco. Thus, in the fourth chapter, I examine a number of legal decisions, primarily from the United States, and seek to articulate and systematize some of the most important semantic objects tacitly invoked in these decisions.

In the case of psychoanalysis, where the object—unconscious intent—is already fixed, I am concerned primarily with the *methodological* issues surrounding this unique sort of inference. In the first section of chapter 4, I set out to define the interpretive techniques available to psychoanalysis and to place these techniques within a more adequate philosophy of mind and action, in part developing insights of writers such as Elizabeth Anscombe and in part examining the relation between psychoanalysis and recent work in experimental psychology and cognitive science. After a brief response to Adolf Grunbaum's powerful critique of psychoanalysis, I illustrate these interpretive principles by a close reading of sections from Freud's process notes (or diary) for the case of Ernst Lanzer, the "rat man," focusing in particular on the sorts of verbal ambiguity stressed by Jacques Lacan.

In the final chapter, I define and illustrate what I take to be the most important variety of intent peculiar to literary study—authorial aesthetical intent—and discuss some methodological peculiarities of its interpretation. Specifically, I argue that there is an aesthetical attitude that we adopt in approaching works of art and that is crucial to our aesthetic response. However, this attitude has been widely misunderstood in Western aesthetics. Drawing upon the notions of *dhvani, rasa,* and *sahṛdaya,* as developed by the Sanskrit aestheticians Ānandavardhana and Abhinavagupta, I seek to formulate a more adequate notion of aesthetic response. This refor-

7

mulation in turn provides a basis for understanding authorial aesthetical intent, which I develop and illustrate in an interpretation of some problematic sections from *King John* and *King Lear.*

Once again, interpretation is important. And for this reason the theory of interpretation is important. Even if they are flawless—and, needless to say, they are not—the following analyses and arguments must leave almost all particular interpretive disputes unresolved. Simply because we know what we are looking for does not mean that we will find it easily or that arguments about its specifics will be readily adjudicable. However, it is only once we have become clear about what we are interpreting for and have made at least some progress in determining how we might look for it that serious argument about the relative plausibility of interpretive hypotheses can begin; indeed, it is only after we have determined the precise object of our interpretive concerns that we can make any lucid, coherent interpretive claims in the first place. The following analyses, then, are not primarily efforts to resolve particular interpretive disputes; rather, they are efforts to diminish the sort of misunderstanding that is common in interpretive disputes, by introducing into discussion a greater degree of conceptual and methodological clarity. This book will achieve its purpose not insofar as it ends interpretive disagreement but insofar as it allows interpretive debates truly to begin and to follow a rational course. Once again, as should be obvious—especially in the areas of civil law and mental health, but even in literary study—this is not and cannot be a matter of indifference, intellectually or practically.

1 STIPULATION AND RATIONAL INFERENCE

On the Ends and Means of Interpretation

WHAT IS MEANING?

The first concern of an interpretive theory is the interpretive object: meaning. Any interpretation aims at isolating the meaning or meanings of some text. Thus the first question of such a theory must be: what is meaning? For example, is it authorial intent? Or is it response? Or is it some sort of autonomous systemic play? Or is it social production? And are these notions clear enough and unified—for example, is there just one sort of authorial intent? And if meaning is intent and there are different sorts of intent, which sort of intent is meaning? And so on.

As we have already noted, the question 'What is meaning?' has been, in one form or another, a topic of serious philosophical controversy for centuries, even millennia. Incompatible alternatives are proposed and debated just as widely and just as intensely today as formerly. And with just as little progress. The reason for this is simple: There is no such thing as meaning in the sense demanded by the question. Specifically, the question concerns how we are going to use a particular word—'meaning'. It treats any statement to the effect that we should use 'meaning' in such-and-such a manner (for instance, as referring to authorial intention) as if it were a *factual* statement that could be true or false in the usual sense. But *definition*—which the question seeks—is necessarily prior to factual assertion. In other words, an utterance is true or false only *after* it means something. Its coming to mean that particular thing, however, cannot be true or false. Though interpreted in all sorts of surprising ways, the doctrine of the arbitrary nature of the signifier means just this: a normative definition of a term is not and cannot be true or false as there is no natural relation between a signifier and a signified (a sound and a meaning) which relation that definition might be said to have or not to have captured. Put another way, there is no connection between word and world unless we put it there.

Let me illustrate by way of an analogy. Imagine a group of hunters who are also philosophers of language. One says, 'The only true object of hunting is goose'. The others demur with more or less vehemence. The first persists, 'But surely the only true objects of hunting are animals. So the question is—what is the true meaning of 'animal', or what *are* animals *really*? It seems beyond dispute that animals are really geese'. The second replies, 'Why, not at all! It is quite clear that animals are, in fact, mammals, and thus that hunting is nothing other than the search for mammals! It is quite naive to think otherwise!' A third, more pragmatic in orientation, joins in the fray, insisting that, though the true meaning of 'animal' is obscure, it is self-evident that hunters have little choice but to concern themselves with felines.

I hope everyone—including those who, like myself, know nothing at all about hunting—will agree that this is an asinine debate. One can (unfortunately perhaps) hunt all sorts of things and all sorts of things can be animals. However, if we like, we can define 'hunt' so as to confine it to one or another object. In fact, this sort of thing occurs implicitly all the time. For example, suppose we all know that Dana hunts nothing but bull moose, and Dana knows we all know this, and so on. When Dana says, 'I'm going hunting', we all infer that he is hunting bull moose. In this context, we take 'hunting' to mean 'hunting for bull moose'. And if Dana changes his target, he must say so: 'I'm off for the hunt, but today it's the wily pard!' More simply, we can merely choose and state what we are hunting at any given time. Thus we can say, 'I'm hunting for bull moose', or ask, 'Want to hunt some wily pard?' or whatever, thereby stipulating the object of our hunt—not discovering any true meaning of 'hunt' or 'animal', any true nature of these, and so forth, but just making a certain sort of stipulative assertion about our goals and actions. Again, an attempt to discover any such entities as true meaning or true nature would be ridiculous. Stipulation is clearly our only choice—whether that stipulation is individual or collective, explicit or implicit. All of this should, I think, be indisputable. Moreover, it should be indisputable that the same holds for cooking, singing, cleaning, peeling, and so forth. (Compare, for example, a group of philosopher chefs; one, perhaps an Oxford professor of South Asian ancestry, begins an intellectual melee with the anticolonial blast: 'The true object of cooking is lamb vindaloo'.)

My point here is that things are also no different for interpreting—though in this case, and perhaps this case alone, people do not find it indisputable. Some writers (for instance, early Stanley Fish and later Norman Holland) feel that meaning, the object of interpretation, is individual reader response (or, at least, a function of such response), as developed in terms of the individual reader's feelings and "identity theme" (Holland) or temporal expectations (Fish). Other writers (for instance, later Stanley Fish) claim that meaning is simply and solely a communal convention—that is, the meaning of an utterance is simply and solely what a given group agrees upon or tacitly constructs. Still others (Steven Knapp, Walter Benn Michaels, and E. D. Hirsch, as well as various psychoanalytic critics) feel that meaning (descriptively) is or (normatively) should be understood as conscious or unconscious authorial intent. A further group (Hans Robert Jauss and certain Marxist critics) believe that meaning is a social and historical phenomenon. Perhaps the largest number (most New Critics, structuralists, and poststructuralists) take it that meaning is the result of a linguistic system or structure, which not only is independent of intent but may be directly opposed to intent. And there are further views as well.

My first claim is that there is no question of fact here, but, as in the case of hunting or cooking, only a question of stipulation. In other words, it is important to say whether one is going to examine individual readers' affective responses, the personal/biographical associations of the author, the changing views of critics as historically and socially 'situated', self-conscious authorial descriptive intent (as given in, say, truth-conditions), and so forth. It is important to stipulate this. But it is senseless to debate which activity is 'really' interpretation, which object is 'really' meaning.

More exactly, there are important semantic reasons that 'what is . . . ?'-questions—such as 'What is meaning?' or 'What is hunting?'—can be answered only stipulatively. Specifically, I take it everyone would agree that a referential term, other than a name, has both a definition and an extension (a set of objects to which it may be taken to refer—the extension of 'dog' being all dogs, for example). My argument is a simple one. A definition can be right or wrong only relative to an extension, and an extension can be right or wrong only relative to a definition. In other words, we can argue that one definition of 'dog' is right and another wrong only to the degree that one definition fits the extension of 'dog'—that is, it applies to all and only things we count as dogs—whereas the other does not. Similarly, we can argue that one extension of the term 'dog' is right and another wrong only to the extent that one extension fits the definition of 'dog' and the other does not. Clearly, then, we cannot decide that *both* definition and extension are right or wrong. Indeed, we cannot even consider the 'validity' of the two conjunctively. One, either definition or extension, must be established arbitrarily. And this means precisely that one or the other must be stipulated (or that some further means of deciding one or the other must be stipulated—as when we stipulate 'ordinary usage' as determining definition or extension—which comes to the same thing).

That said, let us return for a moment to our analogy. Suppose that we have convinced all our hunter-philosophers that hunting moose, hunting duck, hunting rabbit, and so forth are all forms of hunting and thus we merely need to stipulate the object of our hunt. But then a hunter-poet comes along and says that he/she is hunting (or cooking, or . . .) 'unicorn' and a strange fellow—evidently trained on the continent—appears and tells us he/she is out for 'snark' (baking snark and so on). Clearly, there is a difference between hunting moose or duck and hunting unicorn or snark. Moose and ducks exist; unicorns do not—and snarks are not even adequately well-defined to merit discussion. We may, if we like, stipulate the object of our hunt (or cuisine, or . . .) as unicorn or snark—but then we know beforehand that we can never have a successful hunt (or meal, or . . .).

Not surprisingly, the situation is the same with interpretation. Meanings may be stipulated as 'emanations of the solar body on another astral plane', but then there are no meanings (in that sense). Now I think we can all agree that intentions exist. Authors do have conscious descriptive intents (statable in terms of truth-conditions), biographical associations, unconscious identifications—as well as specifically aesthetical intents, as I shall argue in chapter 5. Moreover, it seems indisputable that individual readers have temporal expectations, personal associations, literary associations, and so on and that groups of readers share certain expectations and associations. In other words, any sort of meaning that is specified in terms of intent (including abstraction from intent) is, I think, ontologically unexceptionable. Intents exist, and thus meanings defined in terms of intent exist also. Intents are like moose—and a far cry from snarks. In contrast, any *other* sort of thing commonly proposed as meaning is really on the side of the snarks, or at least the unicorns. As I indicated in the introduction, it will be the burden of chapter 2 to defend this limitation of meanings to intents.

HOW DOES ONE GET TO THE MEANING?

The second task of a theory of interpretation—subsequent to the isolation of the interpretive *object*, meaning—concerns the *method* of inference to that object. A full, detailed answer to this 'how'-question of interpretive theory must be formulated in relation to particular interpretive aims in particular interpretive disciplines. Thus, for example, in our discussion of psychoanalysis we will consider the specific procedures by which one might interpret to an analysand's unconscious intent. However, there are important general principles of interpretation, principles isolable through an examination of ordinary communicative understanding, everyday interpretive inference. Thus, I should like to begin by discussing inference to intent in quotidian communication situations. I should then like to use the conclusions of this analysis to discuss and defend the possibility of valid interpretive inference, in the face of social, historical, and other relativist objections.

In ordinary communication, there are several clear sets of principles that guide our interpretative inferences. Some obvious cases are our idiolectal knowledge of semantics, morphology, syntax, and phonology—which together constitute our linguistic competence for either interpreting or speaking—as well as some general logical or quasi-logical principles.[1] Roughly speaking, our linguistic competence, once acquired, provides us with much of what we would consider data for an interpretation—or, rather, it provides us with a sort of first level of interpretation that serves as data for a second level of interpretation—and the logic helps us to synthesize this for coherent understanding. We are not, most often, in the situation of the field linguist, seeking to fit together utterances and acts in order to get a few basic vocabulary items, some basic morphology and syntax, and such. For the most part, we know what people mean by some ordinary word and thus we unreflectively assume any given utterer of that word to mean the same, unless we have specific evidence to the contrary.

In this regard, interpretation proceeds like any other inferential and constructive activity—such as explanation in the physical sciences (a point made by a number of writers; see, for example, Kiparsky 1987, 187; Staal 1988, 5; Babbitt 1972, 3; Rorty 1991, 79 and throughout). There too prior theories, like linguistic competence (itself an implicit theory of meaning/interpretation), provide data for further constructions by way of logical principles. But data and the principles of logic, though necessary, are not sufficient to the construction of theories in the physical sciences. The Principle of Minimal Interpretation is crucial also. Though conceived of in many different (and often contradictory) ways, this is best thought of as a principle of ordering according to which the theory that accounts for the most data with the least theoretical apparatus is ranked above alternatives.

13

The Principle of Minimal Interpretation is, as I shall argue, crucial not only to theory evaluation in the natural sciences but to all forms of rational inference. Newton went so far as to claim that "truth is ever to be found in simplicity," and Einstein described himself as seeking "truth" in "simplicity" (quoted in Faust 1984, 110). Though I believe that both were mistaken in linking simplicity with truth (rather than with the preferential ordering of hypotheses), their stress on the inferential importance of the Principle of Minimal Interpretation seems entirely right. For example, without this principle, there is no induction. As Ludwig Wittgenstein pointed out, "The procedure of induction consists in accepting as true the *simplest* law that can be reconciled with our experiences" (Wittgenstein 1961, 70). Or, as Kenneth Friedman put it, "a hypothesis, h, is inductive if and only if h is at least as simple as any competing hypothesis that receives as much evidential support" (Friedman 1990, 85), which is to say, if it involves the smallest theoretical commitment—the fewest principles or posits, types of principle or posit, and so forth—for a fixed domain of data. Specifically, if the same type of thing happens over and over, one can construct a theory asserting that the event occurs each time for the same reason—according to the same law, for example. But one can just as easily construct a theory of these events that claims that each event is unrelated to all the others and that all have different causes. Both are logical. Both fit the data. It is only because of the Principle of Minimal Interpretation that we choose the former with its smaller number of principles (or, rather, we choose the former, *ceteris paribus;* the principle is in fact more complex than this implies, as we shall see below).

I should emphasize here that the Principle of Minimal Interpretation, as I am using it, is purely methodological. It concerns what we should do in evaluating theories, how we should order them. Any theory can be rendered empirically adequate. In effect, this is the point of all skepticism— that we can construct an empirically adequate theory claiming that life is hallucination, that other people are automatons, that the universe is made of green cheese, or whatever. Data alone never disconfirm a theory—or, rather, any theory disconfirmed by data may be rewritten and further complicated in such a way as to make it empirically adequate. Simplicity is the only clearly consistent and comprehensible way of ordering the infinity of empirically adequate theories; for this reason, it is what we ordinarily pursue, if inadequately, in everyday 'theorization'.

More exactly, we have no choice but to accept the Principle of Minimal Interpretation for we can just make no sense of its denial, in much the same way as we can make no sense of the denial of the Principle of Noncontradiction (on which see Quine 1976a, Quine 1976b, and Putnam 1983a).[2] Writers such as Friedman (1990, 92–109), McMullin (1993, 66–67), and others have tried to offer positive arguments for accepting simplicity orderings, most often based upon prior success, but I fail to see how any such argument can avoid circularity. Specifically, I fail to see how any formulation of even a very basic or uncontroversial datum can be unequivocal or unambiguously self-evident. But if it is not unequivocal or unambiguously self-evident, it requires an 'interpretation', and that interpretation presupposes an ordering principle—and that ordering principle is simplicity. In other words, we only decide that previous success is indeed previous success (and not, for example, delusion) by implicitly relying on simplicity considerations. Thus previous success cannot serve as evidence for the validity of such considerations. However, for the same reasons, alternatives to the Principle of Minimal Interpretation do not appear to be coherent or even comprehensible. Specifically, to determine whether or not any given ordering criterion applies in a particular case, we need to invoke simplicity. Even if the criterion is uncomplicated and 'objective'—for example, 'of several empirically equivalent theories, choose the one most recently formulated' or 'choose the one with the most words beginning with s'—even in cases such as these, we have to employ the Principle of Minimal Interpretation in order to decide whether or not a given theory was indeed most recent, whether it does contain the largest number of words beginning with s, and so forth. In this way, there does not seem to be any need for positive argument supporting adjudication by simplicity criteria, just as there is no need for positive argument supporting the Principle of Noncontradiction. There just are not any other choices. The only choice is between following the principle well and following it poorly.

On the other hand, there are (as we shall see below) cases in which we may have to choose between various formulations of simplicity criteria or of logical principles. In these cases, we will necessarily rely on our implicit criteria and principles, and we will appeal to such considerations as prior success in order to decide between these alternatives. Such decision is, of course, circular, but not perniciously so. For the point in this case is not to demonstrate that simplicity criteria or logical principles are right but rather to articulate those criteria and principles that we assume to be necessary.

It is important to point out that, in the sense in which I am using the term, 'simplicity' covers what is sometimes called 'consilience' (see, for example, Thagard 1988). Holland et al. state the principle of consilience in the following terms: "From a set of competing theories we should prefer the theory that explains the most classes of facts" (1986, 333). In this connection, they view a theory as *simpler* if "it requires fewer special assumptions than do its competitors" (334). These are widely viewed as distinct considerations. In my view, however, the choice we make between two theories on the basis of the number and complexity of rules and the choice we make between theories on the basis of domains covered are precisely the same. A theory with fewer rules than its competitors all treating a single set of data and a theory with the same number of rules as its competitors but covering more sets of data are preferable for the same reason: they are both *simpler* in the relevant sense.

In a similar way, simplicity is aggregative and contextual. One theory is simpler than another not only because it requires fewer posits or rules or exceptions or because it covers more sets of data, but because it coheres with the general principles of other theories. As Holland et al. put it, "learning based on specific problem types is abstracted to a degree sufficient for use on widely different problem types" (261). If I get a terrible backache for the first time in my life on the same day as seeing a rare tropical plant for the first time, I will not conclude that seeing the plant caused the back pain. It fits the data. It is logically coherent. And, considered in isolation, it is as simple a hypothesis as one that connects my dorsal suffering with some strenuous physical activity—even simpler, if I have engaged in that activity on previous occasions with no ill effects. But given our general principles of causal relations, given all the other sets of causal inference we accept, it is clear that the plant theory is far less simple than the strenuous activity theory. Specifically, though it does not state more rules or posits at the level of the particular causal connection, the plant theory *presupposes* an extra *type* of causal connection. It is, then, less simple than the competing explanation in terms of strenuous activity.

This difference in usage (distinguishing or not distinguishing 'simplicity', 'consilience', and so forth) indicates that the precise definition of *simplicity* is not universally agreed upon. In part, this is not a substantive issue but a matter of stipulation. My point here is that simplicity considerations, construed as a sort of proportion between (types of) posits and principles on the one hand and (sets of) data on the other, encompass the more common construals of simplicity, consilience, and so forth, the name or names being a matter of indifference (as Popper says, "I do not attach the slightest importance to the *word* 'simplicity'" [Popper 1968, 140]);

whatever name or names it is given, simplicity in this sense provides the single theoretically crucial ordering principle for the adjudication of alternative inferences (theories, hypotheses, and such).

On the other hand, not all such disagreements are trivial matters of names. In this context, it is worth taking a look at what are probably the two most common notions of simplicity that are significantly different from mine. The first, advocated by Willard Quine, among others, ties simplicity to empirical likelihood, claiming that the simpler thesis is the one that is harder to disprove because it says less. The second, maintained by Karl Popper and his followers, insists that simplicity is a matter of improbability and ready falsifiability. There are, of course, variations on these approaches. For example, Kenneth Friedman has argued that simplicity is a matter of testability (cf. Popper 1968, 142, where he says that simple theories *"are better testable"*), and Elliott Sober maintains that it is a matter of informativeness, one hypothesis being more informative than another if it yields predictions with fewer auxiliary premises (cf. Popper 1968, 142, where he says that simple theories *"tell us more"* and *"their empirical content is greater"*). Of course, all these writers are free to stipulate their use of 'simplicity' as they like—as long as they do not take their construals of simplicity as exclusive. In other words, we may conceive of theory-adjudication as involving empirical and logical considerations plus some other set of principles, which we may call by one name ('simplicity') or by several names ('simplicity', 'consilience', and so on). Alternative construals of simplicity—such as those just mentioned—conflict with my construal only if they reserve the entire space of nonlogical, nonempirical adjudication for simplicity *in their sense*. Indeed, this is fine too, if their construals of simplicity are adequate for theory adjudication. However, I do not believe that they are.

Perhaps most important, these construals tend to treat simplicity as if it were a matter of hypotheses alone. Thus, Quine gives an example involving two numbers: 5.2 and 5.21. Suppose we are discussing meter readings. In this case, the 5.2, Quine claims, is simpler "because ten times as much deviation is tolerated" (1976c, 257). Writers such as Popper (as well as Friedman, Sober, and others) would give different analyses, also drawing conclusions about relative simplicity—presumably the exact opposite conclusion, at least in Popper's case. (Popper's examples, though more elaborate, are directly parallel, treating linear versus quadratic functions, circles versus ellipses, and so forth, in terms of simplicity [see 138 and 142–43].) However, in my view, it just makes no sense to rank one number over another number in a simplicity hierarchy removed from data, associated posits and principles, and so on. Imagine the following situation: 1) Each of a significant number of meter readings is 5.21. In this case, the claim that all relevant occurrences have a value of 5.21 would be the simplest. Specifically, if we say that something has a value of 5.2, that is, or may be (depending upon the meter), tantamount to saying that its value varies between 5.15 and 5.25, that it might be 5.17 or 5.22, and so on. If, however, we say that it has a value of 5.21, then we say that it is never 5.17 or 5.22, but only 5.21. Clearly, this view is simpler when the data are all 5.21.

But the situation changes in the following case: 2) The meter readings vary between 5.16 and 5.24. In this case, the claim that all relevant occurrences have a value of 5.2 would be the simplest hypothesis. A third case shows yet a further alteration: 3) The meter readings vary between 5.16 and 5.24, *but* the vast majority fall at 5.21, and all other occurrences of the same type have previously been found to have values constant to one one-hundredth of a point, and in previous cases where this sort of variation has been found, these apparent variations have been accounted for by other factors. In this case, the claim that all relevant occurrences have a value of 5.21 would be the simplest hypothesis.

Especially in these last two cases, it is not clear how simplicity can be understood as degree of verifiability or falsifiability (or testability or informativeness). Of course, these authors may claim that their metatheories would lead to the same conclusion as mine, but by way of principles other than (what they call) simplicity. If so, their construals of simplicity are not exclusive and this may be a terminological disagreement after all. Perhaps we do indeed advocate the same principles, only under different names. (Though, in fact, it seems fairly clear that this is not the case.) In any event, it should be clear that the construals of simplicity articulated by Quine, Popper, and others are in and of themselves inadequate precisely at the points where they yield results different from those of the construal I have been defending. Moreover, it seems that the only way they can address this problem is by adding further principles that are, collectively, equivalent to simplicity in my sense.

On the other hand, some issues remain unaddressed even in my formulation. For example, my account of simplicity says nothing about whether all posits and principles of competing theories should be counted equally. Certainly, types of posits and principles are more important than numbers of posits or principles within one type. And certainly type is a relative concept, defined within a hierarchy of theories or subtheories, with judgments concerning the economy for any given level of theoreticity counting *before* (that is, superseding) judgments of economy for any subsequent level (for instance, if we can adjudicate between theories at the atomic level, we typically do so without proceeding to the subatomic level). Beyond this, some authors think that the number of ad hoc principles is the most crucial consideration; some think that the number of principles of all sorts is more important than the number of posits. I am skeptical of most such 'subhierarchizations', in part because they seem to assume hard and fast distinctions where these do not necessarily exist. For example, we can often (always?) reformulate ad hoc principles so that they have the form of general laws; and I suspect that we can often cut down on our principles, including ad hoc principles, by generating further posits (if so, this would seem to render incoherent such extreme views as that of Thagard 1986, 86, which counts principles only, not posits). Fortunately, debates over these subhierarchizations do not bear on the general point, or on any of the interpretive issues we will be considering.

Whatever we decide about the subhierarchization of simplicity considerations, it is important to emphasize that none of this implies anything at all about a supposed simplicity of the world. Indeed, the notion of a 'simple world' does not make too much sense. Simplicity is, again, a relation between competing theories, considered relative to (sets of) data. Moreover, the Principle of Minimal Interpretation, as I am using it, does not even say that the simplest theory is the one 'most likely to be correct'—likelihood being a statistical notion that appears to have no clear interpretation in this context. This last point is of particular relevance in the humanities and social sciences. I suspect that the occasional objections to simplicity criteria voiced by writers in these fields derive at least in part from confusing a preference for simpler theories with an imagined claim about the simplicity of the world. For example, Clifford Geertz maintains bizarrely that anthropologists should not follow the precepts of natural science and seek simplicity but should, rather, seek complexity (Geertz 1973, 34). Evidently, he feels that earlier anthropologists left out too much in their analyses of culture, that they did not recognize the complexity of culture. But this could only mean that their theories were empirically inadequate *or overly complex* (in the relevant, technical sense) through failing to cover broader ranges of data. The problem Geertz has isolated is clearly *not* that earlier anthropologists followed the Principle of Minimal

Interpretation but rather that they did precisely the contrary; hence the problem would not be solved by violating that principle, but only by following it.[3]

Returning to interpretation per se, it should be clear that here too, as in scientific explanation, logic and data are necessary but insufficient. For example, if someone says, 'I think that Ortcutt has a new girlfriend. He's busy every Friday and Saturday night', we may take the two statements to be related and infer that the speaker believes that Ortcutt is seeing this new girlfriend on Friday and Saturday. However, we may equally assume that the two statements are unrelated—so unrelated, in fact, that the 'he' of the second sentence does not even refer to Ortcutt. Both follow the principles of logic and both are consistent with the data. Paul Grice has proposed that there is a set of rules, rules of conversation or conversational implicature, that govern interpretation in these cases. In this instance, for example, Grice claims that we interpret in accordance with the "Maxim of Relation/Relevance" and thus assume the second claim to be *relevant* to the first.

Another case might be the following. Someone says, 'Mr. Ortcutt is looking very unhealthily thin'. We may assume that the speaker is claiming that Ortcutt has lost weight—too much weight. Or we may assume that the speaker, without mentioning anything about mirrors, is claiming that Ortcutt has used mirrors cleverly to devise a way of making himself look fifty pounds thinner, without losing a single ounce. Grice claims that in this case we interpret in accordance with the "Maxim of Quantity," which tells speakers to give as much information as is necessary, and adjures auditors to believe that such necessary information has been given. Thus we assume no mirrors are involved because none are mentioned.

These two maxims, along with two others (which I shall not discuss), comprise the principles of conversational implicature, which, according to Grice, combine with principles of logic and linguistic competence to allow quotidian, communicative interpretation. Clearly, there are no such special rules in the construction of theories in the physical sciences, and thus it might seem that interpretation and theorization diverge in this respect. However, Grice's rules are, I believe, theoretically redundant, and interpretation is fully parallel to 'explanation' in this regard. In the cases cited above, Grice's rules merely tell us to choose the simplest alternative. Given different interpretive possibilities, we tacitly invoke the Principle of Minimal Interpretation and choose the one that appears most elegant. Grice's maxims of relation/relevance and quantity merely spell out some of the consequences of such a choice. Thus, in the case of the first example, it is simpler to assume that there is one topic than it is to assume that there are two—or, rather, it is simpler given our beliefs, or theories, about the way conversations proceed, what sorts of things people say after announcing an hypothesis, what sorts of things people do on Friday and Saturday nights (again, simplicity evaluation operates in the context of a broad range of theoretical assumptions). As to the second case, losing too much weight is the ordinary way of looking unhealthily thin; tricks with mirrors are not ordinary. This makes the assumption that Ortcutt has lost weight simpler communicatively, in large part because it is simpler factually. In other words, this is what we would assume on seeing an emaciated Ortcutt. Thus it is what we assume on hearing of an emaciated Ortcutt. Moreover, in the absence of any expectation that the speaker is trying to deceive us, we assume that he/she would expect us to draw this inference (based on simplicity and so on) and thus would correct it, should he/she know it to be false. We assume this too based on prior theories about communication in general, about this particular speaker, and so forth.

Significantly, we do not always interpret in accordance with Gricean principles. As Grice readily admits, speakers do not invariably follow these principles, and sometimes we notice. In these cases, we straightforwardly interpret in accordance with simplicity considerations; indeed, it is by reference to simplicity that we decide when such cases arise. When a representative of U.S. military intelligence speaks about the Persian Gulf War, we do not (or at least should not) assume that he/she is giving us all necessary information; we do not interpret in accordance with the Maxim of Quantity. If we know that a certain speaker regularly flies off on tangents, we do not (necessarily) assume that his/her contiguous statements are mutually relevant; we do not (necessarily) interpret in accordance with the Maxim of Relation/Relevance. In many ordinary circumstances, we assume that people are violating various principles in order, for example, to 'make conversation'. Consider the following interaction from Sam Selvon's *The Lonely Londoners:* " 'The boat-train come yet?' Tolroy ask, though he know it ain't come yet. 'No,' Moses say, though he know that Tolroy know" (Selvon 1985, 26). Tolroy violates the Maxim of Quantity. Moses recognizes this because he implicitly considers Tolroy's familiarity with the boat-train, the observable condition of the station, the general human awkwardness of beginning a conversation, and so forth, in the context of which it is simplest to assume that Tolroy is perfectly aware that the boat-train has not arrived and is not trying to get information but merely wants to make conversation.

Hudson presents a rather more exotic example. According to Elinor Keenan, in certain parts of Madagascar, the Maxim of Quantity is not followed in certain circumstances. As Hudson reports, quoting Keenan, "if A asks B 'Where is your mother?' and B responds 'She is either in the house or at the market', B's utterance is not usually taken to imply that B is unable to provide more specific information needed by the hearer" (Hudson 1980, 118). Note that this poses a problem for Grice's maxims, but not for the Principle of Minimal Interpretation. Once an interpreter knows that religious beliefs and so forth inhibit full identification of certain referents, it is no longer simplest to assume that a speaker is presenting all relevant known information about such referents.[4] (On the other hand, simplicity considerations along with a knowledge of general human purposes do predict that this sort of situation should be cross-culturally exceptional, as Hudson reports that it is.)

As examples such as these indicate, we clearly employ simplicity criteria and not Gricean principles in cases where the two conflict. And this indicates that it is simplicity criteria that we are employing all along.

This conclusion is further supported by the fact that, in addition to Grice's rules, there are a number of other well-attested principles that guide quotidian interpretation, and these too are instances of the Principle of Minimal Interpretation, specified in particular contexts. For example, Gillian Brown and George Yule point out that "The principles of analogy (things will tend to be as they were before) and local interpretation (if there is a change, assume it is minimal) form the basis of the assumption of coherence in our experience of life in general, hence in our experience of discourse as well" (Brown and Yule 1983, 67). The connection with simplicity here is self-evident (though this connection also indicates that Brown and Yule may have overgeneralized, ignoring those unusual circumstances in which the assumptions of no change or of minimal change would not hold). Similarly, in the interpretation of narrative, they explain: "if there is no cue to the contrary, [we assume that] the first-mentioned event happened first and the second-mentioned event followed it" (125). We assume, in other words, that the temporal order of narrative is the same as the temporal order of the events themselves—unless there is a "cue to the contrary," which is to say, data that render another hypothesis simpler. Along the same lines, Johnson-Laird points out that in interpret-

ing words, we tend to assign meaning based on what fits most easily—
or simply—into our conception (or theory) of the world: "For example,
a listener imagines a shark as an instance of the generic term, 'fish,' since
a shark is a plausible actor in the situation described by the sentence"
(Johnson-Laird 1993, 570).

After Grice's maxims, N. L. Wilson's "Principle of Charity" is perhaps
the most striking case of an interpretive principle that is in part subsumed
and in part superseded by simplicity considerations. In Hilary Putnam's
words, this principle states that "we should assign the designatum that
makes the largest possible number of the speaker's beliefs true" (Putnam
1975, 275). In fact, we assume the veracity of a speaker's statements when
our relevant theoretical principles indicate that it is simplest to do so, but
not otherwise. If someone points out the window to a thunderstorm and
says, "Well, it's stopped raining," we assume that he/she misspoke or was
being ironical. If, in contrast, someone who never studied any physical science gives a muddled account of quantum mechanics, we assume that he/
she is wrong. Like Grice's principles, the Principle of Charity turns out to
be right—that is, to provide a normative guide for our interpretations—
only when it coincides with the Principle of Minimal Interpretation. In
cases of conflict, the Principle of Minimal Interpretation is and should be
preferred. (Of course, this is not to say that Wilson's principle, or Grice's
maxims, do not enter in cases where simplicity is not decidable.)

In keeping with this, writers in experimental psychology, cognitive science, and artificial intelligence have noted the importance of simplicity
considerations in quotidian and disciplinary interpretation, at least in general terms. For example, H. H. Clark has argued that hearers interpret the
referents of someone's speech by recourse to the principle: "use the simplest assumption to posit the existence of such an entity" (Garman 1990,
364). And Jerry Hobbs has argued that, in literature and elsewhere, "we
want to choose the most economical interpretation for the sentence or the
text as a whole" (Hobbs 1990, 48).

In sum, interpreters seek to interpret in accordance with linguistic principles, logic, and the Principle of Minimal Interpretation. This interpretive
approach is identical in structure with the sort of explanatory approach
adopted by everyone in everything from quotidian inference to the construction of theories in the physical sciences. In Clark's words, interpretive
"comprehension is a form of thinking that should not be set off" from
other sorts of problem solving and inference (quoted in Garman 1990,
365). Or, as Geoffrey Sampson puts it (referring to Popper), "There is no

philosophically significant distinction to be drawn between the process by which those particularly general elements of knowledge that we classify as 'science' grow and that by which ordinary men and women learn to understand their everyday world" (Sampson 1980, 9). Indeed, I shall argue in the following chapter that it is precisely these principles of rational inference that the child employs in gaining linguistic competence initially. In this way, everyday explanation, the construction of theories in formal sciences, the acquisition of language (hence the development of basic interpretations and of a basic interpretive theory), and, finally, both quotidian and disciplinary interpretation of larger discursive units, all proceed by the interaction of data, logic, and simplicity. These form the basis of all interpretive method.

There are, of course, writers who have criticized precisely this sort of identification, though it is often difficult to puzzle out exactly what their argument against this identification might be. Consider, for example, Jurgen Habermas. Habermas is probably the most famous theorist to have argued against an identification of the methods of physical science, social science, and hermeneutics. Adolf Grunbaum has argued cogently against Habermas's views (see Grunbaum 1984), and there is no need to repeat his criticisms here. However, even if we were to accept Habermas's claims, they would have little bearing on the methodological issues we are addressing. For example, according to Habermas, a crucial difference between the causal sequences investigated in the physical sciences and those investigated in the human sciences is that "the 'influence' of events on an acting subject is dependent on a specific interpretation" and thus "the behavioral reaction is . . . mediated by a concrete understanding of the meaning of given situations" (Habermas 1988, 35). This is perfectly true, and an important point against behaviorism. But it would seem to show that behaviorism was not fully following principles of scientific method, and thus that it should be replaced by something along the lines of cognitive science. In other words, insofar as behavioral psychology failed to take this into account, it was not being too scientific and inadequately hermeneutic; rather, it was being inadequately scientific. Claims about the importance of interpretive understanding in human behavior—no matter how valid—in no way indicate serious methodological differences between the physical sciences and the human sciences. Of course, there are differences in the way the general principles of rational inference are specified and in the resultant structure of the theories. And Habermas is right to emphasize this, especially as some philosophers of science, as well as some sociologists and psychologists, are far too inclined to take physics—in all of its methodological and theoretical particularity—as a model and standard for every discipline. (Indeed, this is probably one source of the methodological errors in behaviorism.) But even at this level, his division is inadequately discriminating (after all, the specific methods and theories of, for example, law and literature or astronomy and biology differ greatly also), as well as overly dichotomistic (in failing to recognize the broad methodological principles that govern all rational inference).

Hilary Putnam is worth briefly considering in this context as well, for he has come to similar conclusions, despite the fact that his background is almost the polar opposite of Habermas's. Specifically, Putnam argues that

> if a historian reads documents, examines the public actions, reads the diaries and letters, how then does he decide 'Smith was hungry for power'? *Not* by applying 'general laws of history, sociology, and psychology' to the data as positivist methodologists urge he should! Rather he has to absorb all this material, and then *rely on his human wisdom* that this shows power-hunger 'beyond a reasonable doubt' (as the courts say). In effect, he uses *himself* as a 'measuring instrument'; which is pretty much what Weber, Dilthey, etc., urged . . . Sometimes his decision is controversial (even when he is right), but sometimes not (does anyone doubt that *Nero* was egotistical?) (Putnam 1978, 73)

Putnam is no doubt correct that the historian does not and should not seek to formulate deterministic laws—he/she should follow the general principles of rational inference, not their specification in physics or chemistry. But, even granting the simplistic conception of historiography as focusing on such questions as whether Smith was power-hungry or Nero egotistical, Putnam is wrong to argue that the historian does or should use him/herself as a "measuring instrument." What a historian does is consider Smith's behavior (did Smith grab every opportunity to achieve power, choosing power over love, intellectual achievement, and so on), and he/she considers this behavior in the context of general theories about the way people behave, given certain motives, and so forth. In other words, the historian tries to decide what explanation best fits Smith's behavior in such a way as to be consistent with his/her broad theoretical presuppositions about human psychology. In other words, the historian follows (or should follow) principles of rational inference (or scientific method). Moreover, self-intuition is a particularly unfortunate choice as an alternative to rational inference, for, as many psychological studies have indicated, our introspective judgment is highly fallible. Even on ordinary matters, my analyses of myself are as much matters of uncertain theoretical inference as are my analyses of other people (see, for example, Nisbett and Wilson 1977; Nisbett and Ross 1980, chapter 9; and Gopnik 1993; this is a point to which we shall return below). Even if interpretation were closely akin to introspection or self-experience, that would not make it any less like explanation in the natural sciences.

SOME PROBLEMS OF RELATIVISM

Habermas and Putnam stress the putative difference between observation, on the one hand, and meaning or subjective experience, on the other, in order to defend the validity of nonscientific interpretive methods. Other theorists, however, have seen in this apparent discrepancy a reason to question the very possibility of inference to meaning or subjectivity, or even the sense of speaking about facts of meaning or subjectivity at all. Indeed, some authors have maintained that the pervasiveness of meaning undermines or relativizes judgments about physical nature and thus undermines or relativizes the validity of scientific method even within natural science.

This brings us, then, to a further set of problems, which cut across the distinction between object and method in interpretation—problems of the possibility of valid, nonrelativist interpretation. These problems may be divided into two categories: 1) Problems arising between communities, especially those that are historically or culturally separated, and 2) problems arising between individuals within a community. The first give rise to various social relativisms, the second to linguistic solipsism and related skepticisms. I shall argue that though there are serious practical problems in each area, there is no problem of principle that should cause us to believe that rational interpretive inquiry, along the lines just indicated, is impossible or so limited as to be pointless.

The first thing to note in this context is that if our argument against nonintentional, or nonidiolectal, meaning holds up (on which, see chapter 2; see also Chomsky 1980, 117ff.; 1986, 19ff.; and 1988a, 36f.), then historical/cultural—or, more broadly, social—relativism reduces to solipsism. Indeed, some thirty years ago, Ward Goodenough argued that culture is idiolectal. First of all, Goodenough distinguished between "culture 1, the recurring patterns which characterize a community as a homeostatic system, and culture 2, people's standards for perceiving, judging, and acting." He then maintained that "no two persons can be said to have exactly the same cultures 2, because every individual in organizing his experience of phenomena, including the actions and utterances of his fellows, necessarily creates his own" (quoted in Osgood, May, and Miron 1975, 335, 336). Moreover, empirical studies in linguistics, sociolinguistics, and related fields have repeatedly indicated that there is far more similarity across cultures and far more difference within cultures than any of us is inclined to imagine (for an important semantic example of this, see Hudson 1980, 92–94). Indeed, as R. A. Hudson has pointed out, empirical studies indicate that any extreme relativism based on presumed cultural differences is simply "untenable," given the present state of knowledge, for, at the very least, "there are clear restrictions on the nature and extent of differences between people in the concepts that their languages express" (95).

But if language and culture are idiolectal, which is to say, if we do not truly *share* a language or a culture, if we do not, by our membership in a community, have special access to the meanings of some supraidiolectal language, the norms and principles of some supraidiolectal culture— and if, in addition, there are striking differences between people's idiolects within languages or cultures and striking similarities between idiolects across languages and cultures—if all this is the case, then there is and can be no special problem of intercultural or historical interpretation. Rather *all* forms of interpretation, within or across communities, involve the reconciling of individual idiolects. Intercultural and historical interpretation do not involve gaining access to another community's supraidiolectal conceptual scheme—a scheme to which the members of that other community already have access, in some obscure way, a scheme that conflicts with our own supraidiolectal, and also somehow intuited, scheme. Rather, interpretation involves the attempts of individuals to match their never fully identical idiolects in such a way as to allow understanding.

For obvious reasons, this reconciliation is—at least in some superficial ways—much easier within a community than across communities.[5] Interpretation across communities is inhibited by limitations of data, along with lethargy, racism, and other factors. These practical difficulties should not be downplayed, but the important point is that they inhibit precisely the same *sort* of interpretation as is practiced *within* a community. Indeed, even intracommunal interpretation is inhibited by limitations of data, as well as ignorance, lethargy, racism, and other factors.

In sum, there is no difference of *kind* here, but only one of *degree*. Now, this identity of kind between intercommunal and intracommunal interpretation strictly implies that if we cannot in principle be right about one, then we cannot in principle be right about the other. Any *in-principle impossibility* of *inter*communal interpretation—as asserted, for example, in various types of cultural and historical relativism—entails the in-principle impossibility of *intra*communal interpretation. If it is not merely pragmatically difficult, but *in-principle impossible* for me to understand someone from another culture or (the writings of) someone from another period, then it is also *in-principle impossible* for me to understand my neighbor. Indeed, given the fact that I come to understand myself in much the same way as I understand my neighbor, it is in-principle impossible for me to understand myself!

Thus, the problems of cultural, historical, and other similar relativisms reduce to the problem of solipsism—indeed, a sort of hypersolipsism in which one is as isolated from oneself as from the rest of the world. But I take this linguistic hypersolipsism to be a skeptical position of the ordinary, trivial sort. All theories are tentative—including all theories that posit the existence of other minds, causality, the possibility of valid interpretive inference, and so forth. Thus, it is *possible* that other minds, causal principles, and so on do not exist, that all interpretive inferences are false or random. Nothing in interpretation or in natural science or in any empirical discipline is certain. Skeptics merely point out this obvious fact. However, they fail to point out, or to realize, that this fact is trivial, for bare possibility is meaningless and in no way indicates that plausible views—that other minds exist, that rational procedures can and do lead to valid interpretive inferences, and so forth—should be abandoned or should not be preferred to alternatives. In this way, such traditional forms of relativism have no bearing upon the present undertaking, for, again, as arguments about in-principle incomprehensibility of cultures (as opposed to arguments about practical difficulties, even severe practical difficulties), they reduce to hypersolipsism and, thereby, to trivial skepticism.

Before turning to the problem of nonidiolectal theories of meaning, however, I should like to look at two particular contemporary relativisms, the two most powerful of which I am aware. The first, the 'paradigm relativism' attributed to Thomas Kuhn, concerns theory-formulation in the physical sciences, and thus, by the preceding argument, in all forms of inferential reasoning outside of pure logical deduction. The second, W. V. O. Quine's "ontological relativity," as expressed in his "indeterminacy of translation" thesis, has a more narrowly linguistic and interpretive focus. I shall conclude by considering a related topic, Stanley Fish's skepticism about the possibility of "critical self-consciousness," a skepticism that, if valid, would extend to all forms of theoretical reflection, including the present study.

Under one common interpretation of his writings, Kuhn maintains that different theories are *incommensurable*—thus inadjudicable—because there is no place from which they might be compared. One must take up one's position *within* a theory and thus one can never adopt a neutral position from which competing theories might be viewed disinterestedly and with comprehension. Part and parcel of this position is the thesis that any data that might be thought to contribute to adjudicating the competing claims of the theories are necessarily data *for a given theory*. In other words, data cannot be dissociated from the particular theories in which they are formulated; data are always 'theory laden'.

At one level, these claims are quite true. For example, some flashing lights and meter readings may be taken by quark theorists to present data about quarks ('the experiment shows that quarks behave thus and so'), going on to posit specific properties in order to explain these data ('the fact that quarks behave thus and so may be accounted for by positing these types of quark, which may form these combinations'). However, someone else may not accept the existence of quarks at all ('the experiment shows nothing about quarks, but only about protons'). Thus he/she just will not accept 'Quarks behave thus and so' as a datum. Clearly we do not accept as data properties of objects we believe to be nonexistent. In this sense, at this 'level', different theories—in this case a theory positing quarks and a theory denying them—do not share data.

But what is important for our purposes is that, at another level, these theories do share data—possibly data about proton behavior, possibly only data about flashing lights and meter readings, possibly something in between. Thus, while the data are not shared under one formulation, they are shared under other formulations. There are, in other words, levels of theoreticity such that the posits and principles made at one level presuppose the posits and principles of all lower levels but are not presupposed by them. The quark and antiquark theorists share data starting at some lower level of theoreticity, then extending all the way down. Of course, there are often enormous practical problems impeding rational adjudication of theories even though some lower-level or 'background' theory is held in common by the disputants. After all, not all competing theories are adjudicable on grounds of evidence, coherence, and simplicity. But these are, again, only pragmatic difficulties; there is no question of principle at

29

stake. Moreover, *interpretation* of the divergent theories from a common background should not even prove too difficult in pragmatic terms. Problems of principle relating to incommensurability could arise only in cases where no lower-level or background theory is held in common, where the theories diverge at *all* levels of theoreticity—which is to say, where the 'disputants' simply cannot communicate at all, even to the point of recognizing a dispute. First of all, this seems to be a biological impossibility. Secondly, even if it were not a biological impossibility, it would not have any theoretical consequences. Were we to be faced with a case of absolute noncommunication, the whole issue of discrepancies and adjudications could not even arise. Finally, such absolute incommensurability or noncommunication is, in any event, not a problem in real interpretive situations such as those we will be addressing.

Unsurprisingly, most of these points have not gone unnoticed. For example, Alan Musgrave points out that:

> One must admit, of course, that terms change their meanings with different theories, in the sense that, to use one of Kuhn's examples, a Copernican will class the earth as a planet while an Aristotelian will not. But I fail to see why, if this leads to a "communication problem," the Copernican cannot explain that on his theory the earth, since it revolves around the sun like the other planets, must be classed with them. I also fail to see why the Aristotelian cannot understand this, without of course necessarily accepting it—or why he cannot make the Copernican understand his own reasons for classing the earth differently. The same applies to Kuhn's other examples ("element," "mixture," "unconstrained motion"). (Musgrave 1980, 49)

Similarly, Roy Bhaskar argues that "it clearly could come to pass over some scientific transformation that, as Feyerabend and Kuhn have suggested, no meanings are shared in common between two conflicting scientific theories. Can we then still sustain the notion of a rational choice between such incommensurable theories? Yes. For we can allow quite simply that a theory T_A is preferable to a theory T_B, even if they are incommensurable, provided that T_A can explain *under its descriptions* almost all the phenomena that T_B can explain under its descriptions *plus* some significant phenomena that T_B cannot explain." Indeed, "to say of two theories that they conflict, clash or are in competition presupposes that there is something—a domain of real objects or relations existing and acting independently of their (conflicting) descriptions—*over* which they clash. Hence incommensurable theories must share a part world in common" (Bhaskar 1989, 19). John Earman makes the point succinctly: "Even for cases of major scientific revolutions, we can find, without having to go too far downward toward something like foundations for knowledge, an observation base that is *neutral enough for purposes at hand*" (Earman 1993, 16; see also Thagard 1988, 96; Holland, et al. 1986, 333; Thagard 1992, 93, 108, and throughout). (Earman makes the point that Kuhn not only exaggerates the divergence between scientists working in different paradigms but also exaggerates the uniformity of views held by scientists working in the same paradigm [31].)

Perhaps the most important and influential response to Kuhnian and related relativisms is that of Donald Davidson. It is worth considering Davidson's views briefly before going on. In his important essay, "On the Very Idea of a Conceptual Scheme," Davidson argues that "we cannot make sense of total failure" in translation—between languages, paradigms, and so on (1984, 185). If I understand this claim correctly, it implies that the historical nonoccurrence of such a complete failure is a triviality. It is a fact about the way we construct translations, not a fact about the way human beings, languages, and such are. But Davidson's claim, in that case, seems clearly mistaken. We could adopt usual field methods with some newly discovered population and simply never be able to begin the construction of even a basic lexicon, finding our hypotheses continually falsified. The fact of interlinguistic and interparadigmatic translatability is not trivial in the least.

On the other hand, Davidson is certainly right to point to the evident contradiction in most actual conceptual relativist claims, for a writer such as Benjamin Lee Whorf does not merely claim that the meanings of Hopi speakers are opaque. Rather, he shows us that they are opaque by explicating them, quite specifically, in English. And a writer such as Kuhn—if he is to be considered a genuine conceptual relativist—does not merely claim that the meanings of 'pre-revolutionary' theoretical terms are opaque. Rather, he shows us that they are opaque by explicating them, quite specifically, in "post-revolutionary idiom" (Davidson 1984, 184).

Davidson is also correct when he states that arguments about the relativity of truth to conceptual scheme really demonstrate nothing more "than the pedestrian and familiar fact that the truth of a sentence is relative to (among other things) the language to which it belongs" (189). In other words, the meaning of a sentence is a function of the rules of the language in which it is uttered and, without meaning, a sentence can hardly be either true or false. Indeed, this point (somewhat revised) is central to the preceding argument for a stipulative view of meaning.

But, having said all this, it is important to note that Kuhn himself may not in fact advocate the sort of relativism with which his name has been associated. Indeed, many of the points we have been urging are fully recognized by Kuhn. In the "Postscript" to *The Structure of Scientific Revolutions,* Kuhn writes that "since the vocabularies in which [opposed theorists] discuss such situations [of theoretical dispute] consist . . . predominantly of the same terms, they must be attaching some of those terms to nature differently, and their communication is inevitably only partial. As a result, the superiority of one theory to another is something that cannot be proved in the debate. Instead, I have insisted, each party must try, by persuasion, to convert the other" (198). At first blush, this appears to be a relativist assertion. But Kuhn goes on to claim that "nothing about that relatively familiar thesis implies either that there are no good reasons for being persuaded or that those reasons are not ultimately decisive for the group. Nor does it even imply that the reasons for choice are different from those usually listed by philosophers of science: accuracy, simplicity, fruitfulness, and the like" (199); indeed, Kuhn elsewhere maintains that these methodological criteria (simplicity and so forth) are "fixed once and for all" (quoted in McMullin 1993, 63) and "necessarily permanent" (Kuhn 1993, 338). Subsequently in the "Postscript," Kuhn maintains that, despite serious practical difficulties, theorists arguing across paradigms "must . . . have some recourse." Specifically, "the stimuli that impinge upon them are the same. So is their general neural apparatus, however differently programmed. Furthermore, except in a small, if all-important, area of experience even their neural programming must be very nearly the same, for they share a history, except the immediate past. As a result, both their everyday and most of their scientific world and language are shared" (1970, 201).

Kuhn does take this analysis to motivate a denial of the traditional notion that "successive theories grow ever closer to, or approximate more and more closely to, the truth" (206). This too may seem to be a relativist statement. However, I suspect that it is not. I take it, rather, that Kuhn is merely making a claim about similarity relations between posits and reality. Most people unreflectively assume that of two theories the posits of the superior theory are more similar to relevant real existents. Kuhn's point, I take it, is that this assumption is unwarranted. I am not entirely convinced that Kuhn is right on this issue; it depends on how we understand similarity in this context (are we concerned only with posits? with posits and with laws? what about types of posit and law?). In any event, it should be clear that Kuhn's views, thus understood, are not necessarily relativistic or otherwise in conflict with the preceding analyses. Though, again, if Kuhn's views are interpreted in the common, relativistic manner, it then appears that they are unjustified (and, indeed, incoherent).

Like Kuhn, Willard Quine is well aware that empirical data are often inadequate for deciding between theories, including interpretive theories. Developing this point somewhat differently from Kuhn, however, and focusing on more narrowly semantic issues, Quine concludes from this that "rival systems of analytical hypotheses [that is, hypotheses about the meanings of words in a given language] can conform to all speech dispositions . . . and yet dictate, in countless cases, utterly disparate translations; not mere mutual paraphrases, but translations each of which would be excluded by the other system of translation" (1960, 73). More important, for Quine, the claims of these rival theories are inadjudicable and, indeed, this is not merely an epistemological problem. It is just not the case that one or the other of these theories is true. Thus, Quine explains:

It may be protested that when two theories agree . . . in point of all possible sensory determinants they are in an important sense not two but one. Certainly such theories are, as wholes, empirically equivalent. If something is affirmed in the one theory and denied in the other, one may argue that the particular form of words affirmed and denied is itself unlike in meaning in the two cases but that the containing theories as wholes have the same net meaning still. Similarly one may protest that two systems of analytical hypotheses are, as wholes, equivalent so long as no verbal behavior makes any difference between them and, if they offer seemingly discrepant English translations, one may again argue that the apparent conflict is a conflict only of parts seen out of context. Now this account is fair enough, apart from its glibness on the topic of meaning; and it helps to make the principle of indeterminacy of translation less surprising. When two systems of analytical hypotheses fit the totality of verbal dispositions to perfection and yet conflict in their translations of certain sentences, the conflict is precisely a conflict of parts seen without the wholes. The principle of indeterminacy of translation requires notice just because translation proceeds little by little and sentences are thought of as conveying meanings severally. That it requires notice is plainly illustrated by the almost universal belief that the objective references of terms in radically different languages can be objectively compared. (78–79)

Therefore, "The point is not that we cannot be sure whether the analytical hypothesis is right, but that there is not even . . . an objective matter to be right or wrong about" (73).

As I understand him, Quine's idea here is that if a field linguist observes his/her informant saying '*gavagai*' and pointing to a rabbit, he/she may interpret '*gavagai*' as 'rabbit' or 'undetached rabbit part' or 'rabbit stage' or whatever. If he/she goes with 'rabbit', that will have certain consequences for interpretation elsewhere—and the same holds for the other alternatives. Ultimately, with enough tinkering, any of these could be accommodated in a theory perfectly consistent with all the data.

Indeed, one need not go to another language to see this. I could interpret Quine's 'rabbit'—'rabbit' in Quine's idiolect—to mean 'rabbit stage' in my idiolect. When he says, 'But by 'rabbit' I do not mean 'rabbit stage',' I can then accommodate the new data by assuming that, in Quine's idiolect, 'stage' has its normal sense *except* when conjoined with 'rabbit', in which case it functions to change the meaning of 'rabbit' in his lexicon to that of 'rabbit' in my lexicon. Then, when Quine says things like, 'I saw that rabbit when it was born, then three months later, then one year later; I guess you could say I've seen three rabbit stages', I can assume he is just being irrational. And so on. (In fact, for reasons already indicated, I could make the same argument for my own use of 'rabbit'.) All this would be empirically equivalent with the assumption that by 'rabbit' Quine (or Hogan) means *rabbit*. Quine's position appears to be that as these theories are empirically equivalent, we cannot choose between them—and, moreover, there is no fact that would even make one correct and the other incorrect.

But, first of all, empirical equivalence hardly implies an absence of fact. Of course, for Quine, the absence of fact is an absence of meaning. It is not that the world is deficient but that the meanings of our claims—including the meanings of our theoretical or 'metaclaims'—are not fully determinable and thus not fixed. However, as Chomsky has repeatedly noted (see Chomsky 1975, 179–204; and 1980, 14–24), the fact that meanings are not definitively or absolutely decidable does not by itself distinguish the indeterminacy of translation from the ordinary "underdetermination of theories by evidence"; it does not, in other words, differentiate translation (or interpretation) from any other inferential activity. Quine, of course, denies that the evidential underdetermination of a semantic theory is parallel to the evidential underdetermination of a physical theory. But his argument in this regard is unconvincing. Specifically, Quine maintains that "Natural science . . . is underdetermined by all possible observation. However, suppose that we have settled for one of the many over-all theories of nature that fit all possible observation. Translation remains indeterminate, even relative to the chosen theory of nature. Thus the indeterminacy of translation is an indeterminacy additional to the underdetermination of nature" (1987, 10). It is difficult to have anything other than a 'So what?' reaction to this argument, for it shows only that the underdetermination of our semantic theory is not *the same* underdetermination as that of our physics. Certainly we could arbitrarily 'fix' one and the other would remain underdetermined. The same thing could be said about biology and physics. The point seems entirely irrelevant to the issue.

Of course, Quine's conclusion would seem to hold if we (circularly) presuppose a behaviorist linguistics in which mental meanings are merely legislated away *a priori*. But this view is highly implausible, as Chomsky demonstrated twenty-five years ago (see Chomsky 1959). Meaning appears to be as much a part of the world as anything else. In Quine's idiolect (or in mine), 'rabbit' refers to the enduring animal or it does not, and this is a fact about Quine (or me), just as much as eye color or height.

Moreover, Quine's arguments not only fail to show that there is no fact of the matter about meaning; they also fail to show that we cannot choose between the competing theories, even when they are empirically equivalent. For example, it is presumably clear that one theory about Quine's idiolectal meaning for 'rabbit' is *far* simpler than the other. Thus we can choose—and should choose and do choose—the (simpler) theory in which Quine just means *rabbit* by 'rabbit', rather than the other one in which he means *rabbit stage*. Again, simplicity is crucial to the adjudication of *any* claims. As Pierre Duhem observed, and as Quine has emphasized, we can always reconstrue a theory in such a way as to make it fit the data. Thus, we can make 'Human beings are made of green cheese' a perfectly empirically adequate claim. We can make it empirically equivalent to 'Human beings are not made of green cheese'. Without reference to simplicity, we have no way of adjudicating between these claims. Indeed, by Quine's principle that undecidability entails an absence of fact, without reference to simplicity we have no basis upon which to claim that there even is a fact about whether or not human beings are made of green cheese. And since

Quine appears to allow no place whatsoever for simplicity considerations in this context (no doubt owing to his peculiar conception of simplicity, discussed earlier), this would seem to land him in the absurd position of denying that there is a fact about anything—since all pairs of contradictories can be rendered empirically equivalent and cannot be adjudicated without reference to (relative, contextual) simplicity. Quine's only escape from this dilemma is through the insistence that undecidability entails an absence of fact only for mental phenomena and not for physical phenomena. But, again, this is an implausible distinction.

On the other hand, these criticisms may interpret Quine's thesis too narrowly. Jerrold Katz has argued persuasively that Quine did not intend his indeterminacy thesis to be independent of his argument against the analytic/synthetic distinction (see Katz 1988). In his extremely influential essay, "Two Dogmas of Empiricism," Quine maintained that one of the main preoccupations of Anglo-American philosophy, the one from which it drew its name—*Analytic* philosophy—was impossible. We just cannot definitively analyze the semantic constituents of a term, because there is no fact of the matter about what is part of the meaning of a term and what is merely an emprical belief about the objects to which that term refers.

Many writers, such as Chomsky and Jackendoff, feel, understandably, that this is a superficial problem, a mere quibbling over peripheral cases. As Jackendoff puts it, "Unclear cases of doors and tigers do not make the distinction between doors and nondoors or between tigers and nontigers incoherent; why then should such cases be grounds for rejecting the analytic-synthetic distinction?" (1983, 117). But the fluidity of even idiolectal meaning and empirical belief is not confined to peripheral issues. Thus, as Geoffrey Sampson points out, we tend to think that 'male' is just part of the meaning of 'father'. But suppose we are in a society in which a significant minority of men have sex-change operations after begetting a child. In this case, when we hear someone refer to 'Jane's father' and assume the person to be *male,* we are clearly dealing with an empirical belief and not a linguistic analysis. According to Katz, this perceived fluidity causes Quine to conclude that there is no such thing as a correct analytical hypothesis, because there is no such thing as a correct analysis, because there is no firm fact about meaning isolated from empirical belief.

Unlike many of Quine's critics, I agree that the analytic/synthetic distinction is almost hopeless. But I do not see that, ultimately, this helps Quine out any on indeterminacy. It does follow that in translation/interpretation one should not formulate analytical hypotheses in the technical sense, because there is no fact of the matter about semantic analysis as such—and this is not insignificant. But then, even according to Quine, there still should be facts about strongly and weakly held empirical beliefs. So 'male' is not technically *analytic* of 'father'—but most of us have a strongly held belief about fathers being male. And that is all we need.

More exactly, recent work in semantics has emphasized that idiolects are formed in such a way as to incorporate hierarchies of rules—formed through the usual generation of hypotheses, revision, and so forth—that govern our use or interpretation of terms. Jackendoff discusses these under the rubric of "preference rule systems." As Jackendoff explains, "a preference rule system has the correct formal properties to account for the characteristics of word meanings—in particular, to cope with the gradation of judgments [of centrality or 'definitionality'] and with the existence of exceptions to many apparently defining conditions" (139). Similarly, Holland et al. understand all cognition, including meaning, to operate through a complex of rules arranged in a "default hierarchy" (for instance, a father might be female—after a sex-change operation—but, given no information about an operation, the "default" assumption for 'father' is 'male'). As Holland et al. explain, "people will induce a rule cluster corresponding [for example] to the category or concept 'dog'. Such a category may be regarded as a set of probabilistic assumptions about what features go with what other features and what consequences are to be expected given various antecedents" (1986, 17). Thus, Quine's critique of analysis in no way implies that there is no fact of the matter for interpretation/translation but only that there is no strictly *analytic* fact of definition. We should not hypothesize absolute and definitive meanings in idiolects. But this is no reason to avoid hypothesizing complexes of hierarchized rules—which, in fact, we have every reason to do.[6]

Thus, once again, we do not seem to face any special problems with interpretation, any problems of principle, but only practical problems—however serious these may be. Moreover, the fact that these problems are practical, if often serious, indicates the importance of theoretical rigor in interpretation. Practical difficulties can, most often, be lessened by rational procedures. In-principle impossibilities, however, are irremediable. As a number of researchers have shown, unreflective, everyday inferences turn out to be seriously flawed in complex cases (see, for example, Nisbett and Ross 1980; Holland et al. 1986, 165ff.). Inferential procedures can, however, be modified by adherence to explicit procedures of the sort we have sought to isolate. In other words, it would at least seem that practical difficulties, including tacit biases, may be limited by a sort of critical self-consciousness about one's inferential procedures.

Recently, however, Stanley Fish has articulated a third variation on the theme of inadjudicability, a variation aimed at precisely this notion of critical self-consciousness. In, for example, "Critical Self-Consciousness, or Can We Know What We're Doing?" and elsewhere, Fish contends that any hypothesis of critical self-consciousness "requires . . . a mind capable of standing to the side of its own ways of thinking in order to critique them" (1989, 437), and this, Fish maintains, is just not possible. Specifically, there is no "objective standpoint" that does not "presuppose some set of already-in-place distinctions, hierarchies, values, definitions," and so on (440). And thus there is no neutral ground upon which self-conscious self-criticism could take place.

There seem to be at least three different issues here. The first concerns the degree to which there is a practical problem with rationality; it concerns the degree to which interpretations and so forth that claim to be rational or objective are in fact rational or objective. (For instance, is irrationality a matter of occasional flukes, or is it systematic and pervasive?) The second and third concern matters of principle. In one case, the question is whether or not absolute objectivity is possible and is related to the issue of whether or not we can get our conceptual scheme right, whether or not there are rational criteria for evaluating the referential accuracy of our conceptual scheme, and so forth. In the other case, the question is whether or not we can rationally evaluate and adjudicate particular alternatives in particular areas.

As to the first issue, I believe that there is an enormous and very important practical problem in this regard, a pervasive and systematic problem (see Hogan 1990a, chapter 5; 1993). Let us take a simple case. We all have a cognitive bias toward confirmatory data, data that support strongly held beliefs (see Nisbett and Ross 1980, chapter 8; Mahoney 1977; Mahoney 1987). For example, many people have a strong stereotype about the relation between mathematical abilities and gender. Such people will have a general tendency to see women who fail mathematics as failing (in large part) because they are women and men who succeed as succeeding (in large part) because they are men. Thus, if over the course of several years, a person with such a strong stereotype sees half the men in a certain mathematics program fail and half the women fail—the other half of each group succeeding—his/her (unreflective) inclination will be to take the successful men and unsuccessful women as confirmatory of the stereotype, with the other cases being classed as exceptions. Thus he/she will tend to dismiss what is in fact strongly disconfirming evidence and tacitly reconstrue a disconfirmatory set of data as confirmatory of his/her prior hypothesis (or prejudice). The problems only become worse when the situation is more complicated. This raises the obvious question: what can be done about such biases? And this leads us to the two issues of principle.

As to the first issue of principle, that of absolute objectivity, the very notion makes no sense to me. As already mentioned, it seems to mean something like beginning with a correct conceptual scheme—what Milton's God presupposes when He congratulates Adam for having "rightly nam'd" the animals (*Paradise Lost* 8.439). But the notion of getting one's conceptual scheme right makes sense only on the presupposition of essentialism, which, as I argue in chapter 2, is at best ontologically implausible and epistemologically obscure (at least in our lapsarian condition). Thus Fish's arguments in this regard, though lacking something in scope and rigor, have a certain point. If writers such as Stephen Toulmin—one of Fish's main targets—mean to claim that we can divest ourselves completely of beliefs, interests, and such and just observe naked reality, reality as it 'really is organized and classed in and of itself', then Fish is right to point out that such writers are mistaken.

But what of the second question of principle, what of the view that one can indeed rationally evaluate particular principles, that one can retreat to a level of common belief and debate alternatives, constructing valid or invalid arguments and so on, as argued above, contra Kuhnian relativism? As far as I can tell, Fish has not presented us with any reason to believe that this is not possible. He has pointed to the in-principle impossibility of having *no* presuppositions and he has pointed to practical difficulties with various sorts of adjudications. But he has given us no reason to believe that it is not possible to become aware of certain of one's relevant presuppositions and therefore to think more rationally about a certain issue. Moreover, since there at least seem to be many cases of just this sort of self-reflection and self-criticism, the burden of proof would appear to be on him. John Earman has made much the same point in connection with a perhaps related assertion of Kuhn's. Specifically, Kuhn has claimed that "there is . . . no theory-independent way to reconstruct phrases like 'really there'; the notion of a match between the ontology of a theory and its 'real' counterpart in nature . . . seems . . . illusive in principle" (quoted in Earman 1993, 18). Earman replies, "I need not demur if 'theory' is understood in a *very* broad sense to mean something like a conceptual framework so minimal that without it 'the world' would be undifferentiated Kantian ooze. But I do demur if 'theory' is taken in the ordinary sense, i.e., as Newton's theory or special-relativity theory or general-relativity theory" (18).

Let us return to the more ordinary case of sex and mathematics, as we have considered broader theory/language issues already in connection with Kuhn and Quine. One person's intuitive feeling about the situations he/she has observed may be that they prove men have mathematical ability and women do not. Suppose, however, that such a person becomes aware of confirmatory bias and decides actually to determine, by explicit and self-conscious calculation, the percentages of males and females who have failed the mathematics course in question. Suppose, further, that this person discovers that the same percentage from each group failed. Even without previously changing his/her general stereotype, such a person would have critically reflected on a belief (that women had a greater tendency than men to fail a given mathematics course), examined the evidence through explicitly formulated procedures, and changed that belief.

A slightly more complex and historically realistic example may clarify the point further. Men have traditionally done better on the mathematics SAT. For a long time, virtually everyone assumed that this meant that men have greater mathematics abilities. This was certainly a possible hypothesis. But a rational and self-critical inferential procedure involves the generation and examination of alternative hypotheses. And very few such hypotheses were generated and examined. After many years, several researchers hypothesized that perhaps this discrepancy might be a matter not of men having greater ability but of men having spent more time studying mathematics. This gave rise to further investigations, as early studies did not control for this variable. As Anne Fausto-Sterling reports, "work that attempted to control for both the number of math courses and the number of related courses in areas such as mechanical drawing and drafting sometimes found only small sex-related differences favoring boys" (1985, 55). These remaining differences have most often been interpreted to mean that men do indeed have superior mathematical abilities, but in lesser degree than was previously thought. Other studies indicate, however, that, owing to a number of factors, boys and girls who have taken the same number of math and math-related courses will not in fact have *studied* mathematics the same amount. (The reasons range from differences in parental pressure to differences in instructor's attention [see Fausto-Sterling 1985, 57–59].) Thus existing research has yet fully to control for the crucial variable. In any case, what seems to have happened here is that an obvious, and evidentially well-supported hypothesis—that math skill varies not with sex but with amount of math studied—was for many years not brought forth or investigated because of ideological bias. The eventual generation and examination of the new hypothesis evidently involved a questioning of that bias, a recognition of certain presuppositions—not *all* presuppositions about *everything* but certain presuppositions about what sorts of factors might go to explain certain differences in SAT scores. (Note that even those who maintain a belief in superior male mathematical abilities now tend to see them as less in degree and as only one factor in the SAT discrepancies.) Moreover, the generation of further hypotheses, the recognition that even the recent studies have significant uncontrolled variables, indicates a project for future research that may further revise standard views on gender and mathematics. Fish has given us no reason to believe that the self-conscious critics who generated the alternative hypotheses are no more rational than the earlier analysts who unquestioningly posited sex-based abilities; he has given us no reason to believe that critical self-consciousness did not involve the isolation, criticism, and rejection of false prejudices—still less, that such critical reflection did not occur at all. The point holds for interpretations of speech and writing no less than for the explanation of test results.

Fish does acknowledge that certain sorts of argument might be accepted by an antagonist, and that someone previously opposed to a given thesis might have a change of heart (see 1989, 461). In this connection, Fish emphasizes, correctly, that arguments inducing such a change of heart will rely on principles to which the person in question already holds. But, again, nothing follows from this about critical self-consciousness. The point indicates once more that *absolute* critical self-consciousness (whatever that might be) is impossible. But that is all. In the case just cited, we can observe critical self-consciousness about a belief in superior male ability. This is not in the least affected by the fact that there are and can be no cases of critical self-consciousness about this and all other beliefs simultaneously. As Clifford Geertz has put it, "I have never been impressed by the argument that, as complete objectivity is impossible . . . (as, of course, it is), one might as well let one's sentiments run loose. As Robert Solow has remarked, that is like saying that as a perfectly aseptic environment is impossible, one might as well conduct surgery in a sewer" (Geertz 1973, 30).

Of course, Fish's point would indeed hold if there were no fact of the matter about any issue, if there were no such thing as a claim that is true or false independent of our beliefs. Granted this, Fish's position makes more sense. If there just is no fact as to whether or not gender is a causal factor in mathematics success, then reexamining one's views in this regard, generating more adequate hypotheses, and so forth cannot be considered a matter of critical self-conscious overcoming even 'local' bias. It is change but not critique, alteration but not advancement. However, the relativist view of truth is logically incoherent and based on trivial skepticism. As we have already discussed, even the strongest arguments in its favor rely on implausible premises. The position cannot be disproved (after all, the relativist is free to deny all our methodological principles). But we have no reason to accept it. Nor is it even completely clear what it might mean truly to accept such a logically inconsistent and wildly unsimple view of the world.

Thus we have seen that the *object* of interpretation is stipulative and that the first task of a theory of interpretation is not to discover the 'true nature' of meaning but to specify what sort or sorts of meaning actually exist (the topic of chapter 2) and which of these are of concern to a certain discipline, project, or whatever (the topic of chapters 3 through 5 with respect to law, psychoanalysis, and literary criticism). We have also seen that the most general *method* of interpretation is the most general method of theorization: hierarchical explanatory construction based on data, prior construction (or theory), logic, and the Principle of Minimal Interpretation. Finally we have seen that, despite widespread beliefs among humanists, there is no problem of relativity or of in-principle inaccessibility that faces theorization in general or interpretation in particular. There is, rather, only the usual problem of uncertainty, the problem of possible error, which affects any empirical judgment in greater or lesser degree, and which should only encourage us to follow the principles of rational inference more self-consciously and more rigorously.

2 THE LIMITS OF STIPULATION

On the Possibility of Nonintentional Meaning

In the preceding chapter, I argued that meaning is purely stipulative. It is merely a matter of decision (explicit or implicit, individual or collective) whether we take 'meaning' to refer to authorial intent, or common reader response, or whatever. But, again, it does not follow that *anything* can be stipulated as meaning, for the simple reason that not everything exists. Or, rather, though anything can be called 'meaning', there are some things we cannot examine in a text—because they do not exist, because they are like unicorns or snark. Indeed, certain sorts of things commonly claimed to constitute meaning are, in my view, ontologically worse off than unicorns. We can, after all, imagine a situation in which unicorns would be found. Though we have no reason now to believe that they exist, we could imagine finding such a reason—and, indeed, finding such a thing. In the following pages, however, I argue that the situation is different with the four most commonly championed sorts of extraintentional meaning. Not only do we have no reason now to believe that they exist, the entities themselves are so conceptually obscure and so hazy as explanatory principles that it is hard to imagine a situation in which we could have reason to believe that they exist, for it is hard to imagine what it would mean for them to exist or how their existence could make any difference to us.

I take the most widely accepted varieties of nonintentional meaning to be: 1) social, 2) autonomous, 3) essentialist, and 4) what I shall call 'representational'. It is worth saying a word about each before beginning my criticisms. Social meanings are the meanings of language insofar as it is understood to exist as a 'social object' in some sense independent of individual intents, a social object of which individual intents are mere approximations. Some (though by no means all) Marxist and sociological thinkers implicitly hold to this view, but it has been explicitly defended by English and American philosophers of language and logic, such as Michael Dummett and Saul Kripke (in his interpretation of Wittgenstein). Thus,

I shall concentrate my criticisms upon the arguments presented by these two writers, especially Kripke.

Autonomous meaning is meaning conceived of as part of an extra-intentional, sometimes even counterintentional, abstract linguistic system. Along with social meaning, this view has probably had the most important place in and greatest influence upon the theory and practice of interpretation. This is indicated by the fact that the best-known contemporary autonomist is also the most influential literary theorist—Jacques Derrida. However, Derrida, like most autonomists, assumes linguistic autonomy without any explicit argument, or even any explicit formulation of the position, though he does offer hints as to what his argument might be. As far as I am aware, Jerrold Katz is the only autonomist (or "Platonist," as he prefers) who has offered explicit arguments for autonomism. As I have discussed and criticized Derrida elsewhere (see chapter 2 of Hogan 1990a), I shall concentrate on Katz's arguments in this section.

The next variety of meaning I should like to consider is essentialism, the position that the meaning of a referential term is given in the essence of the object to which it refers—the essence of water for the term 'water', that of gold for the term 'gold'. This position has been vigorously defended by Saul Kripke, as well as Hilary Putnam, and has serious ramifications for the entire preceding argument—in that it should affect the term 'meaning' just as it affects 'water' and 'gold'. Clearly, however, Kripke's argument relies upon the assumption that there are essences. I shall argue that all of the data Kripke cites in support of positing essences are explainable by reference to intent and matter alone, without essences—and thus that essences are redundant. Moreover, I shall further argue that the notion of an essence is so vague as to be of no explanatory value anyway. Even if the data Kripke cites were problematic, essences would provide no solution.

Finally, I shall turn to representationalism. Having brilliantly examined and analyzed a wide range of linguistic data, Noam Chomsky has concluded that such data are inexplicable without the positing of nonintentional, mental processes involving the application of rules to absolutely introspectively inaccessible mental representations. I shall argue that in fact the data Chomsky cites are for the most part explicable by reference to intention and some general cognitive capacities, and that even in the few cases that remain unexplained, representationalism provides no adequate account because of the obscurity of the causal connections it posits.

SOCIAL MEANING

The majority of linguistic theorists today explain language by reference to idiolect, refusing to grant nonidiolectal language—social, autonomist, and so forth—any ontological or epistemological status. The most famous and influential arguments against the positing of some sort of language over and above idiolect have been made by Noam Chomsky. As Chomsky puts it, "a person's language should be defined" in terms of "the grammar represented in his/her mind" and "if one wants to try to reconstruct" the "vague everyday notion of language," this "should be explained in terms of the real systems represented in the minds of individuals [that is, idiolects] and similarities among these" (Chomsky 1980, 120). Elsewhere, he explains that "E-language," which is to say, nonidiolectal language, "was the object of study in most of traditional or structuralist grammar or behavioral psychology" but it "is now regarded as an epiphenomenon at best" (Chomsky 1986, 25). In addition, writers from such non-Chomskyan fields as sociolinguistics and discourse analysis concur. For example, Hudson points out in his introduction to sociolinguistics that "society consists of individuals," and thus "both sociologists and sociolinguists would agree that it is essential to keep the individual firmly in the centre of interest." Indeed, "we can be sure that *no two speakers have the same language*" (12). In other words, no autonomous language, no dialects, and so forth, exist, or, more generally, "varieties [of language] do not exist"; rather, "all that exists are individuals and [idiolectal] items" (Hudson 1980, 40). Brown and Yule make a similar point when they assert, as a basic principle of discourse analysis, that "it is speakers and writers who have topics, not texts" (Brown and Yule 1983, 68, see also 94), a point made earlier by philosophers of language, such as P. F. Strawson and John Searle (see Strawson 1950; Searle 1979, 155).

In sum, meanings are things individual speakers mean. Grammatical and other rules of language exist only in the minds of individual speakers/hearers; they are solely and simply idiolectal rules. The notion of an independent language is merely an abstraction, a generalization, from a set of extensively reconciled idiolects, idiolects which share many rules, and even more practices (for identical practices can result from distinct rules), and which individual speakers try regularly to reconcile further still. Clearly, there is a 'social' aspect to our knowledge and use of language. We learn language through social interaction and use language communicatively. Indeed, the noncommunicative functions of language are, it seems, subsequent to and derivative of the communicative functions. (We will return to this point in the section on representationalism.) In this sense, my view of language is extremely 'social'. But none of this indicates that there is, beyond individual idiolects, some social language, some shared conceptual scheme or common semantic space in which members of a community participate, or which provides normative linguistic principles for members of such a community. Advocates of social meaning, in the sense in which I am using the phrase, maintain precisely this—that meaning is an actual social phenomenon distinct from individual meaners, that grammatical principles are not idiolectal, that idiolects are defined with respect to language and not vice versa.

As already noted, the social position has been widely held by interpretive theorists. For example, Clifford Geertz views the nonidiolectal, social existence of language as firmly established and urges his readers "to see to it that the news . . . reaches anthropology" (Geertz 1973, 12). Though writing after the relevant developments in linguistic theory, he cites as self-evidently ludicrous the idea that "the progressive form of the verb" is "a characteristic of someone's mind . . . cognitive structure, or whatever" (13). In fact, far from being self-evidently ridiculous, this is probably a pretty accurate picture of what the progressive form of the verb actually is.

The general view that Geertz and others espouse, but most often do not defend, is well articulated by Michael Dummett: "A language, in the everyday sense, is something essentially social, a practice in which many people engage; and it is this notion, rather than that of an idiolect, which ought to be taken as primary. We cannot, indeed, dispense with the notion of idiolect, representing an individual's always partial, and often in part incorrect, understanding of his language; but it needs to be explained in terms of the notion of a shared language, and not conversely" (Dummett 1993, 30–31). Unlike many advocates of this position, Dummett offers at least one reason for construing the relation between idiolect and 'social language' in this way—"the phenomenon called by Putnam the 'linguistic division of labour'" (31). Putnam's notion concerns the fact that when we do not know the meaning of a word, we defer to experts to discover that meaning. Thus we defer to physicists to discover what a 'cathode ray' might be and to zoologists for the precise definition of 'marsupial'. Clearly, however, when we defer to such an expert, we are asking the expert how he/she and others like him/her use the term in question. In other words, when we ask a zoologist about 'marsupial' we are asking about his/her intent and his/her judgment on the common intentional/

idiolectal meaning of the term for a certain number of people, the 'experts'. Moreover, these people are considered 'experts' not because they have special knowledge about nonintentional or nonidiolectal, social meanings, but rather because they deal with people whose mutually reconciled idiolects actively include 'marsupial', people who talk about, read about, write about, and work with marsupials. (Putnam might add that experts know what marsupials 'really are'. This bears not upon questions of *social* meaning but upon questions of *essential* meaning. We shall turn to these below.) Thus when we seek to adjust our idiolect to the 'social language', we are merely seeking to adjust our idiolect to the idiolects of others. There is nothing but the idiolects, the individual intents, and these are all that we need to explain the facts.[1]

Thus 'social language' is, at least in this case, redundant with respect to idiolect or intent. Moreover, it is inscrutable with respect to these. Anyone who speaks of 'social meaning' or 'social language' must conceive of it as identical with common features of intents or not, that is, as an abstraction from idiolects or as something in addition to those idiolects. If proponents of social meaning conceive of this meaning as identical with common features of intents, as merely an abstraction from idiolects, then they are merely claiming that there are common features of individual intents, that one may abstract from partially reconciled idiolects, that individual idiolects may be judged by their degree of reconciliation with the idiolects of others in the community. If this is all Dummett wishes to claim, there is no substantive disagreement but merely a trivial terminological discrepancy.

If, on the other hand, social meaning or social language is thought by its advocates to *differ* from common intent, if it is thought *not* to be a mere abstraction from idiolects, there is substantive disagreement, and the question arises as to whether or not such an entity would help us to explain anything even if there were unexplained data. Let us imagine, then, that there is a nonintentional, social language, a social language distinct from common intent, irreducible to idiolects. Suppose then that we defer to experts on the meaning of 'marsupial'. Once again, the experts are going to be familiar with the common intentional meaning of the term in their group or profession. In each case, the expert we query will give his/her own intentional meaning as he/she understands that to be reconciled with the intentional meanings of other 'experts'. Similarly, when he/she speaks, he/she will undertake to make his/her intentional meaning accord with the intentional meanings of those with whom he/she is speaking. In whatever manner the nonintentional, social meaning might be said to exist, there is no obvious way in which it could be made accessible to perception or inference. Even if we could not explain our deference to experts in terms of common intent or abstraction from idiolects, social meaning would provide no solution for it is not clear how anyone, including experts, could have access to it—except insofar as they have access to common intent.

The point can be made most clearly by a somewhat silly example. Suppose that the social meaning of 'marsupial' is *lampshade*. Now, when a zoologist-in-training is introduced to the term 'marsupial', it is defined as a sort of animal lacking a placenta and having, instead, a pouch. It is defined in this way because this is the way zoologists use the term, that is, their common intentional or idiolectal meaning. Furthermore, when out in the field, he/she sees people running after wombats and shouting, 'Catch that marsupial!' or cuddling baby bandicoots and cooing 'That's Mama's little marsupial.' Or perhaps our trainee hears a colleague, about to move Down Under, allude to the kangaroo by repeating the words of old Mrs. Roxburgh, from Patrick White's *A Fringe of Leaves:* "There are compensations for living in Van Diemen's Land—some very quaint marsupials" (see White 1976, 78). However, he/she pretty much never sees anyone shading his/her eyes before a bright, naked bulb, and saying, 'That light is too bright. Why don't you get a marsupial for it?' Though, if he did, it would indicate that 'marsupial' meant *lampshade—in that speaker's idiolect,* independent of what it might mean in social language. Thus he/she learns common intent, and judges others' usage by common intent, but has no way, or no obvious way, of learning or judging by reference to any social meaning distinct from common intent, which is to say, distinct from the idiolects whose common properties constitute common intent.

Thus, social language is an epistemologically useless notion, whether or not intent or idiolect might be adequate to resolve the problems raised by its advocates. In other words, whatever inadequacies there may be in an intentional or idiolectal notion of language, social language or meaning cannot be a solution, for it, evidently, has no explanatory capacity.

This point is, I believe, well-illustrated by Dummett's invocation of "social practice" as explanatory of nonidiolectal social meaning. Dummett fully acknowledges that a theory of meaning must involve a theory of "implicit knowledge" on the part of individual speakers/hearers and cannot be reduced to an account of "social practice" (Dummett 1993, 103–4). However, he also believes that some notion of an idiolect-independent "social practice" is necessary for a theory of meaning. "I am urging," he explains, "an adaptation of Alice's picture, according to which words have meanings in themselves, independently of speakers. Of course, they do not have them intrinsically, and hence independently of anything human beings do. They have them in virtue of belonging to the language, and hence in virtue of the existence of a social practice. But they have them independently of any particular speakers" (quoted in Gorman 1993, 223). Donald Davidson, who has defended a strongly intentionalist position (see Davidson 1986) has characterized those who put forth such views in the following terms: "There are those who are pleased to hold that the meanings of words are magically independent of the speaker's intentions" (quoted in Gorman 1993, 225). Davidson is, I think, basically right in referring to such views as "magical" in that they discount relatively clear descriptions and relatively comprehensible explanations as inadequate, only to replace them with obscure descriptions and opaque explanations. The notion of "social practice" illustrates the point. The most obvious meaning of "social practice" is something like the following: 'the activities of individual men and women, construed in terms of their intentions, beliefs, and so on, and the current (and perhaps historical) relations between these'. But, in the case of language, this definition is, precisely, idiolectal. It posits only speech practices based on the intentions of (interacting) individual speakers. Yet Dummett presents social practice as something different from idiolect. What, then, could it be? In what sense is there an activity engaged in by individual people yet different from the interacting (cooperating, contradicting, mutually adjusting) practices of those individual people? I can see no way of making sense of the idea. Far from explaining something about language, it seems only to muddle up what is otherwise a clear and perfectly adequate account.

It is worth noting that these points are generalizable to social accounts of other sorts—for example, class analyses. To say that a class has certain interests can mean nothing other than that the individuals comprising that class in general share those interests. To say that a class acts in a certain way is to say nothing except that subjects in a certain group generally act in that way. If the notion of class is thought of as anything other than a generalization across individuals then it becomes both redundant and opaque. This is not to say, of course, that there are not statistical properties that apply to groups. There certainly are such properties. Nor is it to say that individuals should be thought of as acting for entirely private reasons and in utter isolation—quite the contrary, as I have already stressed in the case of language. Nor does it mean that we should stop talking about classes and instead name and describe each relevant individual. What it does mean is that when we speak of a class in this sense we are not speaking of anything *in addition to* the individuals who comprise that class (compare Kripke 1980, 50).

Returning to the issues at hand, Michael Dummett is not, again, the only writer to have argued that meaning is necessarily social rather than idiolectal. In recent years the most important and influential work in this area has probably been that of Saul Kripke, specifically his explication of Ludwig Wittgenstein's "private language argument" (Kripke 1982). I should like to define the problems raised by Kripke/Wittgenstein and then briefly criticize Kripke/Wittgenstein's solution to these problems, before going on to propose an alternative analysis.[2]

Kripke spends considerable time trying to establish the relevant problems in order that readers might get a feel for what is at stake. I cannot seek this effect and thus can only refer the reader to Kripke's excellent second section. In any event, the crux of the argument is this: Suppose that I am adding two numbers. I feel, believe, claim that I am following a rule in doing this addition. Moreover, I feel, believe, claim that I have for some time followed that rule and will continue to follow it in the future (barring disaster). Finally, I feel, believe, claim that the rule I am following is the right one. But how can I possibly justify any of these feelings, beliefs, claims? I might think I'm following a rule in adding two numbers, but, in fact, I might just be generating a third number randomly. Similarly, I might be following a rule, but one different from that or those I followed in the past, and, moreover, different from the rules followed by others. I certainly cannot have recourse to consistency of past behavior, for *some* rule can be construed that would be accurately instantiated in any set of 'additions'. Thus, given '1 + 1 = 2', '2 + 2 = 4', '8 + 14 = 22', and many similar formulae of two digits or less, I can find a rule that yields '102 + 104 = 206', but I can also find a rule that will yield '102 + 104 = 7'. For example, the rule might be the 'normal' rule of addition qualified as covering only numbers of two digits or less with all numbers of three digits or more summing to seven.

The point here is that absolutely any counting behavior on my part will be consistent with *some* rule. Thus absolutely any behavior on my part— for instance, adding 102 and 104 and coming up with 7—will be justifiable as rule-governed. Moreover, as this is true of every one of us, and of every set of possible additions, the notion that one or another rule is the 'right' rule of addition, and thus the notion that any given rule any of us might be following is right or wrong, loses any sense it might have had. So too, it would seem, does the notion of addition.

I should emphasize that this problem of rule-following applies across the board. Crucially, it applies to reference. Thus absolutely anything I might today call a 'hamhock'—not only hamhocks, but marsupials, lampshades, or whatever—can be reconciled with my past behavior and thus judged justified. In other words, it is not only criteria for, say, mathematics that are at stake, but reference quite generally.

Kripke/Wittgenstein's solution to this is somewhat peculiar, I think. According to Kripke/Wittgenstein, we can make claims of meaning, and even of some individual's meaning, only in the context of a "form of life." This form of life defines "assertability conditions" for attributions of meaning. For Kripke/Wittgenstein, there is no time when attributions of meaning are true. However, there are times when such attributions can be uttered in the language game. In this case, such assertability comes with agreement. Thus, if I say '2 + 2 = 4' and you say the same, and I say '6 + 8 = 14' and you say the same, and so on, then either of us may say of the other that he/she is now adding and that he/she is doing it correctly. As Kripke puts it, "Any individual who claims to have mastered the concept of addition will be judged by the community to have done so if his particular responses agree with those of the community in enough cases" (1982, 91–92). It should be emphasized that in speaking of 'concepts' here "we depict no special 'state' of [others'] minds"—and thus, presumably, no fact about idiolects. Rather, in these attributions, we merely "take [others] into the community, as long as further deviant behavior does not exclude them" (95). I take it, then, that correctness—in addition, reference, or whatever—is, according to Kripke/Wittgenstein, some sort of nonidiolectal social practice.

But there are serious problems with this account. Judging agreement and deviance is itself a rule-governed activity in the relevant sense. If I say '3 + 2 = 5' and you say something, I judge it to be the same or not the same by following rules. Even such a simple matter as understanding regional and foreign accents shows that utterances of the word 'five', for example, are not self-evidently identical (think of a Boston accent, an Alabama accent, a Chinese accent). The same holds for script. Moreover, judging this equation to be a single unit, rather than a series of unrelated sounds, is rule-governed. Judgments of agreement are saturated with such rule-governed inferences. Thus, if Kripke/Wittgenstein's argument is successful against *addition,* it is equally successful against *agreement.* Indeed, it is successful against *assertion,* or, for that matter, against the references of 'reference', 'community', and all the other terms that go to make up the argument. There is absolutely no reason to substitute an agreement rule for an addition rule. Either the argument works, in which case both rules are useless—and meaningless, along with the argument itself—or the argument does not work, in which case we may as well stick with the (idiolectal) addition. As Wittgenstein—not Kripke/Wittgenstein—says, "it is no use . . . going back to the concept of agreement, because it is no more certain that one proceeding is in agreement with another, than that it has happened in accordance with a rule" (quoted in Baker and Hacker 1984, 44).

I should emphasize that I am not merely saying that we can make mistakes about agreement. That is obvious, and relatively unimportant. Rather, my point—and, I think, Wittgenstein's point—is that, granting Kripke/Wittgenstein's claims, there just can be no criterion of agreement whatsoever. And there can be no imputation of any sort either. Nothing can legitimately be termed 'agreement', 'imputation', 'recognition of agreement', 'criteria of assertability', 'taking into the community', and so forth, *unless* 'addition', 'reference', and so on may be defined and applied independently. If there is no addition except by agreement, then there is no agreement, except by agreement. But if agreement can only be established by reference to itself, then it cannot be established (similar points have been made by Blackburn, Hoffman, and others).[3]

Thus, Kripke/Wittgenstein's solution to the skeptical dilemma is inadequate, and the dilemma cannot be seen as lending support to the positing of social meaning. First of all, social meaning can have no normative or explanatory value relative to this dilemma as there is no way to exempt it from the skeptical argument, if the latter is at all valid. Indeed, the introduction of social meaning, here as elsewhere, merely renders the issue more obscure, the justificatory process more opaque. Second, and more important, Kripke/Wittgenstein's dilemma is not in fact a genuine problem. Rather, it is an ordinary skepticism based upon the possibility of generating empirically equivalent theories—in this case theories about what rules a given individual follows. Kripke's argument is merely that there are infinitely many theories that account for an individual's behavior in terms of rules. Thus, for addition, there is the 'ordinary' rule; the 'ordinary' rule plus the qualification 'except subtract 10 from all sums on 12 July 1997'; the ordinary rule plus the qualification, 'except all numbers over five billion, which sum to seven', and so on. Now, Kripke/Wittgenstein concludes from the existence of mutually contradictory empirical theories to the absence of any corresponding fact. Thus, for Kripke/Wittgenstein, as there can be different, empirically adequate *theories* of what rule I am following in addition, there is no *fact* as to what rule I am following in addition. But this is a *non sequitur* of the sort we have already encountered in discussing Quine's indeterminacy of translation thesis. The actual or possible existence of empirically equivalent theories about a state of affairs has no bearing on the determinacy or indeterminacy of the state of affairs itself. Kripke/Wittgenstein's argument has no serious ontological consequences. It says nothing at all about what there is or might be.

But do they say something about what we might know? In other words, do they indicate that, even if there is a fact of the matter about what rule we are following, we can never know what that rule is? Or, more to the point, do they indicate that we cannot proceed by rational means plausibly to evaluate competing hypotheses? Is there no way we can choose between imputing to ourselves or others the simple addition rule and imputing to ourselves or others that rule plus some temporal or other qualifications? Does Kripke/Wittgenstein's argument have serious *epistemological* consequences?

It will probably come as no surprise that I think not. I should immediately explain, however, that this is not owing to the supposed introspective accessibility of our rules (as, for example, Mulhall maintains). Once again, our knowledge about the rules we are following is inferential in precisely the sense that our knowledge of other people's rules is inferential. For this reason, we can ignore introspection and treat only the case of discerning the rules others are following. Clearly, if we resolve the problem with respect to others, we resolve it with respect to ourselves also—even outside of any concern for introspection.

So, the question is—are there rational, nonempirical means of adjudicating rival hypotheses regarding the rules other individuals are following? There seem to be two main contexts in which such adjudication might take place. One is that of cognitive psychology, or another scientific endeavor where the aim is accurately to *formulate* the rule or rules some person or people are following. The other is learning, usually childhood learning, where the aim is to *assimilate* the rule or rules some person or people are following, in order to follow such rules oneself. Once again, the situation is the same in each case: there are infinitely many, mutually contradictory theories consistent with the data.

To take an example from language acquisition, a child might infer from hearing 'churches', 'bridges', 'kisses', 'wishes', and so on that words ending in sibilants form plurals by postfixing the sound [əz]. But it is equally consistent with the data for him/her to infer that such words form the plural by postfixing the sound [əz] before 14 January 2010, and by prefixing the sound [kwa] thereafter. So, is there no rational procedure for decision? Certainly there is—choose the simpler alternative, hence the one lacking the temporal qualification. Maybe this will turn out to be the wrong choice, but, again, the *possibility* of error is part of any empirical judgment and its presence here is trivial. Adjudication by simplicity just is the rational procedure in this case. Moreover, it is apparently the method children actually use (see Holland et al., 1986, 79f.).

Of course, this is, and should be, the method cognitive psychologists, linguists, and other investigators use as well. A linguist investigating someone's linguistic competence might conclude from hearing 'churches' and so forth that the speaker follows a rule telling him/her to form plurals of words ending in sibilants by postfixing [əz], or he/she might conclude that the speaker follows a rule telling him/her to form such plurals by postfixing [əz] before 14 January 2010, and by prefixing [kwa] thereafter. Again, both are consistent with the data. But the linguist chooses the former, and for the same reasons as the child, only in this case with the added consideration that language acquisition itself seems to proceed by simplicity adjudications, at least in clear cases such as this. (There could, of course, be more difficult cases where the grammatically simplest hypothesis is not at all easy for a child to infer; in these cases the simpler choice for the investigator would be a somewhat more complex but more readily accessible rule. Once again, simplicity is contextual.)

Readers familiar with Nelson Goodman's writings will have recognized a close connection between Kripke/Wittgenstein's reflections and Goodman's "New Riddle of Induction." Indeed, Barry Allen has gone so far as to claim that "the skeptical argument [of Kripke/Wittgenstein] *is* Goodman's riddle of induction, tailored to field linguistics rather than mineralogy" (quoted in Hacking 1993, 284). As Goodman's views on induction have been widely influential, it is worth considering them briefly before continuing. Goodman begins by defining a predicate 'grue', which "applies to all things examined before t just in case they are green but to other things just in case they are blue." As Goodman explains, "we have, for each evidence statement asserting that a given emerald is green, a parallel evidence statement asserting that that emerald is grue. . . . Thus . . . the prediction that all emeralds subsequently examined will be green and the prediction that all will be grue are alike confirmed by evidence statements describing the same observations" (Goodman 1978, 74). But this is problematic, because we would never say that emeralds are grue. We would only say that they are green.

Goodman seeks to solve this riddle by appeal to a predicate's degree of "entrenchment," which is to say, roughly, the degree to which it is common, ordinary, widely used in our everyday practices. We choose to say that emeralds are green rather than grue because 'green' is a better entrenched predicate than 'grue' (see 94–98). One wonders why Goodman thinks that this is any kind of solution. First of all, it is not a justification of our choice of 'green' over 'grue', but merely a statement that we tend to be conservative. It is hard to see how the assertion 'We've always done it that way' could be a justification, except by reference to past success—but past success is relevant only if we draw inductive conclusions, and drawing inductive conclusions is precisely the problem. Second, and more important, our judgments about patterns in the world are shot through with inductive reasoning. Our inferences about people's use of the word 'green' are based in part on inductively derived beliefs about speech, about what people mean by what they say (not only 'green' but everything else), about how they refer to the world, and so on. If there is a real problem with induction, we cannot solve it by reference to entrenchment, because without induction, we cannot figure out what's well entrenched.

My solution, of course, is recourse to simplicity criteria. We choose 'green' because all of our theories about emeralds make it simpler to impute constancy of color; moreover, a wide range of our theories would have to be revised and greatly complicated to accommodate the possible shift in emerald color on a certain date. 'Emeralds are green' is, thus, a vastly simpler hypothesis than 'Emeralds are grue'. Goodman considers and denies this solution on the grounds that we can always make 'grue' and 'bleen' (blue before t, green after) our basic predicates, defining 'green' as 'grue before t, bleen after' (80). But this makes no sense. Simplicity is not a matter of which terms we use to define other terms. If this were so, we could define away all ad hoc qualifications to a given theory. Suppose one theory predicts the behavior of all particles of a certain sort, while another theory, with comparable posits and general principles, predicts the behavior of the same particles but requires two ad hoc qualifications (relating, for example, to the speed at which the particles are traveling and the substances through which they are passing). The former theory is clearly simpler. By Goodman's analysis, we could make the principles of the second theory 'basic'. Then, we could define the first theory so that it has to include 'qualifications'. These 'qualifications' would state that the predictions of the first theory need not be modified according to the speed at which the particles are traveling or the substance through which they are passing. But this definitional trick would hardly change the relative simplicity of the two theories. Returning to 'grue' and 'green', the difference here is not a matter of definitions but of the fact that all our theories indicate that emeralds will consistently reflect light from one part of the light spectrum and (under constant conditions) this reflection will not shift. Sure, we might someday change our minds about this—or about the structure of the color spectrum. Nothing in what I have said indicates that it is impossible for 'grue' to become a simpler hypothesis in certain circumstances—for example, if we have good reason to expect some strange astronomical event that will shift the color spectrum or permanently affect human color perception. But in no case will our simplicity orderings be determined by direction of definition (by whether 'grue' is defined by reference to 'green' or vice versa), as Goodman seems to imagine.

In sum, there seem to be no problems, either ontological or epistemological, arising from Kripke/Wittgenstein skepticism about rules or Goodman's related riddle of induction—and thus this skepticism appears to provide no difficulties for an idiolectal limitation of meaning and a generalized approach to inference by way of logic, evidence, and simplicity. Moreover, even if there were skeptical problems of the Kripke/Wittgenstein variety (or problems arising from the 'linguistic division of labor', as suggested by Dummett) the positing of social meaning would be useless. Social meaning is not only ontologically redundant but epistemologically inscrutable, and thus could have no explanatory or normative function in any case.

AUTONOMISM

By 'autonomism', I mean the doctrine that language has some extraindividual, nonsocial existence, that language, as a system, has its own independent being. Historically, this view extends back at least to Plato (see Ong 1982, 167–68 and citations), continues through such later classical writers as Quintillian (see Kenner 1987, 221), becomes crucial for the development of modern philosophical systems, such as that of Hegel (see Hogan 1980), and so on. In its contemporary development, there are two main forms of autonomism, one 'Platonist', the other 'structuralist'. The

THE LIMITS OF STIPULATION

former has found its most articulate expositor in Jerrold Katz. The latter has not been explicitly defended, as far as I am aware; however, it has been developed thoroughly and influentially by Jacques Derrida. (In fact, Derrida's position is not univocally autonomist, but his work certainly has many elements of autonomism.)

These positions differ in several ways. First of all, as to ontology, the linguistic Platonist position, a revision of Chomskyan linguistics articulated by Katz (1981), claims that a language exists as a series of abstract sentential objects, much like numbers in Platonistic mathematics. In this scheme, a language is constituted by a specific set of abstract sentences, along with all the structural relations these imply (see, for example, Katz 1981, 6, 206, and elsewhere). Structuralists, on the other hand, building upon Saussurean linguistics, tend to ignore sentences and concentrate on unanalyzed morphemes, or even words, claiming that each morpheme is defined in a 'system of differences'. In this scheme, it is a specific (autonomous) system of morphemes (and phonemes)—or, as these writers usually prefer, 'signifiers'—that constitutes a language. Thus, Derrida defines language in terms of "differance," which he in turn defines in these systemic/autonomist terms: "*Differance* is the systematic play of differences, of the traces of differences, of the *spacing* by means of which elements are related to each other" (Derrida 1981, 27).

There is a further, epistemological difference as well. Katz, following Platonistic mathematicians, insists that a subject can gain direct and immediate access to the Platonic realm of sentences through a faculty of 'intuition'. Derrida, on the other hand, claims that access to meaning is always partial, that the language always to a degree resists intent (see, for example, Derrida 1981, 158; and de Man 1983, 11). Katz's claim concerning a faculty of intuition is serious and well defended; however, I shall argue, it is ultimately inadequate. As I have already indicated, as far as I am aware, Derrida makes no argument defending the partial access he assumes—or the differential conception of meaning that is at the very foundation of his project; for this reason, and because I have already analyzed and criticized Derrida's principles at some length in another context (see Hogan 1990a), in the following I shall consider the position of Katz only.

Before going on to this, however, I should like to recapitulate the principle considerations that are guiding this examination. First of all, intention is, presumably, disputed by no one (except eliminative physicalists; we shall consider this view below). Thus the positing of autonomous meaning—or social or representational or essential meaning—is justified only insofar as it helps to account for data unexplained by intentional accounts, or possibly data explained in an inelegant manner by intentional accounts. If autonomist and related accounts do not increase the explanatory capacity of our theories, they are redundant with respect to intentional accounts. These are the *ontological* considerations.

Second, intentionalist accounts, positing no difference between intent and meaning, pose no problem concerning the possibility of intentional access to meaning, whether this access is conceived of as introspective or inferential. When I learn a language, I learn what certain speakers mean when they say certain things, what they will understand when I say certain things, and so on. There is no difference between our various intents on the one hand and 'the language' on the other. All nonintentional accounts, however, posit some extraintentional meaning. Thus, in each of these accounts, there *is* a difference between the various intents on the one hand and 'the language' on the other. This poses a problem of reconciling the two. It is my contention that no such reconciliation is possible. If the two are not reconciled, then we have no access whatsoever to 'the language per se' and thus it is entirely irrelevant to our speaking, interpreting, and so on. In other words, if we cannot get at 'the language', then 'the language' has no function for us. Therefore, it is theoretically, interpretively, explanatorily useless. Even if it turns out that intentional accounts are inadequate to the data, extraintentional accounts are of no value if intent cannot be reconciled with the extraintentional entities, if autonomous language and so on are inaccessible to intent. These are the *epistemological* considerations.

As to the ontological considerations, Katz presents two arguments that Chomsky's idiolectal representationalism—or, as he terms it, "conceptualism"—is empirically inadequate. These may be applied *pari passu* to intentionalism. The first argument concerns "the general epistemological distinction between knowledge that we have of something and the thing(s) that we have knowledge of" (1981, 77). Katz's argument here is, roughly, that the grammar known by the individual speaker cannot merely be the speaker's grammatical competence for, were this the case, the crucial epistemological distinction would be lost.

As Chomsky has indicated, arguments such as this derive at least in part from a systematic ambiguity in his own and related uses of the term 'grammar' (see Chomsky 1986, 28ff.). However, Katz's objection can be maintained independently of the resolution of this terminological ambiguity. Fundamentally, this, like many objections to idiolectal accounts, is a *criterial* objection. The problem is one of establishing criteria for grammatical validity. This is clear from Katz's comparison of grammars with mathematical theories or formulae. Katz points out that "We take Fermat's statement that no whole numbers exist such that $x^n+y^n=a^n$ (where n is a whole number greater than two) to be about *numbers*. Would anyone for a moment think of claiming the Wolfskehl prize for a demonstration about human mathematical competence or performance?" (77). For Katz, then, what makes (idiolectal) knowledge of a language actual *knowledge* is that it satisfies nonsubjective criteria defined by reference to the language itself, independent of individual speakers, which is to say, independent of idiolects. This, he maintains, is assimilable to the case of mathematical knowledge, which is actual knowledge insofar as it satisfies nonsubjective criteria defined by reference to numbers and so forth, independent of individual mathematicians.

Once again, however, the criteria for any particular grammar are given in the grammars of the community. The object of my knowledge is the common properties of the grammars of those in the community in which I am seeking to communicate—to understand and to speak understandably. As long as we have a notion of common intent, or language as an abstraction from extensively reconciled idiolects, there is no criterial problem for intentionalist accounts.[4]

Katz's second argument concerns analyticity and necessary truth. For Katz, there are certain sentences that are true analytically and a Platonist or autonomist meaning must be posited to account for this fact. For example, Katz claims that "Nightmares are dreams" and "If one succeeds in convincing Jones that his wife is dead, then Jones will believe that his wife is dead" are analytic statements and thus necessarily true. Their truth has nothing to do with "self-observation or observation of the external world" and is unrelated to psychological certainty (178). Following mathematical arguments put forth by Gottlob Frege and Edmund Husserl, Katz argues that this datum goes to indicate the inadequacy of idiolectal accounts. Leaving aside the serious problems with the very notion of analyticity, discussed above, and granting the analytic/synthetic distinction for the sake of argument, it should be clear that 'Nightmares are dreams' can count as analytic not if nightmares are in fact dreams, but if and only if 'nightmare' *means* a certain sort of dream. This is what analyticity is about. Now, 'nightmare' does mean a certain sort of dream *in the common intent of English speakers*. Thus, in ordinary English, 'Nightmares are dreams' is analytic—and it is analytic for precisely intentional/idiolectal reasons, for reasons having to do with what *people mean* by 'nightmare'. A similar analysis holds for the relation between convincing someone of something and that person believing that thing. Thus it would seem that Katz's data are easily accounted for by reference to intent or idiolect and without reference to autonomous language.

However, Katz claims that an account along these lines is inadequate. Specifically, following Husserl, Katz points out that if the truth of 'Nightmares are dreams' is contingent upon the truth of any empirical fact—in this case the communal intents regarding the terms—then 'Nightmares are dreams' is not necessarily true but only contingently true, even though it is analytic. For Katz, this is a *contradictio in adjecto* demonstrating the inadequacy of the idiolectal account.

But it is not a contradiction. All analytic statements are contingent in this sense. Whether one adopts an idiolectal account or not, it is still true that 'Nightmares are dreams' is analytic if and only if 'nightmare' means a certain sort of dream—and this is clearly a contingent fact. Katz's claims can be true if and only if 'nightmare' could not mean anything else, if and only if 'nightmare' *necessarily* means a certain sort of dream. But we can only make sense of this notion if we assume that the sound represented by the marks 'nightmare', or the marks themselves, are necessarily connected with the meaning, *a terrifying dream*. But this is obviously wrong. Not only might any given sound have meant something else, pretty much all of them have meant something else. (At one time, 'nightmare' referred to an evil spirit.) Again, no term is necessarily linked to any given meaning.

Of course, there is a certain necessity in analyticity. Given that 'nightmare' means 'a terrifying dream', then it is necessarily true that nightmares are dreams. But the necessity here has nothing to do with 'nightmares' meaning 'terrifying dreams'—this is a contingent empirical fact. Rather, the necessity concerns the relation between terrifying dreams and dreams. It is necessarily true that terrifying dreams are dreams. But this has no consequences for an intentional or idiolectal limitation of varieties of meaning.

Thus it seems that Katz's arguments from the nature of knowledge and the necessity of analyticity are both unsuccessful. Insofar as Katz points to real data in need of explanation, an intentional or idiolectal account seems entirely adequate.

The question remains as to whether autonomism would be of any explanatory use even if the data remained inexplicable. As we have already remarked, Katz, virtually alone amongst nonintentionalists, proposes a manner of reconciling intent and nonintentional, in this case autonomous, meaning—the "faculty" of intuition. According to Katz, there are three sorts of objects in the world—physical, mental, and "abstract." The first comprises everything from chairs to quarks. The second comprises intentional phenomena, as well as Kantian or Chomskyan 'mentalistic' phenomena. The last comprises numbers, sentences, and other Platonistic entities. In connection with these three ontological types, and permitting access to them, are three "faculties"—perception, introspection, and intuition (193). Through perception, we gain access to the physical world. Through introspection, we gain access to ourselves. Through intuition, we gain access to the Platonic realm of abstract objects.

Katz must recognize, however, that there are crucial differences between these faculties. Perception may be claimed to allow access to the material world as there are causal relations that obtain between the objects on the one hand and the faculty of perception, or some physiological correlates thereof, on the other. Introspection is in some ways hazier, but it does directly concern our own intents. Perception poses a relational problem because in it material objects are to be brought under intention. In introspection, in contrast, there is no difference between the intent and its object. The object is equally the subject (as the German Idealists were fond of saying). In this case, what appears puzzling is not that the two can be brought into relation but that this relation often fails, that introspection appears frequently to be mistaken. Indeed, introspection is probably best understood as a form of perception—in this case a perception of something subjective, such as a memory or desire, rather than something worldly, such as a chair or a tickle. The degree to which we can know or be certain about the objects of one or the other sort of perception, the degree to which we must use each sort of perception as the basis for inference, and so forth seem pretty much the same. Introspection can fail, then, for the same reason that external sensation can fail. First, in neither case do we directly perceive principles, regularities, and so on; these must be inferred, and such inferences are fallible. Second, even our perceptions of particulars (worldly or subjective) occur in the context of theories (expectations and such) and thus are themselves partially inferential, and thus fallible, if in lesser degree. (We will return to these points in chapter 4.) In any event, the point about causal continuity still holds. However limited introspection may be, the fact that we have some subjective perception of subjective phenomena does not seem causally opaque.

However we deal with introspection, though—whether we limit it, as just suggested, or grant it a broader scope—it is clearly different from

Katz's Platonistic intuition. Platonistic objects and intent are not of the same type. Indeed, that is Katz's whole point. So the problem of how the subject and object might be related arises here, as it did in the case of worldly perception. In the latter case, this relation was accounted for in terms of causal relations between objects and sense organs. Now, Katz could posit some nonphysical causal nexus operating from autonomous language to individual minds, though this would only change the problem from 'How are autonomous language and intent related?' to 'What is the nature of this nonmaterial causal relation?' It would change the terms of the debate without advancing the investigation. In any case, Katz assumes that any relation between intent and autonomous language must be noncausal, so the issue does not arise. But he still has to explain this relation. In order to do so, he posits a considerable mentalistic apparatus that allows the mental construction of an autonomous language from relatively little data—all of it gathered in the usual way (observation of interaction with fluent native speakers, explicit instruction, and so forth). In the process of construction, the sentences of the language are "depsychologized" and represented as abstract objects. As Katz puts it, a conception along these lines, "characterizes actual intuitions as a result of projections from an *a priori* enumeration of systems of competence which corrects and depsychologizes complexes of grammatical information and casts them into concrete form as concepts of sentences modelled on the notion of an abstract object" (206).

I may be failing to grasp Katz's point here, but I see no way in which this leads to abstract objects and intuition thereof. Even if we grant Katz's elaborate mentalism, the faculties he posits can function only to generate mentalistic entities which, through "depsychologization" are *thought of as* abstract. In other words, Katz's apparatus puts minds in touch not with abstract objects but, rather, with mental objects that are thought of as abstract. Autonomism thus becomes a species of representationalism—which Katz has rejected. In any event, the problem of access to Platonic entities remains unresolved.

There are further problems here as well. For example, what defines a language for Katz? Is there a Platonic realm of Black English, and Hiberno-English, and Indian English? How about Pidgins and Creoles? And is there a Platonic realm for each stage of each of these? And, if so, must there not be a Platonic realm for each idiolect? And how do these Platonic realms come into existence? Are they the product of historical developments, the results of changes in dialects and periods, hence the results of changes in idiolects? Or were they established in all their detail at the beginning of time by a divine being who, from the perspective of eternity, could foresee all the seemingly contingent developments of all languages?

It appears that little sense can be made of the notion of autonomous language. It is, in short, explanatorily vacuous. Moreover, it is, as we have seen, theoretically redundant, for all the relevant data are perfectly well explained by reference to intention or idiolect. Katz is no doubt right that many, perhaps most, people conceive of language in this 'depsychologized' way (or at least most literate people do—see Ong 1982, 78ff., on writing and the idea of "autonomous discourse"). Certainly many people talk about language as if it were autonomous. Indeed, Chomsky has pointed out that some notion along these lines dominated linguistics for many years (see, for example, Chomsky 1986, 19–20, 25). It has certainly dominated literary theory and practice from New Criticism through Deconstruction (as, for example, E. D. Hirsch has pointed out; see Rorty's discussion in Rorty 1991, 89). But this does not make autonomism any more plausible. It only makes it more important—more consequential— to recognize that the notion of autonomous language lacks both function and perspicuity.

ESSENTIALISM

In Book I, chapter 5, of the *Topics,* Aristotle wrote that "a definition is a phrase signifying a thing's essence" (Aristotle 1984, 169). This is the basic premise of essentialist theories of meaning, and like the other nonidiolectal views of meaning we have considered, it has a long and distinguished history. The tradition extends from "Plato's supposition in the *Cratylus,* that some power more than human gave things their first names, and that names are therefore mysteriously related to essences" (Kenner 1987, 325) through Husserl's normative view that "the eidos itself is a beheld or beholdable universal, one that is pure, 'unconditioned'—that is to say: according to its own intuitional sense, a universal not conditioned by any fact. It is *prior to all 'concepts',* in the sense of verbal significations; indeed, as pure concepts, these must be made to fit the eidos" (Husserl 1973, 71). Locke characterized this as the doctrine according to which *"Names of substances [are] referred . . . to real essences that cannot be known"* (Locke 1992, 263). William Carter characterizes contemporary essentialism in similar terms: "Semantic *determinateness* can be parsed in terms of a *favored semantic path*—roughly, a 'path' representing all and only correct applications of a given word. . . . [A] term's favored semantic path is fixed by real essence" (Carter 1986, 58–59). Clearly, the essentialist view has been of widespread and longstanding importance. (Indeed, some of my compatriots even appropriated this conception of language for nationalist purposes, maintaining "that Gaelic was descended from the only tongue to escape the miscegenation of Babel, and was consequently traceable by uninterrupted etymology back to Adam's speech which corresponded with the essences of things" [Kenner 1987, 349].)

Saul Kripke is no doubt the most significant contemporary essentialist. In his writings, essentialism is part of a broader conception of reference, which is nonstipulative, at least in certain aspects. Kripke's ideas are important to consider not only because they are directly opposed to those presented above and not only because they represent an important recent version of a longstanding tradition; they also bear examination because they have significantly influenced a range of current semantic and interpretive theories (such as in cognitive science [see Lycan 1990, 279], legal and literary interpretation [see Hirsch 1988]).

Specifically, Kripke distinguishes between two sorts of referential terms —those that designate their referent or extension "rigidly" and those that do not. The former group consists in proper names and natural kind terms, which is to say common nouns defined by some essence. For Kripke, a term rigidly designates its referent or extension if that referent or extension is identical in all counterfactual situations or "possible worlds." This identity, for Kripke, may be determined intuitively. It is my view that intuitions provide no evidence for new ontological categories of posits, such as essences; that we have no other reason to posit essences; and finally that, even independently of essences, we have no reason to believe that singular reference must be guided by intuitive identities in counterfactuals or that such identities reveal to us the 'true nature' of reference. In other words, reference is, once again, stipulative and idiolectal and Kripke's arguments provide no reason to think otherwise.

Let us begin with Kripke's notion of "possible worlds." For Kripke, a possible world is a "counterfactual situation" or a "possible state (or history) of the world" (Kripke 1980, 15). As Kripke explains, a possible history or counterfactual situation is merely a situation that might have occurred but did not. As Kripke puts it, "One is given, let's say, a previous history of the world up to a certain time, and from that time it diverges considerably from the actual course" (113)—this hypothetical divergence defines the possible world. Similarly, Kripke explains that "ordinarily when we ask intuitively whether something might have happened to a given object, we ask whether the universe could have gone on as it actually did up to a certain time, but diverge in its history from that point forward so that the vicissitudes of that object would have been different from that time forth" (115). In asking such a question, we are asking about a possible world, focusing on one particular object. For example, one might ask, 'Could Ronald Reagan have lost the 1984 election?' or 'If Reagan had lost the election, would Mondale have behaved decently towards Nicaragua?' These are questions about a possible world—specifically, one in which Ronald Reagan did indeed lose the 1984 election. In the same way, one could ask 'Could gold have been blue?' or 'If gold had been blue, would we still use it for jewelry?' These too are questions about a possible world—specifically, one in which gold is blue. Or, rather, the first question in each case asks if a certain counterfactual world is indeed possible and the second asks about certain properties of that world.

Now, according to Kripke, some terms or phrases do not refer to the same object or set of objects in all possible worlds. Thus, for example, 'Ronald Reagan' refers to the same object (Ronald Reagan) in all possible worlds. But 'the president of the United States in 1988' does not refer to the same object in all possible worlds, for this phrase might have referred to someone else—Mondale, for example. According to Kripke, we know this because we know that 'The president of the United States in 1988 might not have been Ronald Reagan' is true, whereas 'Ronald Reagan might not have been Ronald Reagan' is false (see 49).

In defining his terms (by stipulation), in relation to examples such as this, Kripke writes, "Let's call something a *rigid designator* if in every possible world it designates the same object, a *nonrigid* or *accidental* designator if that is not the case" (48). According to this definition, then, all proper names are, for Kripke, rigid designators, and so are all natural kind terms—such as 'gold'—for names refer to the same particular object in all possible worlds and natural kind terms refer to the same type of object in all possible worlds. Now since many properties of each can vary across possible worlds—Ronald Reagan might not have been president— the question arises as to what defines this identity. In the case of proper names, it is, for Kripke, an original act of naming—for example, a baptism—as linked to the present by a "causal chain" of use. In the case of natural kind terms, it is the *essence* of the kind. In consequence, origin and essence constrain, respectively, the reference of proper names and the meaning/extension of natural kind terms.

But the nature of this constraint—and thus the entire point of a *theory* of reference, an attempt to explain what reference 'really is', how it works, and so on—is unclear. Sticking to names for the moment, Kripke admits that one can stipulate referents pretty much as one likes. For example, he says that someone may determine the referent of a term by saying, " 'By "Goedel" I shall mean the man, whoever he is, who proved the incompleteness of arithmetic,' " and then explains, "Now you can do this if you want to. There's nothing really preventing it. You can just stick to that determination. If that's what you do, then if Schmidt discovered the incompleteness of arithmetic you *do* refer to him when you say 'Goedel did such and such' " (91). Of course, he goes on to claim that "that's not what most of us do" (91)—but this does not matter, unless we have *stipulated* that our notion of reference will be guided by most common usage. Once Kripke has admitted that a name may be stipulated to refer to an object other than that given in a causal chain leading back to an original act of naming, the function of that chain in a *theory* of reference has been lost. The causal chain becomes merely *one* way of *stipulating* reference. Indeed, when Kripke formulates his 'theory', he indicates that the causal chain defines reference *only* when causally-defined reference is what one seeks—which is to say, stipulates. As Kripke puts it: "A rough statement of a theory might be the following: An initial 'baptism' takes place. Here the object may be named by ostension, or the reference of the name may be fixed by a description. When the name is 'passed from link to link', the receiver of the name must, I think, intend when he learns it to use it with the same reference as the man from whom he heard it" (96). Clearly, to baptize by ostension or description is to stipulate a referent. Moreover, to intend to use a term with the same reference as one's predecessor is merely to stipulate (implicitly) that one is using the term 'causally'. But this makes the conclusion—that the referent of the term in question is causally defined—trivial, for reference here is stipulation all the way down. 'Causal' stipulation may be the most common sort of stipulation, one of particular epistemological or other importance, and thus one that we should be grateful to Kripke for isolating, but it is a stipulation nonetheless—indeed, it is doubly stipulative, for it refers back to an earlier, 'baptismal' stipulation or its equivalent.

Turning to common nouns, we find a similar, though more complex situation. Natural kind terms are rigid designators fixed by the essences of the objects to which they refer. Thus, for Kripke, gold is necessarily an element with atomic number 79; water is necessarily H_2O—and so on.

"If there were a substance . . . which had a completely different atomic structure from that of water, but resembled water" in "feel, appearance and perhaps taste," Kripke asks, "would we say that some water wasn't H_2O?"—answering, "I think not." Because, for Kripke, being H_2O is an essential property of water, whereas feel, appearance, and taste are merely contingent properties of water. But none of this indicates that we cannot stipulate the meaning or extension of 'water' so as to include similar tasting but differently structured substances. In fact, we can stipulate the meaning/extension of 'water' however we like. Kripke would probably even admit this—just as he admitted that we may stipulate a nonoriginary, noncausal referent for a name such as 'Goedel'.

Indeed, this point is explicitly granted by Hilary Putnam in "The Meaning of 'Meaning.'" Defending the view that 'water' essentially refers to H_2O, Putnam asks us to imagine a twin earth that is absolutely identical to our earth down to every detail of every person's physiology (for instance, there is a twin Pat Hogan identical with me down to molecules). There is, however, one difference: on Twin Earth, there is no H_2O, but instead there is some substance, XYZ, which is indistinguishable from water in taste, appearance, and so on. Does this mean that 'water' on Twin Earth has a different meaning than 'water' here, because the meaning of the term is fixed by the essence of its referent (H_2O in our case, XYZ in theirs)? The two would certainly be different, if we stipulate that our use of 'meaning' is confined to—or even just includes—the molecular properties of referents. The two would sometimes be different, but not always, if we stipulate that our use of 'meaning' covers people's idiolects; in this case, the meanings would be different for those whose internal lexicon linked water with molecular structure or with some vaguer scientific criteria, but not for those whose lexicon defined 'water' solely in terms of taste. The two would not be different at all if we simply stipulated that we would define 'water' perceptually or functionally. The case of Twin Earth does not seem to provide evidence against any of this. Thus, despite the fact that Putnam's thought experiment has had broad influence, I don't see that it has any significant consequences for our understanding of meaning. Indeed, Putnam himself readily admits that "a speaker may sometimes refer to XYZ as water if one is *using* it as water" (Putnam 1975, 239), and in later writings Putnam develops the implications of this admission, maintaining that an essentialist theory of reference cannot "get off the ground" because reference is a function of "intentions" (Putnam 1983b, 221).

It seems, then, that there is no constraint upon us to stipulate essences as the meanings of natural kind terms. But here another question arises, one equally important for the present study—is it even *possible* to stipulate essences as meanings? do essences even exist? For, if they exist, then they will have a special place in our stipulations, including our stipulation of 'meaning'. In other words, even though we can choose alternative ways of stipulating the meaning of a term, if there is some essence that determines what the referent of that term 'really is', it would seem that that essence is the most important aspect of that referent. In other words, if essences exist, then they will have powerful normative force, even if they do not in fact determine our meanings or stipulations.

As we have already indicated, Kripke's evidence for the existence of essences is intuitive. He intuits his (and our) reactions to certain counter-factual claims and on the basis of this infers essences from transworld identities. Kripke speaks of "the linguistic intuitions" he adduces "on behalf of rigidity" (10), "the intuitive test for rigidity" (11), the role of intuitions about truth conditions (12), and so on. He writes, "It's a common attitude in philosophy to think that one shouldn't introduce a notion until it's been rigorously defined. . . . Here I am just dealing with an intuitive notion and will keep on the level of an intuitive notion" (39). Finally, he goes so far as to say: "Of course, some philosophers think that something's having intuitive content is very inconclusive evidence in favor of it. I think it is very heavy evidence in favor of anything, myself. I really don't know, in a way, what more conclusive evidence one can have about anything, ultimately speaking" (42).[5]

Intuitions certainly show something. The question is—do they show essences? Indeed, even if there are essences, would intuition show them? Well, it seems clear that intuitions are formed in social interactions ranging from language acquisition to formal education. Moreover, these inter-actions are guided by certain abiding concerns with causality. In other words, it is in general most *useful* to discover properties of objects that are relevant to causal sequences into which those objects might enter; thus we have a propensity to look for such (causal) properties. In a sense, all of our problem-solving activities aim first at answering the question 'Why?' or the question 'How?'—and thus at uncovering causal relations. Modern physical science has advanced our understanding in these areas to such a degree that we may isolate certain properties—such as chemical structure—as causally relevant in almost any context. Moreover, the results of this work in the physical sciences are taught in our schools, from first grade on, as absolutely certain truths. For example, many of us—and probably everyone who grew up to read Kripke—learned in tender youth that water 'really is' H_2O.

Thus, it seems indisputable that we are concerned with causally relevant properties for good, pragmatic—even adaptive/biological—reasons. It also seems indisputable that we are taught from childhood that the relevant conclusions of physical science are absolutely true. It appears reasonable to conclude that these and related factors combine to determine our intuitions. We intuit that water 'really is' H_2O precisely because we have been taught that water 'really is' H_2O and because we have serious, general concerns with isolating causally relevant properties. This seems a perfectly adequate explanation for the intuitive data Kripke cites, which, then, cannot be invoked in defense of the positing of essences. Moreover, this avoids the very serious problem of whether or not Kripke's intuitions are rightly considered to be definitive. That after all depends on whether or not Kripke could provide rational criteria that would determine his intuitions to be valid, while at the same time determining anyone else's contradictory intuitions to be invalid. As is no doubt obvious, there is a relatively small number of people in the history of the world whose intuitions about counterfactuals are governed by such criteria as molecular structure or atomic number. The most obvious and simplest way of explaining the presence of such criteria in some cases—as well as their absence in other cases—does not in any way involve essences. Indeed, it is hard to see how essences could be considered relevant to this distinction at all. The difference between Kripke's intuitions and those of, say, Aristotle is not that Kripke has better 'essence-receptors'; it is just that Kripke knows about the researches of modern chemistry while Aristotle did not. In other words, the difference pretty much has to be a matter of education—as I'm sure Kripke would admit. But if the difference between intuitions is a matter of education, then the intuitions considered alone must be a matter of education—and in that case, it is difficult to see how they could have any probative value.

Finally, it is not clear that essences would be of any use even if the data of intuition were not explicable by reference to education and so forth. Specifically, we have no reason to assume that our intuitive preferences even might, somehow, reflect essential properties of the world. We have no reason to assume that intuition might allow access to essences. It is not even clear what it would mean for us to have such intuitive access. The problem here is the same as it was in the case of Katz. Intuition is supposed to concern a relation between intent and something different from intent—essence—but the connection is not causal. Thus intuition is assimilable neither to perception nor to introspection, and its supposed relation to essences seems totally fanciful.

Moreover, by Kripke's principles, it would seem that any decisions about essences necessarily rely on the conclusions of natural science. First of all, this should allow Kripke only the circular intuition that the essence of a substance, such as water, is whatever the essence of that substance ultimately turns out to be. Secondly, it puts Kripke in the position of making intuition both superior and inferior to empirical research. Specifically, scientists hypothesize properties of objects (substances and so on)— for example, that the molecular structure of water is H_2O. But in and of themselves, such hypotheses do not define essences. 'The molecular structure of water is H_2O' means only that the molecular structure of water is H_2O—*not* that H_2O is the essence of water. Any such claim about the essence of water must rely on some further intuition that goes beyond the chemistry. But this seems contradictory. On the one hand, the intuition is entirely dependent upon the research of chemists; it has no capacity to determine essences alone (think, again, of the great premodern thinkers, such as Aristotle—none of them even could have gotten water 'right'). But, on the other hand, this same intuition must go beyond the chemistry to determine that certain hypotheses of chemistry pick out essences. It is extremely obscure how intuition could recognize an essence once it is thrown up by empirical science, even though it could tell us nothing about that essence independently of the empirical science.

Thus, though we may often wish to stipulate reference in causal terms— either those of a (causal) chain of speakers leading back to an historical 'baptism' or those of (causally) relevant chemical or other properties of the referent in question—and while we can be grateful to Kripke (and Putnam) for analyzing the ramifications of this sort of stipulation, we see again that there is no *need* to stipulate reference in this way. Causality no more provides the 'true nature' of reference than anything else. Moreover, even if we do decide to stipulate reference in causal terms, such a stipulation involves nothing beyond intents and a material world. It involves no essences; these, like autonomous and social meanings, appear both redundant and inscrutable. Once again, there seems to be no further sort of meaning or reference beyond the idiolectal, no third entity between or beyond minds and things.

Style Secrets
of the Rich and
Famous

It seems like every star out there always looks stellar, but how do they do it? Here are some tips from

ETER ..../STARMAX, BILL DAVILA/RETNA. STEVE GRANITZ/RETNA.
.........../RETNA; (m...dle ro.......ROUGH/CELEBRITY,
.........LOCO........

Tips Control-Under-t

1. **Don't stop eating completely. Your body needs fuel.**

2. **Don't restrict any particular food—it will make you crave it even more.**

3. **Always push yourself to work out for at least 10 minutes. Once you get past that first 10, the rest won't seem so bad.**

4. **Get a workout buddy to help motivate you when you don't want to work out.**

5. **Buy a cute dress or jeans in a realistic goal size, and use it as a motivator.**

6. **Instead of checking your progress on the scale, check your measurements.**

February 1999

I lost so much weight the first month, but now my weight loss has slowed down. This month I lost 12 pounds. The best news is that I haven't gained any back. It's been tough since I always found so much pleasure in eating, but I've come so far that I just can't let myself return to my old habits. In some ways, eating is actually more enjoyable now. I don't fear food as much.

Lately, I've been comparing myself with everyone else, which can be dangerous. I didn't lose any weight for two weeks and thought, This is too hard. I wish I were someone else so I wouldn't have to deal with this. I even thought about going back to my old ways, just for a week, so I wouldn't have to worry about my weight. But then I thought, What are you talking about? Look at you! You've already come so far. You look and feel great! That helps me stick with it. So does all

Picture perfect: Now a size 12, Kate has signed with Main Line Models in Pennsylvania.

10 minutes went by, I'd think to myself, I might as well stay 15 more minutes. And it worked.

I made a ton of great progress, but I gained 3 pounds at first. That freaked me out because it was the first time I gained any weight since I started this. I thought I must have gotten off track with my eating, but the trainer at the gym assured me it was muscle. Three weeks later, the 3 pounds were gone. In fact, I dropped even more weight because building muscle speeds up your metabolism. My total weight loss adds up to 70 pounds. Time to go shopping again. It seems like I've been buying new clothes every two weeks because nothing fits anymore.

October 2000 During the past year or so, I've basically been sticking with the same food and exercise routine. I walk briskly on the treadmill for 25 minutes, and then I do some free get back on track.

May 1999 I can't believe the way everyone at school is treating me. People who never talked to me before are suddenly saying hi to me in the halls. It's kind of upsetting. I feel like saying, "You didn't talk to me before, so why now?"

I've finally started incorporating exercise into my diet. We had tryouts this month for the cheerleading squad, and I made it. Cheering is not that popular where I live, but I do have to get fit for it, and I'm realizing how out of shape I am. Right now it takes me a little over 13 minutes to jog a mile, so I'm trying to go to the gym three or four times a week. I've always had a membership, but I've never been committed to working out.

September 1999 I survived the gym this summer. Sometimes it was so hard to get motivated to go. I just wanted to be lazy and hang out like everyone else. But I forced myself to go and, once I got there, I'd tell myself to do just 10 minutes on the treadmill and then go home. But by the time

incredibly well for me. I've lost a total of 94 pounds in almost two years. I still struggle every day, and I think it's always going to be hard because I can't eat what everyone else can. I'm not lucky enough to have a fast metabolism like other people.

I'm still eating well and I find ways to make the food I eat nutritious and tasty, like having an apple with peanut butter or eating a veggie burger instead of a regular burger. I never really feel deprived. In fact, I've found that by eating more healthful foods, I can eat more and consume fewer calories. It's really what you eat, not how much you eat.

My self-confidence has skyrocketed. I've even started modeling, which is something I never thought I'd be able to do. I will never let myself weigh 264 pounds again because I worked so hard to get rid of all the extra weight. There were so many times I wanted to quit. But I learned that if you stick with something, you will eventually see the rewards. I'm glad that I did this, and most important, that I did it for myself.

Kate's Keep

your workout — makes burns more calories than fat.

8 Be realistic. If you're 5 feet 11 inches, there is no way you're going to weigh 100 pounds.

9 Don't get discouraged if you only lose a few pounds at first. A couple of pounds at a time will add up and, before you know it, you will have reached your goal.

10 Be proud of all the progress you make, no matter how insignificant it may seem. All progress is worth praise.

on what keeps them
looking their best.

LeAnn Rimes "I like being able to walk out
of the house without makeup on. And although
I watch what I eat, I never deprive myself."

Charlize Theron
"I'm fifty-fifty on glamour
stuff. I'd rather put on
a pair of jeans, get
on my Harley and act
like a guy."

Shirley Manson "If I could,
I'd dress tip to toe in cashmere.
I want cashmere underwear.
I don't want to look like everyone.
I see trends and try to do the
opposite just to be a devil."

Jason Biggs
"For chill-wear, I'm
big on cargo pants
and sneakers. For
an audition, it's
jeans and John
Fluevog shoes. For a
premiere, plain-front
black Gucci pants, a
gray V-neck sweater
and black shoes. Black is
my color. And since I've lost
some weight, I like wearing
nice-fitting clothes."

Anna Paquin
"I wear sunscreen
365 days a year. I don't
ever tan. I love scarves
and hats. I love pink,
but nothing too bright
or obnoxious."

Alicia Witt "I like looking
natural during the day, so
I just use an eyelash curler
and a little bit of waterproof
mascara. I think it really
makes my eyes pop."

...ise from top right: JOHN ...ALLO/RETNA, ST... ...ORBIS ...

REPRESENTATIONALISM

By 'representationalism'—sometimes called 'conceptualism'—I mean a mentalistic theory of language or speech that is nonintentional. Such a theory conceives of mind not as intention or experiential subjectivity, but as an objective entity of some sort, a kind of sophisticated machine in which 'representations' (the name given to mentalistic objects) are manipulated by various rule-governed computational processes. These processes and objects are in principle closed to introspection or intentional experience, except in their 'outputs'. Nonlinguistic representationalism (and mental objectivism) found its most articulate expression in Kant. The most rigorous linguistic version is due to Chomsky, though it has also been developed by, for example, Jerry Fodor and others working in cognitive science. I shall confine the present discussion to Chomsky's writings.

As is well known, Chomsky posits a complex "underlying" structure or, rather, sequence of structures, for every utterance. Specifically, there is a "base component" that generates a "D-structure." The D-structure may be thought of as the first version of the sentence to be uttered. It is somehow represented in terms of constituent structure (with constituents such as *determiner, noun, noun phrase* marked). Thus we might think of 'Who did Mary excoriate?' as starting out more like 'Mary did excoriate who', with 'Mary' marked as a noun phrase, 'did excoriate who' as a verb phrase, and so on.[6] This D-structure is then sent through a "transformational component" encompassing the rule "move a," a generalized movement rule, and constraints that limit the operation of that rule. The "transformations" effected by this component result in the restructuring of the D-structure. In combination with a further "case component" that functions principally to assign case and filter out structures with faulty case markings, they then yield "S-structures." These are much closer to what we actually say. In the preceding example, it is the transformations that get the 'did' before 'Mary' and the 'who' before 'did'.

Often, however, this is not enough. For example, the D-structure of 'the man that I met' would be 'the man that I met who'. Transformations yield the S-structure, 'the man who that I met'. To get to the syntactic structure of what we actually say, the "surface structure," we must delete the 'who'. This is done by further, highly constrained deletion rules. Finally, we have some "output filters" to eliminate any final ungrammatical structure that might have otherwise slipped through. In addition to this, there are entirely distinct semantic and phonological components.

The first functions to determine co-reference relations (for instance, when a pronoun and a noun phrase, or two pronouns, refer to the same thing); the second functions to effect further phonological transformations, which ultimately yield a form of our actual utterance, abstracted from physical features irrelevant to the grammar—sound of voice, agility of tongue, and so on. All of these combine to yield, at last, the real utterance.

The detail and intellectual complexity of Chomsky's accomplishment is staggering, especially in the "government and binding" form of his "Extended Standard Theory." However, like the less subtle and less brilliant positions examined above, its posits ultimately appear both redundant and obscure. Let us begin with the former. Certainly no one would deny that Chomsky has invoked quite a mental apparatus here. For example, in terms of extent and structural complexity, Chomsky's representationalism goes far beyond anything to be found in Kant, whose own mental posits were hardly simple and limited. Presumably all would agree that we should avoid these complex posits if possible, admitting them only to the degree that they appear to offer us the simplest account of linguistic phenomena. Moreover, this is true of *all* transformational and related theories, for in the present context the question of simplicity enters more crucially with the *type* of account Chomsky proposes than with its details.

Chomsky claims that there are two crucial sets of data that require the introduction of transformational and related components, the distinction of various levels of (intentionally inaccessible) structure, and so forth. The first concerns certain facts of grammaticality. There are facts about what we can and cannot say that, Chomsky argues, cannot be easily explained—or cannot be explained at all—in nontransformational theories. The second concerns language acquisition and "universal grammar." The nature and speed of ordinary language acquisition and the ubiquity of certain linguistic principles are such as to require the positing of universal, innate grammatical properties, themselves best defined in transformational and related terms. I should like to consider these arguments briefly in turn.

As to the 'facts of grammaticality', I should begin by proposing an alternative construction of the process of sentence-generation. Let us take, 'Who did Mary excoriate?' Usually, this sentence manifests an intent to elicit from an addressee a certain piece of information—specifically, some identification of the person who was subjected to Mary's excoriation. In asking this, then, I presuppose a particular context, certain knowledges on the part of the addressee, and so on. I construct the question in such a way as to assure the addressee's comprehension. And I do this by following rules. (I have no disagreement with Chomsky on the issue of *genera-tive* grammar—with his contention that, in Jackendoff's words, linguistic "judgments must be based on a set of *rules* rather than on some finite set of templates to which patterns are rigidly matched" [45].) Moreover, I tac-itly project an answer of the general form, 'Mary excoriated x'. I think Chomsky would not disagree with any of this.

Of course, none of this goes to indicate that 'Who did Mary excori-ate?' does not have a D-structure form along the lines of a structure-marked 'Mary did excoriate who'. However, neither does a Chomskyan analysis indicate that a nontransformational analysis is inadequate for this sentence. We shall turn to a sentence of this type in a moment. What is important here is that the communicative analysis, like the transforma-tional analysis, indicates that there is indeed a profound relation between, in this case, an interrogative and a related indicative or indicativelike form. (The D-structure is not strictly speaking an actual indicative form, but the structures are parallel to the degree required for the following analysis.) However, the communicative analysis does this by relating the question to a tacitly projected response, to the tacitly projected fulfillment of the aim of the questioning. A transformational analysis, on the other hand, does this by deriving the question through a long and complex series of computational processes. Moreover, the communicative account is, I take it, admitted by the transformationalist/representationalist in any event. Thus, insofar as the crucial data of questions are explicable by way of inter-rogative/indicative relations, the communicative account is superior to the transformational account on grounds of parsimony (parsimony being the most straightforward type of simplicity relation).

Let us look, then, at a phenomenon that has been important to re-cent debates in transformational grammar—'wanna'-contraction. Chom-sky claims that: 1) 'Who do you want to win the race?' and 2) 'What do you wanna win?' are grammatical, but 3) '*Who do you wanna win the race?' is not. Chomsky explains these data in roughly the following man-ner. The D-structure of both 1 and 3 would be something like, 'You do want who to win the race'. The 'who' gets moved out front by 'move α', but leaves a "trace," a sort of marker saying "*Who* was here in the ini-tial structure'. Thus you get something like 'Who do you want [phoneti-cally unrealized trace] to win the race?' This trace, then, blocks contrac-tion between 'want' and 'to' (makes it ungrammatical). Contraction can occur only between contiguous elements, and the presence of the trace makes 'want' and 'to' noncontiguous. Number 2, on the other hand, has a D-structure something like, 'You do want to win what'. Again, the wh-word is preposed (moved to the front), but this time no trace is left between 'want' and 'to', for somewhat more complex reasons than may at first appear. In any event, this makes 'want' and 'to' contiguous, even in underlying structure, and thus the contraction is not blocked.

The first thing I should remark on here is that Chomsky and I are by no means in complete agreement on the facts. In general, I think that speech is far more chaotic than he seems willing to admit. Recall that the relevant notion of grammaticality here is not normative. Thus it should be something along the following lines: a sentence is grammatical for a particular meaning whenever anyone could use it under ordinary circumstances with that meaning and not evoke a spontaneous sense of grammatical oddity in his/her auditors. Indeed, even this is too strict, for many sentences that fit the rules of a language may appear grammatically odd if they are merely unusual or unidiomatic or too complex and thus difficult to parse. We would probably do well to drop the notion of grammaticality and speak instead about degrees of comprehensibility, degrees of ordinariness or idiomaticness in phrasing, and so forth. Patrick Suppes has maintained, plausibly, that "the grammatical rules of our speech are not at all like the rules of chess. They are like the rules of a children's game that is not codified and is continually changing" (Suppes 1986, 116). And Donald Davidson has influentially developed a theory of speech communication based on "passing theories," which is to say, interpretive theories worked out in particular communicative contexts, relying not on "rules in any strict sense" but on "rough maxims and methodological generalities" (Davidson 1986, 173).[7] Linguists such as Talmy Givon have reached similar conclusions: "language—within the minds of speakers, rather than as some abstract system of *langue*—is always in the middle of change in lexicon/meaning, syntax, morphology and phonology" (quoted in Croft 1990, 257). William Croft elaborates: "speakers are constantly involved with a dynamic, unstable system, not a fixed, static one. Therefore, speakers have cognitive competence of dynamic processes—not static arrangements" (257).

Indeed, even if we do not adopt such a fluid conception of language, it seems likely that many of Chomsky's crucially 'ungrammatical' sentences are used every day by many people—including those who judge them ungrammatical—and are not even felt to be deviant by speaker or auditor. Grammaticality judgments are simply not very reliable (a point made by a number of writers; see, for example, Hudson 1980, 19 and citations; and

THE LIMITS OF STIPULATION

McCawley 1979, 218ff. and citations). Indeed, it is worth looking at a few cases of this before returning to 'wanna'-contraction.

Chomsky claims, for example, that "we can form 'the dancing bear' (corresponding to 'the bear that dances'), but not 'the eating man' (corresponding to 'the man who eats'" (Chomsky 1986, 9). In a footnote, Chomsky refers the reader to his early essay, "A Transformational Approach to Syntax," and explains, "in early work, such facts were used to motivate an analysis of intransitives such as *eat* as derived from corresponding transitives by a system of ordered rules that excluded the unwanted cases" (14), thereby indicating the absoluteness of this judgment and its importance in theorization. But I clearly remember often referring to my father as "the incredible eating man," when he would merely hoist the entire pot of stew to his place, rather than confine himself to a more modest second helping. Unlike 'dancing bear', 'eating man' is pragmatically odd—all men eat, so it sounds peculiar, redundant to speak of the 'eating man'. But it is hardly ungrammatical.

Similarly, Chomsky claims that 'John didn't realize that the fool had left his lights on' cannot mean that John didn't realize that he, John, had left his lights on (Chomsky 1986, 79). However, I have certainly gotten sentences like this from students. These are speakers who are fluent in English and only English and have reached the final stage of language acquisition, in Chomsky's sense. Moreover, in context, such a sentence is comprehensible and need not sound odd. Again, I suspect that sentences such as this are fairly frequent in ordinary speech.

There is a striking case of this sort relating to the "theory of control." For Chomsky, I believe, a sentence such as 'She returned to console me for having missed the plane' or 'She returned to chastize me for having stolen the cheese-loaf', must mean that I, and not she, was the one who missed the train or stole the loaf. Specifically, I take it, there is an underlying "PRO"—one might think of this as an inaudible pronoun—which is "bound" to 'me' by the rules of "control" for co-reference. Thus we have, 'She$_i$ returned to chastize me$_j$ for PRO$_j$ having stolen the cheese-loaf'. Thus 'She returned to chastize me for having hit myself' is okay, but 'She returned to chastize [or console] me for having hit me' should be ungrammatical. However, I find in Masud Khan's *Alienation in Perversion,* the following sentences: "To this day I cannot figure out why she had come back for those few sessions. My hunch is that it was to say 'thank you' and also to comfort me for having tried to fool me for two years" (Khan 1979,

184). Here Khan intends, and everyone understands, that *she* is the one who essayed deception, not he. Someone might object that Khan's native tongue is not English, but that isn't really to the point. Khan teaches and writes in English and has taught and written and studied in English for decades. His written English is articulate, readily comprehensible, and idiomatic. Moreover, this book went through readers at a press and probably other readers as well, almost certainly native speakers, who appear to have had no trouble with the sentence. The point is not that the sentence is perfectly normal. It may or may not be. The point is just that grammaticality intuitions are frequently inaccurate and much that is thought to be forbidden by strict rules is not only not forbidden but spoken and written without hesitation, communicative difficulty, or even any spontaneous sense of oddity or inappropriateness.

Returning, finally, to 'wanna'-contractions, my feeling is much the same here. I have absolutely no doubt that people say 'Who do you wanna win the race?' all the time, in appropriate circumstances. On the other hand, it does seem clear that, isolated and decontextualized, 'Who do you wanna win the race?' sounds awkward in a way that 'Who do you want to win the race?' does not. Recall that Chomsky's complex method for explaining this—his invocation of underlying structures, transformations, contraction-inhibiting "traces," and the like—fundamentally relied on establishing a relation between the interrogative and a related, indicativelike form, 'You do want who to win the race'. As we have already remarked, however, insofar as a transformational solution to an interrogative sentence problem relies on an indicativelike D-structure, this solution may be recapitulated in communicative terms by reference to a projected indicative response.

Specifically, when I ask, 'Who do you want to win the race?' I project an answer presupposing the form, 'I want x to win the race'. This is also the case if I ask, 'Who do you wanna win the race?' Thus if I contract, there is a discrepancy between the form of the question and the projected form of the response. Note that this is not the case for 'What do you wanna win?' Here the projected response is 'I wanna win x' and there is no discrepancy. I think Chomsky would deny none of this. Furthermore, it seems perfectly adequate to explain our inclination to find 'Who do you wanna win the race?' somewhat queer in comparison with 'Who do you want to win the race?' and 'What do you wanna win?'

The situation is of the same sort, though more complicated, with regard to 'Bimbo is the one that I want to/*wanna win'. Again, I do not find 'wanna' ungrammatical in this context, but merely awkward. And this feeling of awkwardness can be explained by several factors. For one thing, we are likely to think of the independent, sentential form, 'I want him to win', as more 'basic' than the dependent form, 'the one that I want to win'. First of all, we learn the sentential form earlier and learn how to construct the dependent form in relation to it. Second, the sentential form remains the most common. It is likely that my auditor would, for example, recall my preference as 'Hogan wants Bimbo to win'—and, after all, the whole purpose of my saying this is to communicate information. Moreover, I utter this sentence in a communicative situation in which my auditor might respond, 'You want *him* to win?' or the like. These considerations could be developed but the point is that there are numerous factors—here relating not only to communication but to language acquisition as well—factors that Chomsky would presumably accept and that appear entirely adequate to predict that sentences such as 'Bimbo is the one that I wanna win' will not sound right in comparison with sentences such as 'Bimbo is the one that I want to win'. Thus there seems to be no need to invoke the massive apparatus of transformational grammar to explain this fact.

Of course, a Chomskyan might justifiably object that, even granting my account of 'wanna'-contractions, this is only one small part of the data Chomsky invokes in defense of his theses. This is certainly true. However, as the main focus of this volume is not upon the construction of grammars, I can only indicate, through some illustrative analyses, the sort of approach one might adopt to the wealth of data Chomsky and his followers have gathered in forty years of research. Indeed, a complete response to Chomsky could be made only by a group of researchers who were themselves engaged in a comparable research program based on intentional/communicative principles. As far as I am aware, no such program is currently under way. The same constraints necessarily affect my examination of Chomsky's arguments concerning language acquisition and universal grammar.

Chomsky's argument concerning language acquisition is roughly the following: Children learn language at a rate beyond what is justified on the basis of data available to them. Specifically, they simply never make some particular generalizations consistent with available data, yet mistaken. The speed with which they acquire language is a product of this capacity to avoid particular errors. And as the avoidance of these errors is not empirically determined, it must be determined by innate principles. From this, and on the basis of various related studies in acquisition, Chomsky goes on to construe these innate principles in representational and computational terms. Crucially, the general outlines of the above transformational model, and certain specific transformational principles (the "move a" rule, as well as some general principles of government and binding), go to constitute this innate structure.

The general hypothesis concerning innate linguistic principles is separable from (though clearly related to) representationalism and, more generally, an objectivist conception of mind. However, I should like briefly to indicate why I reject Chomsky's innatism and thereby dispute his representationalism and objectivism even more vigorously. First of all, I would maintain that there is no paucity of data available to the child. Rather the data *appear* inadequate because they are badly organized by linguists. Specifically, linguists most often ignore the communicative aims of the utterances that constitute the data. For this reason, they fail to recognize the most obvious ways of grouping these data—the ways in which a child would in fact be most likely to organize them, because of his/her pervasive concern with communication. In addition, linguists occasionally ignore significant formal similarities as well.[8]

Some of the standard sentences cited in this context are: 4) I wonder who the men expected to see them; 5) 'The men expected to see them'; 6) 'John ate the apple'; 7) 'John ate'; 8) 'John is too stubborn to talk to Bill'; 9) 'John is too stubborn to talk to'. Briefly, the problem is that sentences such as these make us expect that children will make certain mistakes that in fact they never make. Thus sentence number 5 and part of sentence number 4, though seemingly identical, are interpreted differently— and children (it seems) never assume otherwise. Similarly, numbers 8 and 9 do not follow the analogy of numbers 6 and 7. Number 7 means 'John ate something', whereas 9 means 'John is too stubborn for someone to talk to John', not 'John is too stubborn for John to talk to someone'. But this too causes no problem for children. Finally, sentences 5, 8, and 9, taken in isolation, involve peculiarities of interpretation—concerning the subject of the infinitive—that children apparently never have difficulty grasping.

We should begin by eliminating numbers 6 and 7 as in any way inductively relevant to numbers 8 and 9. 'Eat' can be intransitive. The child learns this easily enough by hearing 'I ate', 'We eat', and so on. 'Talk to' is not and cannot be a single intransitive verb. No one ever says, 'I talked to'. (Of course, 'talk' is an intransitive verb, but then 'John is too stubborn to talk' *is* parallel to 'John ate' in the relevant way.) Thus children would have no reason to group sentences such as 6 through 9 together and thus there is no potential error that we should be surprised they avoid.

In a similar way, we should eliminate number 4 in its relation to number 5. It is obvious either communicatively or formally that 4 concerns a state of affairs about which the speaker lacks one bit of information. This missing bit of information is indicated by the 'who'. Moreover in ordinary dialogue, this assertion functions like the question: 10) 'Who did the men expect to see them?' The appropriate sorts of responses for both are, 'Ronbo', or 'They expected Ronbo to see them'. Indeed, the assertion 4 is related to the question 10 just as 11) 'I wonder who he is' is related to 12) 'Who is he?' And as 13) 'I wonder where that came from' is related to 14) 'Where did that come from?' And so on. By the time the child acquires a sentence of the complexity of 4, he/she is unlikely to connect it with 5. Rather, he/she would most probably connect it with 10 and see it as fitting the pattern of sentences such as 11–14.

On the other hand, if a child did connect 4 with 5, that would merely turn 4 into gibberish. If 'the men expected to see them' in 4 means the same thing as 'The men expected to see them' in 5, then the 'I wonder who' in 4 makes no sense. Clearly, a child would never have occasion to utter such a sentence; for him/her it is just a complex form of nonsense with no redeeming qualities (for instance, regular meter or alliteration). In other words, if the child did make this mistake, there would be no way of knowing, for it is not a mistake that could generate any utterance or any other evidentially relevant behavior.

So only the three isolated sentences remain—numbers 5, 8, and 9. The problem is: Why don't children take a very long time to learn these sentences? Why do they so readily interpret these sentences to have the range of meanings they do in fact have?

The first thing I should remark in this connection is that, in general, an absent bit of information—for instance, the agent performing an act represented by a stated verb—must be readily available to an addressee. If this information is not readily available, the communication will be unsuccessful. Thus an unnamed agent or patient of an act—usually an unnamed subject or object of a verb—must either be named elsewhere *or* be some nonspecific agent or patient, 'someone', 'anyone', 'something', and so on. In a few cases, the context for the named agent/patient may extend to the previous sentence—principally in answers to questions. Most often, however, an absent agent/patient must be indicated in the very same sentence. There are some obvious communicative reasons for this, into which, I believe, it is not necessary to enter. In any event, the notion should be easily learnable. Thus the only question that remains is why is a nonspecific agent/patient interpretation ungrammatical in some cases, but necessary in others? In other words, why must we interpret, for example, number 5 as meaning, 'The men$_i$ expected the men$_i$ to see them' and not as 'The men expected someone to see them?'

First, I should like to eliminate number 8 from this problem. I believe that we *could* intend or interpret number 8 to mean, 'John is too stubborn for anyone to talk to Bill', given the proper context. This should be clearer from a parallel sentence. Consider the context: 'We might have to call Bill to help us with the desk'. 'Yeah—well, let's go see how heavy it is. Maybe we can move it ourselves'. 'Hmmm. Not too heavy. What do you think? Should I get on the horn or no?' 'Nah. This is too light to call Bill. Especially at this hour'. Of course, the sentence sounds better if we add 'about'; it avoids a comic ambiguity, and we would probably encourage composition students in this direction. However, it seems clear that the sentence under this interpretation is 'part of the language' in the descriptive sense.

Thus only numbers 5 and 9 remain. As to 'The men expected to see them', I simply see no reason why a structure like this—in which the subject of the verb must also be taken to be the subject of the infinitive—should be difficult to learn. First of all, it is captured in a very simple hypothesis—one subject, not two—and thus it is a likely hypothesis for a child to form on the basis of the Principle of Minimal Interpretation alone. Second, and perhaps more important, by the time the child is able to say, 'The men expected to see them', he/she has heard 'Billy expected to go to the circus', 'Johnny wants to play with the GI Joe with Kung-Fu grip', and 'Sally does not like to eat brussels sprouts'. And the child learns sentences such as these in contexts that are perfectly adequate to indicate that it is the subject of the main verb, and not some unmentioned indefinite noun, that is the subject of the infinitive as well. Thus, the child sees Sally hiding her brussels sprouts, feeding them to the dog, slipping them under the carpet, weeping and shouting, 'I'll die before I eat brussels sprouts'; then he/she hears, 'Sally does not like to eat brussels sprouts'. He/she has no reason to infer 'anyone' as the subject of the infinitive and lots of reason to infer 'Sally'. The child has a wealth of data, linguistic and nonlinguistic, which seem perfectly adequate to account for his/her acquisition of sentences such as 5.

Our final sentence is similar. Evidently, we speak English in such a way that prepositions must have their objects named in the context; the object of a preposition cannot be the unnamed, nonspecific 'someone'. Put differently, 'talk to', 'fly from', and 'eat at' cannot be used as intransitive verbs in English. (I leave aside seeming exceptions, such as 'walk around', for in these cases the preposition does not most often function as a preposition but rather as part of an idiom; when not functioning idiomatically, these prepositions too require a named object.) For this reason, 'John' must be the object of 'to' in number 9. However, it cannot be the subject of 'talk' as well because reflexives in English must be marked and if 'John' were the subject of 'talk', a reflexive would be unmarked. In that case, the sentence would have to read, 'John is too stubborn to talk to *himself*'.

Now, are these principles—that reflexives must be marked and objects of prepositions must be explicit—easy enough to acquire in context? In my view, they are relatively simple principles and thus provide no great difficulty for understanding relevant aspects of language acquisition. Moreover, contextual clues would seem to be unambiguous in many relevant cases. When Sally says to Bobby, 'You're too disgusting to sit with', Sally is the one gagging and running away, while Bobby is the one picking his nose and consuming the fruits of his labor. When Janie says to Lucy, 'You're too stupid to play with', Janie is the one who has been trying to teach Lucy how to play 'tag' for the last six hours.

In his argument against Chomsky's innateness hypothesis, Hilary Putnam maintains that, to account for language acquisition, all we need assume are "generalized learning strategies" and not any specifically linguistic principles, transformational or otherwise. (See Putnam 1971 and 1980. More detailed proposals have been put forth in Sampson 1980; Billman 1983; Maratsos and Chalkley 1980; Anderson 1983; and others—though in some cases these authors reject Chomsky's innatism only to advocate another form of representationalism. See also the response of Holland et al. to Jerrold Fodor's modular notion of mind.) Chomsky's response is that such a statement about 'generalized learning strategies' is vacuous until filled in with some specific proposals. In the preceding analysis, I have assumed that Putnam is correct and, in addition, that these "generalized learning strategies" are precisely the principles of rational inference, as discussed above.[9] This identification is plausible, not only in relation to Chomsky's data but also in relation to broader studies of child cognition. As Thagard has noted, "a growing number of developmental psychologists argue that changes in children['s cognition] are better described in the same terms that describe the growth of scientific knowledge" (Thagard

1992, 251). Moreover, A. Samarapungavan has found that children adjudicate between rival theories by appeal to evidence, logic, and simplicity in the above sense. As Thagard summarizes, "elementary school children tended to prefer theories that explain more, lack ad hoc explanations, and are consistent internally and with the evidence" (258).

Turning to universal grammar, we find a similar situation: a large body of data has been cited in support of representationalism, but these data appear adequately explicable in terms of communication and rational inference without recourse to objectivist mentalism. Specifically, Chomsky and others have isolated a number of features or principles that they take to be instantiated in all languages (or, in some cases, in all languages of an appropriate type). These constitute universal grammar (a portion of which, in turn, constitutes the putatively innate linguistic capacity of humans). A number of these features and principles attributed to universal grammar concern underlying (nonsurface structure) representations or related phenomena. These are thus intratheoretic data, data of transformational theory; in other words, they presuppose the validity of the theory. I will not consider any of these. Other principles are of such obvious communicative function as not to require further analysis in those terms.[10] In addition, as Goodman has pointed out (see Goodman 1971), it is not incumbent upon a theory to explain every statistically unlikely relation between members of a given set, for in any given set it is statistically likely that some statistically unlikely but still random phenomena will appear. However, there remain many interesting principles, or at least tendencies, that appear to be universal and significant and that are not self-evidently open to nonobjectivist (for instance, communicative) explanation. I should like to consider two of these.

The first example concerns mutation. In several Celtic languages, certain words effect a change—or 'mutation'—in the initial consonant of a subsequent word. Most often, these words must be contiguous (and stand in a particular syntactic relation). However, there are some cases in Breton (and Irish) in which contiguity is not a condition for mutation. In these cases, a single element may intervene between the 'trigger', or word effecting the mutation, and the affected word. Moreover, the intervening element must be taken from a finite—indeed, quite short—list of named elements.

Gregory Stump has argued that the 'unmarked case' for mutation is contiguity and that a single, named intervening element is the limiting, marked, and historically unstable case. For Stump, as I understand him, it is just downright impossible for two elements to intervene in a mutation. And this impossibility is a linguistic universal, explicable in terms of government and binding principles. I disagree with Stump's conclusion on two counts: 1) The data do not warrant any conclusions of impossibility. Rather, the data indicate that the tendency of any language is very strongly toward limiting or eliminating intervening elements in mutations, as Stump points out. This said, the data are accounted for and the further, exclusionary statement is redundant. 2) I just do not think languages work that way. Languages are exclusionary in this manner only if the innateness hypothesis is correct, if the universal properties of language are the result of innate, highly constraining linguistic principles. Otherwise, we are free to construct our languages as we like—within the limits of general memory capacity and so forth—and universal properties cannot be spoken of as exclusionary. Moreover, I can make little sense of the exclusionary claim. I see no reason why a group of people could not decide to name two intervening elements, with children learning the two-element intervention as they now learn the one-element intervention. If it is to make any empirical sense, an exclusionary statement of this kind should cover any possible, learnable first language, and not merely actual languages. Thus the exclusionary claim seems baseless.

I emphasize this seemingly minor point because it is important to the points at issue. If the datum is the exclusionary one, then, it appears, we shall need innateness and, possibly, representationalism. But the datum appears to be exclusionary only because innateness and representationalism are assumed. Thus it cannot provide evidence for either.

Our task, then, is not to explain why we *cannot* have two elements intervene in a mutation but rather why, when mutation occurs, there is a *strong tendency* for it to occur between contiguous elements, such that two-element interventions are unknown and one-element interventions are limited and unstable (likely to degenerate and be lost in, for example, variant dialects). But this seems easy to explain. It is merely the instantiation of a simplicity-criterion, aimed at facilitation of communication. For various reasons, other things being equal, degree of simplicity will equal degree of contiguity in the case of mutation. Thus a child will, in general, learn the contiguous cases most easily. This is not to say that contiguity instantiates a Platonic ideal of simplicity, but merely that, in our everyday reasoning, other things being equal, simplicity ranking for causality is directly parallel to proximity ranking (that is, we assume that causes and effects most often occur close together, as is clear from the studies on covariation perception, reported by Holland et al.). And mutation is a causal relation in the relevant sense. Thus no special posits, representationalist or innatist, are necessary to account for the tendency. There are, of course, other factors as well—most obviously, a sort of conservation of mental energy. It would not be easy to keep track of mutations with four or five intervening elements. In fact, it could greatly impede fluency, given the limits on our 'working memory'. (We can keep in mind or 'rehearse' only about seven words at any one time; see Garman 1990, 322–23, for a discussion of the relevant research.) These only make the case for an intentional and communicative account stronger. (Of course, this leaves open the question as to why any language has mutations at all. But this problem goes beyond the present dispute on both sides.)

A similar, covertly communicative example may be found in Mark Baker's "mirroring principle" (Baker 1985). Baker's primary formulation of his principle is in terms of parallel or "mirroring" morphological and syntactic processes and presupposes the very representationalism we are disputing. The basic principle, however, is simple and may be stated in terms that are neutral between our different theories: the meaning of a morpheme is a function of the order in which affixes are added to the stem.

Before explaining this notion, there are a few terms I should explain. The notion of adding affixes to a stem concerns relations of logical and not temporal succession. Thus we would say that 'nondiscriminatory' is formed by adding '-ory' to 'discriminate', forming 'discriminatory', and then adding 'non-' to 'discriminatory'. We would not say that we first add 'non-', giving 'nondiscriminate'. Thus the addition of 'non-' logically presupposes, and in this sense 'follows', the addition of '-ory'. Another way of putting this is to say that 'nondiscriminatory' has this structure: [non-[[discriminate]-ory]].

Certain languages—called 'concatinative'—have very complex word formations that in effect do with single words what English does with sentences. Thus in Chamorro, Quechua, and other such languages, a single word with a stem and a series of tense, person, and other morphemes, will translate into a rather lengthy English sentence. For example, in Quechua, one says "He is causing them to beat each other" by taking the stem for 'beat', adding the morpheme that indicates reciprocity, adding the morpheme that indicates durative aspect, adding the morpheme that indicates causation, and finally adding the morpheme that indicates third person singular. Thus the Quechua word, 'Maqa/naku/ya/chi/n', may be translated, morpheme by morpheme, as: 'beat/reciprocal/durative/causal/3 singular'.

84

(The 'them' of the grammatical English translation is understood for reasons that are unimportant here.)

Let us suppose, then, that we alter the order and place the causative by the stem rather than the reciprocal. Simplifying somewhat for exposition, the result of this is that the meaning changes to 'They are causing someone to beat each other'. In other words, the reciprocity applies to the causing and not to the beating, leaving the third person singular morpheme to take up the act of beating.

Baker explains this and much related data by arguing that order of morpheme addition—which is identical with proximity to the stem in this and most of the other cases he considers—is always identical with the grammatical order and order of interpretation. Thus if the reciprocity morpheme precedes (is closer to the stem than) the causative morpheme, then the reciprocal action indicated in the stem is caused. If, on the other hand, the order is reversed, then the causing of the action indicated in the stem is reciprocal—whereas the action itself is not. Similarly, many languages have an agreement morpheme for subject and verb. Many have passive morphemes as well. Clearly, passivization changes the grammatical subject of a verb. In the relevant languages, Baker explains, the agreement morpheme will not always agree with the subject in passives. Specifically, if the passive morpheme is added before the agreement morpheme—if it is closer to the stem—then the agreement will be with the grammatical (passive) subject. If, on the other hand, the agreement morpheme comes first, then it will *not* relate to the grammatical (passive) subject but to the agent, which is to say the subject of the correlated active sentence.

It is difficult to say whether this is in fact strictly universal or merely overwhelmingly the most common case, as Baker points out (citing some recalcitrant data). In any event, the tendency toward identifying grammatical or interpretive sequences with morpheme-addition sequences is clear. It is also clear that this tendency is precisely what one would expect from simplicity and communicative considerations. Clearly, if the rule governing morpheme-addition and that governing interpretation or grammar are the same, then there is only one relevant rule, and only one form of that rule. In all other cases, there are two or more rules, or the existing rule is given two or more different forms. The simplicity of identifying the rules clearly facilitates both expression and understanding. Imagine the difficulties of either utterance or interpretation if the interpretation rule were something along these lines: 'Take the third morpheme first; then, if there are more than four morphemes, take number five; if not, take number two'; and so on. Interpreting even the simplest sentence would take all week—as would figuring out how to say it. But even less complex cases—for example, 'Add morphemes in this order: a, b, c . . .' for the morpheme-addition rule and 'interpret morphemes according to the morpheme-addition rule, but in reverse, thus: . . . c, b, a', for the interpretation rule—are significantly less simple and thus significantly more difficult to interpret, or learn, than the actual, single-rule case. This is particularly clear when one keeps in mind the broader context of such constructions. For example, it may seem simpler to make both morpheme-addition and interpretation matters of temporal ordering (if you hear causative first, then you apply it first). But this is not simpler, as it obscures the relation between embedded morphological structures and their free-standing equivalents. Consider again 'nondiscriminatory'. To interpret this by temporal sequence would lead us to form 'nondiscriminate' into some sort of unit and not to form 'discriminatory' into such a unit, despite the fact that 'discriminatory' is an independent word, whereas 'nondiscriminate' is not. To interpret in the order of morpheme addition is to preserve a broad set of linguistic relations, such as those between embedded morpheme sequences and independent morpheme sequences. And this is overwhelmingly the simplest alternative.

Thus the universal tendency Baker has isolated is precisely what one would expect, given concerns for simplicity, communication, and so forth. It does not appear to require either innateness or a representational, computational, or objectivist explanation.

Of course, here too, we have been able to look only at isolated examples of the data Chomsky cites in support of his account. However, I hope to have indicated how an intentional account, based on communicative aims and rational inference—an account based on principles that I assume Chomsky would accept in any event—might be made adequate to the data in question. If this project is in general successful, then Chomsky's posits are redundant.

As we have emphasized communication to such an extent in the preceding arguments, we might respond briefly to Chomsky's objection to intentional/communicative 'theories' of meaning. Chomsky's position is that one can very well use words in their usual meanings and not intend to communicate anything but rather aim to clarify one's thoughts or whatever (see, for example, Chomsky 1975, 66ff.; 1980, 229f.). Chomsky has in mind the early writings of the "theorists of communication intention" (Strawson 1979) such as Austin (1962; 1971), Strawson (1950; 1971), and Searle (1969), who defined meaning in terms of communicative intent of a particular sort. Clearly, I have not claimed that meaning *is* communicative intent (any more than it *is* anything else). Moreover, my references to communicative aims have been fairly broad and need not be tied in any way to the detailed and rigoristic formulations of these theorists (their account of an utterer's meaning in terms of his/her intention to cause an auditor to believe such-and-such in virtue of the utterer having said such-and-such, and so on). Nonetheless, these theorists seem to me clearly right to assert the primacy of the communicative function of speech. Even if one does not accept their specific formulations, their emphasis on communication (which, by the way, did not involve a denial of other sorts of meaning; see, for example, Grice 1989, 112–16) seems entirely reasonable and appropriate. After all, even the 'purest' case of noncommunicative language—that used in interior monologue to clarify one's thought—is most often aimed at subsequent communicative expression. Indeed, at least in my case, that interior 'monologue' is almost always structured as communicative speech aimed at some imagined addressee. Moreover, as we have known since at least the time of Vygotsky's seminal researches (see Vygotsky 1962—first published in 1934), the communicative function of speech is primary, and so-called 'ego-centric' speech (see Piaget 1969) is derivative. In language acquisition, communicative considerations are, again, critical; after all, acquiring a language is just getting one's own rules to match up with those of people around one. For these reasons, one should expect communicative considerations to be central to almost any explanation of linguistic phenomena.

Up until now, we have concerned ourselves with the possible redundancy of Chomsky's representationalism and innatism. I should like to conclude with a look at the question of the degree to which underlying structures and other representations posited by Chomsky could be of explanatory value even if they are not redundant. This will also allow us to consider more thoroughly the differences between an objective and an intentional or subjective/experiential view of mind.

As we have already remarked, computational processes and the representations upon which they operate function entirely independently of intent, which is to say, independently of actual or possible subjective experience. The rules are wholly and necessarily nonintentional and the representations are *in principle* inaccessible to intent (see, for example, Chomsky 1988b, 111f.). This differentiates Chomsky's 'unconscious' from, for example, Freud's. For Freud, the 'contents' of the unconscious are inaccessible, but only contingently. Once repression is lifted, then those contents may become intentionally accessible, at least following a process of 'working-through' (see Freud 1963). For Chomsky there is no such process as 'working-through'; there is no possibility of intentional access (or introspective 'perception', as discussed above). On the other hand, these nonintentional processes and inaccessible representations must issue in a surface structure, which is the direct result of these processes and the manifestation of these representations, but which is also an intent. The surface structure must in this way be continuous with nonintentional/objectivistic representations and thus it must be representational itself. However, at the same time it must be intentional.

Two problems arise here. The first problem concerns the possibility of reconciling objective/representational mind with intent. This is a version of the problem we encountered with the social, autonomist, and essentialist conceptions of language considered above: won't we be faced with a situation in which intent and representation are not only distinct but different in kind? In other words, doesn't this make me or you, as intentional subjects, spectators to the production of representations that our nonintentional, thus nonsubjective, computational processes generate and interpret in isolation? Are we, as subjectivities, not as removed from the operation of this representation-generating "organ" of language, as Chomsky calls it (see, for example, Chomsky 1980, 39), as we are from, say, our adrenal glands, or from any external, material object that is similarly independent of our (internal or external) perceptions? The second problem concerns the comprehensibility of extending the notion of the mental to encompass in principle nonintentional and intentionally inaccessible or introspectively imperceptible entities. In general, this sort of in-principle independence from intentionality or perception is definitive of our conception of the physical; it is what we mean by something's being an object.[11] The exact ontological nature of Chomsky's posits, hovering as they do between the mental and the physical, is obscure—which is, of course precisely because his is an objectivist view of mind. Mind is understood as nonphysical, but at the same time it is not experiential subjectivity; it is an object, but it is simultaneously mental. The problem is, in short—does it make any sense to speak of the mind in such objectivist terms?

Chomsky makes reference to the first problem in various places. For example, distinguishing between the "mind" (an objective entity of some sort) and the "*person*" (roughly intentionality, in our sense), Chomsky remarks that "once the system of language and other cognitive structures are developed by the mind, the person has a certain range of choices available as to how to use these systems. . . . A person . . . chooses to follow the rules that . . . belong to the cognitive state his mind has produced." And, further on, "we put to use the system of rules the mind has developed" (1975, 77). But, first of all, the person does not use these rules at all, in any ordinary sense. Rather, it is the "mind" that 'uses' them. The problem then is, so to speak—how do I know what my mind means once it has used the rules to generate the representations that I am to utter?

In other words, the nonintentional/objective mind generates a sequence of representations. These representations are interpretable by nonintentional mind as well. However, for the speaker as intentionality, they are merely representations—just as they are merely representations for any *other* intentionality. As intent and mind are not the same, it is clear that intent cannot know mental meaning as 'its own'—as what it (or the 'person') *intends*—for that meaning is *not* its own, is not intended. Furthermore, mind cannot, so to speak, 'tell' intent the meaning of the representations. In order to do this, mind would necessarily have recourse to further representations, which would only compound the problem rather than solving it. Moreover, there is no clear way in which intent could infer to mental meaning. One infers to the intentional meaning of others by connecting utterances with actions, events, and such. But this only counts as an inference to nonintentional mental meaning as well if the mental and the intentional are somehow already linked. But linking the mental and intentional is precisely the problem.

Thus it is very difficult to see how intent and representation can be reconciled. If this is so, then it would appear that the computationally processed representations of 'mind' could never enter into our speech except haphazardly. We would simply speak and interpret and act on the basis of intentional criteria and inferences, no matter what useless and uninterpretable strings of representations our minds might be generating. In other words, it would appear that even if intentional and communicative considerations are inadequate to the data isolated by Chomsky, a computational representationalism is of no help in explaining these data, for such representationalism is necessarily irrelevant to the intents with which we are concerned in the first place.

Of course, Chomsky believes that intent and representation can be reconciled—in particular, by way of the brain and by a certain conception of the relation between mind and brain, which leads to our second problem. (Chomsky is never explicit about the function of intent here, but I think it might be inferred.) Specifically, for Chomsky, all talk of mind—and, presumably, intent as well—is merely "abstract" talk of brain. As Chomsky puts it, grammatical "knowledge is . . . represented in our minds, ultimately in our brains," and all talk of mental phenomena involves merely an "abstract characterization of certain physical mechanisms" (1980, 5; see also, for example, 1972, 80; 1975, 36; and elsewhere). Thus there really is no problem of reconciling mind and intent, for both are merely abstractions from biological systems that are either identical or in standard causal relation.

But, in fact, a problem does arise. Chomsky presumably wishes his computational and representational grammars to be open to mentalistic descriptions that are not simply identical with physicalistic descriptions. Let us suppose, for a moment, that they are identical. Thus *having D-structure 'Mary did excoriate who'* just means *having such-and-such a brain-state*. Now, if all mentalistic reference is reduced to physicalistic reference, then all meaning itself is reduced to physical states. In other words, if D-structure, surface structure, and so on, are identified with brain-state a, brain-state β, and so on, that is because D-structure just *is* brain-state a, and surface structure just *is* brain-state β. (Or *some* brain-state, anyway; it does not matter whether we are speaking about type-type identity [such that a given D-structure would reduce to the same sort of brain-state at all times in all people] or token-token identity [such that each instance of each D-structure would reduce to some brain-state, but not necessarily the same one at all times in all people].)

Thus our statement of mind/brain identity itself *is* just such-and-such a brain-state as well. The ultimate result of this is the ultimate result of all reductive physicalism—its claims cannot be true, because, if true, they would be nothing but brain-states, or sound-waves, or marks, and thus they would have no truth-conditions, any more than a plunk, a scrape, or a stain has truth-conditions. (I have discussed this at more length in Hogan 1990b.)

But, again, Chomsky, does not claim precisely a relation of identity. Rather, he claims that mind is an *abstraction* from brain. Now, usually, one description is 'abstract' with respect to another when it is more general and covers the same objects, as well as some other objects. Thus 'finger' is more abstract than 'pinky'; 'body-part' is more abstract than 'finger'; and so on. There is, however, no obvious way in which this notion of abstraction may be applied to the relation between descriptions of 'underlying structures' and descriptions of brain-states. Moreover, Chomsky never explicates the idea. It appears to be empty, the sort of thing Chomsky often refers to as 'mere handwaving'.

The vacuity of this notion is well demonstrated in the slippery use to which it is put early on in *Knowledge of Language*. Here, Chomsky argues that the underlying structures generated by individual transformational grammars are real objects of study because they are "abstractions" from brain processes (1986, 23). A few pages later, however, we are told that autonomous language is no real object at all, but merely an "artificial . . . construct," because it is nothing but a mere "abstraction" from individual grammars (27); in fact, this latter use is normal, comprehensible, and correct. Thus, Chomsky argues that B is real because it is an abstraction from A (which is real), but that C is not real, is a mere artificial construct, because it is (merely) an abstraction from B! I do not think that this is a mere slip on Chomsky's part. Rather, I believe that it indicates that his concept of 'abstraction', as applied to mind and brain, is so indefinite as not to count as a concept at all—it has only vague suggestiveness, with no precise meaning. As such, it is entirely useless in reconciling intent and representation.

But Chomsky claims that the notion does have content in that 'abstraction' is precisely the relation between a computer program and the mechanisms that 'underlie' that program. As Chomsky puts it, "linguistics is the abstract study of certain mechanisms, their growth and maturation. We may impute existence to the postulated structures at the initial, intermediate, and steady states in just the same sense as we impute existence to a program that we believe to be somehow represented in a computer" (Chomsky 1980, 188). This computing analogy for mind is nearly ubiquitous today (in literary study, see, for example, Norman Holland 1985, and in anthropology, see Geertz 1973, 44; for another example from the philosophy of mind, see Putnam 1975, xiiif. and elsewhere; for a treatment of cognitive science that clearly indicates the centrality of this analogy, see Johnson-Laird 1988; on its use in psychological functionalism, see the articles and introductions in Block 1980–81). It is the most recent in a long series of technologies employed to analogize mind. And it is no less flawed.

First, there is no such thing as a program in Chomsky's sense. Rather, there is merely a series of machine-states that a programmer is able to manipulate in certain useful ways. Thus, if I program a computer to, say, add, what I am doing is setting up an initial machine-state, which I can then alter by pressing certain keys, in order to arrive at a final machine-state—all of which I may correlate with stages of addition. Thus, when I program the machine and then type in '2 + 2 =', I am merely altering the initial machine-state. So to speak, as far as the computer is concerned, all that has happened is that some buttons have been pushed. Now, when '4' appears on the screen, this again is just a machine-state with the screen illuminated in a particular manner. I have simply designed things so that the illumination will be a numeral, hence systematically correlatable with a word, hence a meaning, hence an answer.

Thus, talking of programs is merely a simple and elliptical way of speaking about intents (of programmers and users) plus mechanisms. Clearly, this is of no use to Chomsky, for even if he were to accept the analogy in these terms—with representations reduced to brain-states conjoined with intents—it is clear that the relation of my intent to my brain is not even vaguely analogous to the relation between my intent and my computer, and thus that the analogy is pointless.

On the other hand, let us suppose that the states of a computer involve various representations, distinct from our intents, or even any computer-intents, if we were to accept such things. If there were such computer representations, they would be analogous to the nonintentional representations of an individual's transformational grammar. But, they would be entirely inaccessible and there would be no way in which we could infer to their existence or properties. We would in any event operate with programmers' (and users') intents, and the uses to which we put the machine and its states would be a function of these. Nonintentional representations here would be as problematic, as inconsequential, and as redundant as they are anywhere. Thus their putative presence and function in this context could not be invoked to account for their putative presence and function elsewhere.

There is a great deal that is obscure about the nature of mind and of language. And thus there are many important topics for further research. But in the present context, where we are concerned with the principles and possibilities of interpretation in ordinary life and in specialized interpretive disciplines, what is most important is that there are intents, that intent is well enough understood to allow us to interpret for various specific types of intentional meaning (legislators' policy aim, speaker's unconscious belief, or author's aesthetical intent, to take examples from each of the following chapters), and that there are not, in addition to such intents, *representations* or other objectivistic mental entities. Representationalism, it seems—like essentialism, autonomism, and theories of social meaning—is redundant with respect to intent. Moreover, even if intent were not adequate to the data, representations, like essences, would, it appears, provide no help. Only idiolectal intent is neither ontologically superfluous nor epistemologically opaque. Thus we are left with intents alone for our stipulations of meaning and intents along with some general principles of rational inference for our investigations of the objects and methods of legal, psychoanalytic, and literary interpretation—to which we may now turn.

3 LEGAL INTERPRETATION

Extension and Definition in the Legislature,
the Community, and the Judiciary

I hope it is uncontroversial that a theory of law should encompass both an interpretive part and an evaluative part. Certainly all theories of law with which I am familiar—even the positivist theory of law—encompass both parts, though the two are not always equally developed. In this chapter, I shall, of course, be concentrating upon the interpretive part of legal theory. However, as the two parts are closely related and as evaluative considerations arise, necessarily and often crucially, in legal interpretation, I should like to preface my more detailed examination of the one part with a brief outline of both parts.

INTERPRETATION AND RATIONAL INFERENCE

The interpretive part of legal theory concerns, roughly, the meaning of written law and of precedents. More exactly, in the case of statutes and other written law (hereafter, I shall refer to all written law through the abbreviation, 'statutes'), it involves the determination of the events or states of affairs to which general statements apply. A statute may be understood to forbid or limit or enjoin a certain type of behavior, act, or state of affairs. For example, a statute might limit the operation of motor vehicles on public roads to speeds not in excess of 55 MPH. Similarly, a statute might require that signatories honor legal contracts or it might forbid the possession of certain substances, such as heroin (cf. Greimas 1990, 110; obviously, demands may be rephrased as limitations, limitations as condemnations, and so on). Statutory interpretation involves, first, the determination of satisfaction-conditions—or, rather, nonsatisfaction-conditions—for the statute (the determination of the general conditions under which the statute would be violated) and, second, the determination of the degree to which these nonsatisfaction-conditions are or are not fulfilled in any particular case under consideration. (I say 'nonsatisfaction-conditions' rather than 'satisfaction-conditions', as the former are much narrower and thus much easier to define and apply; for example, there are innumerable ways to satisfy the speed limit law, such as sitting at home, but many fewer ways to violate it.)

To take the first example, interpreting a statute concerning maximum speed involves isolating criteria that define when an automobile is traveling in excess of 55 MPH and then applying these criteria in particular cases, determining if such-and-such an automobile was traveling in excess of 55 MPH. In a case such as this, it may seem that no interpretation whatsoever takes place and that, hence, no theory of legal interpretation is even relevant. This is, however, untrue. Every decision involving the application of statutes involves interpretation, often of a remarkably complex sort. Indeed, even in this case, the relation between the general criteria and any particular case under consideration is mediated by evidentiary considerations, themselves governed by further, procedural principles involving the judiciary as a whole, the police, and so on.

Thus the general form of statutory interpretation is roughly deductive. As we shall discuss below, this oversimplifies the situation greatly, but it is nonetheless the tendency of statutory decisions, and, in any event, our concern at the moment is only to indicate the general area of interpretive and evaluative studies in the theory of law.

The interpretation of precedent, however, moves in the opposite direction. Statutes tell us that a certain *sort* of thing is forbidden or enjoined or limited. They do not tell us which *particular* things are forbidden or enjoined or limited. Precedents, in contrast, provide us with a number of particular judgments, a number of condemnations of, demands upon, and limitations of particular behaviors, acts, or states of affairs, without a general, exactly formulated, uniform, and binding statement of the category under which these particulars fall. Certainly judges cite general principles in their decisions. However, insofar as the principles are not part of the explicit legal code of the judge's jurisdiction, they are not legally binding in the judge's phrasing. Moreover, when a number of judges decide a case—for example, when the Supreme Court decides a case—even those judges who concur in their judgment may cite different principles in support of their decisions. Similarly, related cases may be judged in a related manner by different judges, but these judges may then go on to defend their related decisions in unrelated ways. Thus particular precedents are indeed accompanied by generalizations, but these generalizations are of a problematic status and, more important, may be incoherent with one another for any given precedent or across related precedents.

Thus the interpretation of precedent involves the construction of generalizations out of particulars in such a way as to make these generalizations cohere with at least certain of the generalizations cited in the precedents, and more crucially with the body of explicitly formulated law. Hence, the interpretation of precedent is not deductive, but—again, roughly—inductive. And it is inductive within a larger system, which, like the larger system of a theory in physical science, defines the framework within which the induction is to take place.

(As should be obvious, the conceptual distinction outlined here does not imply a practical separation. Specific acts of legal interpretation most often involve the interpretation of both statutes and precedents. They involve both 'deductive' and 'inductive' considerations.)

Finally, it is important to point out that determining the relevance of particular statutes or precedents to a particular case is a complex problem. Legal interpretation involves not only something like induction from precedents and something like deduction from statutes but a concurrent determination of the set of relevant precedents and statutes from which such induction and deduction are to proceed. Thus neither the interpretation of statutes nor the interpretation of precedents is a straightforward matter in which the statutes and precedents are held fixed and only their truth-conditions and so on are to be ascertained. Rather, the entire process reacts back upon the statutes and precedents. Our interpretations function not only to determine the legality or illegality of certain behaviors, or acts, or states of affairs, but equally to determine the relevance to the case at hand of the statutes and precedents being interpreted.

EVALUATION AND ETHICS

There are many sorts of evaluation germane to law. Three, I believe, are of particular importance. The first and in my view primary sort of evaluation is moral.[1] It asks after the degree to which rights are protected and the fulfillment of obligations is supported by a given law or set of laws. The second sort is pragmatic. It asks after the degree to which desirable ends—themselves sometimes moral or open to moral evaluation—are being effected by a given law or set of laws. Moral evaluation considers the degree to which, for example, a national speed limit of 55 MPH is morally justified or unjustified. It concerns the degree to which it is morally permissible to abridge or inhibit freedom of movement toward the end of preventing traffic deaths (itself a moral end) or to reduce U.S. dependence on foreign oil (a 'policy' end). Pragmatic evaluation, in contrast, concerns the degree to which a national speed limit of 55 MPH does as a matter of fact reduce highway fatalities or decrease U.S. dependence on foreign oil. The final sort of evaluation is strictly judicial. It concerns the coherence of a statute or legal judgment with the precedent body of law, statutory or customary, and, most particularly, in the United States, the Constitution.

I should like to set aside the second and third—pragmatic and judicial evaluation—on the grounds of their relative simplicity, and look instead at the first, moral evaluation. It is certainly true that problems arise in pragmatic evaluation, but these are merely the usual problems of evidence and generalization common to all disciplines, and not peculiar to law. Similarly, judicial evaluation involves sometimes insuperable problems. However, I would maintain that problems of judicial evaluation are for the most part problems of legal *interpretation*. In other words, I take it that once the problems of interpretation have been solved—including the problems surrounding the relevance of statutes and precedents—the problem of judicial evaluation is also solved. In cases where judicial evaluation is aimed at statutes and seeks to judge, say, constitutionality, the problem is one of the degree to which the statute under consideration does or does not forbid acts, behaviors, or states of affairs protected by the Constitution, or specifically permit acts, behaviors, or states of affairs forbidden by the Constitution. Judicial evaluation thus judges the coherence of consequences deduced from the new legislation with consequences deduced from the body of the law, most particularly the Constitution. The work here is clearly in the interpretation, not in the evaluation. The same holds when judicial evaluation is aimed at particular cases, as when the Supreme Court rules to affirm or reverse the decision of a lower court. Judicial evaluation here is a matter of judging the coherence of the lower court decision with the relevant precedents and statutes. Once again, the crucial and difficult work is interpretive, not evaluative.

Moral evaluation is, however, far more thorny. There are two important and difficult questions that arise in its regard and to which I should like briefly to attend. The first and primary question concerns the manner in which the law should be subjected to moral scrutiny. It concerns how and when we should examine the rectitude of laws or of the legal system, what sorts of moral standards should be employed in such evaluations, and

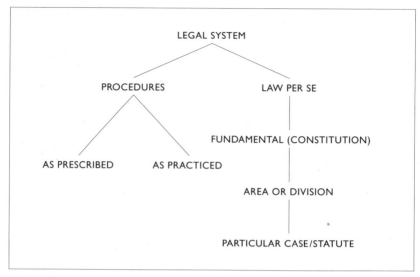

Figure I

so forth. The second and to some extent derivative question concerns the degree to which the law itself has moral force independent of the consideration of moral principles per se. The first question concerns, for example, the manner in which we should evaluate the morality of a statute limiting the speed of motor vehicles or a court decision permitting abortion. The second concerns the degree to which a statute establishing a speed limit or a decision forbidding restrictions on abortion becomes not only legally but *morally* binding *by becoming law.* As we shall see, the two are related and bear significantly upon the interpretive concerns we shall examine below.

As to the former question, I should first of all like to separate the evaluation of legal procedure from the evaluation of the law per se. Within the law per se, I should like to distinguish: 1) the evaluation of fundamental legal principles (primarily those enshrined in a Constitution), 2) the evaluation of more specific areas or divisions of law (for instance, contract law), and 3) the evaluation of particular statutes and precedents. (These are perhaps better viewed as points on a continuum than absolutely discrete levels.) Finally, it is worth distinguishing legal procedures as actually practiced from legal procedures as prescribed in the legal system. (See figure 1.) Some distinctions roughly along these lines are commonplace in discussions of legal theory.

My contention—already hinted at in this anatomy—is that moral evaluation of the law should proceed hierarchically and systematically. The question we should ask ourselves in evaluating a legal system is "To what degree is this legal system morally superior or inferior to anarchy (not in the sense of 'anarchist community' but in the Kantian sense of natural lawlessness), to what degree does it protect rights more or less fully than they would be protected in a state of nature, to what degree does it foster the fulfillment of obligations more—or less—fully than would be the case in its absence?" This question clearly involves a range of issues.

For one thing, it concerns the actual functioning of the legal system. In some ways, it is first of all a judgment about the 'actual practice' of legal procedures. It also, more important for our purposes, refers to the ways legal procedures are prescribed and, more broadly, to the body of law itself. Though the fundamental principles would be of primary importance to such an evaluation, the various (hierarchized) areas of law and the range of specific statutes are obviously crucial as well. In all these cases, our concern is, again, the degree to which the Constitution or some provision of the Constitution, an area or division of law or some statute within that area, fosters or does not foster the protection of more rights and so forth than would be the case without that Constitution, provision, area, or statute. Note, however, that this is not merely a judgment about these legal structures or elements considered in isolation. It is equally a judgment about their place in the legal system as a whole. Thus, for example, a particular law concerning contracts is open to evaluation both in itself and by reference to its place in contract law generally; contract law is in turn open to evaluation both in itself and by reference to its place in the legal system as a whole, and so on. In this way, a law concerning contracts, morally neutral in isolation, may prove damnable or laudable in context. Evaluation is, then, both particular and systemic; it operates at every level from isolated statutes through complexes of laws and precedents to the legal system as a whole and, most important, all these levels must be integrated, each part contributing to the evaluation of the whole—and thus to the evaluation of the other parts.

All of this leads us to our second question, concerning the moral force of the law as law, independent of particular moral considerations. Clearly, the sort of evaluative wholism that I have just been urging necessarily allows law some independent moral force. However, it at the same time limits and qualifies that force. Specifically, our wholism indicates that a law lacks moral force if it is in itself morally wrong by independent moral standards or if it contributes to a legal system or to an area or division of the legal system, the effects of which are not superior to those of anarchy. However, a law as law does have moral force insofar as it is not itself morally wrong and insofar as it contributes to a legal system or area or division that is superior to anarchy. (Obviously, a law has moral force if it expresses a moral principle.) Furthermore, this moral force is a function of the degree of value that may be attributed to the system or area/division. In other words, we have a *moral* duty to obey a given law, if it is not itself vicious, insofar as it contributes to the legal system or an area/division of that system and insofar as that system or area/division is virtuous. Similarly, we have a moral duty to disobey a given law, if the law is not itself virtuous, insofar as it contributes to the legal system, etc., and insofar as that system, etc., is vicious.

Legal interpretation not only tells us what a law is but, in conjunction with judicial evaluation, explains how that law fits into various encompassing categories in the legal system as a whole. Thus legal interpretation is absolutely crucial to moral evaluation. In order to evaluate a specific law, one must know the claims of the law; one must know its place within the system of law; and one must know the claims of related laws. It is, of course, precisely the claims of various laws and sets of laws that interpretation seeks to reveal. Thus, logically rigorous, patient, and scholarly legal interpretation—in short, interpretation that follows the principles of rational inference—is not only pragmatically desirable but morally obligatory. Without it, serious moral evaluation of the law—or, indeed, serious pragmatic and judicial evaluation of the law—is impossible.

Few, I think, would deny that careful, accurate interpretation of statutes and precedents is a difficult task. Yet few would deny that accurate interpretation is an undertaking quite possible at least in principle, and that at the very least some interpretations will be more careful and accurate than others, even if none will be perfect. However, Stanley Fish has recently argued that careful and accurate legal interpretation is just not possible at all, in that accuracy in interpretation is not possible generally and does not even constitute a meaningful ideal. Fish makes these claims in the context of a debate with Ronald Dworkin. Before beginning a more detailed analysis of legal interpretation, then, I should like to turn briefly to this important debate and the assumptions that underlie it.

THE POSSIBILITY AND NATURE OF INTERPRETATION

Ronald Dworkin has developed a theory of legal interpretation based not so much upon explicit rules—the most commonly accepted basis for theories of legal interpretation—as upon more general ethical principles. These principles, according to Dworkin, derive from "the soundest theory of law that can be provided as a justification for the explicit substantive and institutional rules of the jurisdiction in question" (Dworkin 1978, 66). A theory of law, then, must not merely describe but must "try to *justify* the settled rules" by reference to "political or moral concerns and traditions" (67). In other words, a theory of law is, for Dworkin, a sort of moral rationalization of the law or legal system in question, and legal interpretation is a matter of developing and specifying legal principles in accordance with the moral principles germane to this moral rationalization. As Dworkin puts it, "an interpretation of any body or division of law, like the law of accidents, must show the value of that body of law in political terms by demonstrating the best principle or policy it can be taken to serve" (Dworkin 1983a, 264). This principle, in turn, serves to guide further interpretations. To say that one interpretation is "better" than another, Dworkin tells us, is just to say that "it states a sounder principle of justice" if both "fit doctrinal history" (Dworkin 1983a, 266). (For reasons that will become clear in the following section, I believe that Dworkin's notions of 'fitting doctrinal history' and 'adjudication by moral principle' fail to discriminate between some importantly different varieties of interpretation and evaluation—though I also believe that he is completely correct to stress the interpretive, and not merely evaluative, function of moral precepts.)

Thus, for Dworkin, statutes and precedents do constrain interpretations to some degree. In other words, for Dworkin, some interpretations are, indeed, just plain wrong. A statute stating, "The maximum speed limit on all public roads, highways, etc., may not exceed 55 MPH" just does not mean that cheese may not be sold to minors. The self-incrimination clause of the Fifth Amendment just does not mean that everyone should go to church on Pentecost. However, statutes and precedents are not univocal on all cases. When faced with several interpretive choices, Dworkin tells us, we should adopt the one that most clearly conforms to the most elevated moral principles that could be used to justify the statutes or precedents being interpreted. Thus, for example, Dworkin might say that an interpretation of the due process clause of the Fourteenth Amendment in relation to abortion laws should not recur to the intents of the legislators or to any similar considerations. Rather, it should concern the moral justification of such a clause and the relation of that justification to abortion laws. If the most *just* construal of the clause—the construal that gives to the law its greatest moral force—would restrict abortion laws, then such laws should be restricted in accordance with that clause; if the most just construal of the clause would not restrict abortion laws, then these need not be restricted.

Thus, for Dworkin, any legal interpretation is partially constrained and partially free as a matter of fact; as a matter of principle, he adds that the free interpretations should themselves be further limited by specific sorts of moral considerations. To elucidate these concepts, Dworkin uses as an analogy a serial novel, where one author writes chapter 1, hands it over to a second author for chapter 2, who in turn brings the manuscript to a third author, and so on. In this situation, Dworkin tells us, "every novelist but the first has the dual responsibilities of interpreting and creating" (Dworkin 1983a, 262). Moreover, the interpretive constraints will, in general, increase as the novel progresses. "Deciding hard cases at law," Dworkin concludes, "is rather like this strange literary exercise" (Dworkin 1983a, 263). The crucial difference is that the novelists create by reference to interpretation and *aesthetical* principles whereas the judges create, or should create, by reference to interpretation and *ethical* principles.

This description involves a concept of law familiar in the history of legal theory. It is, for example, similar to Kelsen's notion of "concretization," summarized by W. Friedman in the following terms: "The judgement . . . marks a . . . stage in the process of concretization. It at once applies and creates the law. The freedom of creative function is progressively narrowed down in each successive stage, although it never quite ceases. Every judgment contains an act of creation in choosing one of several possibilities of interpretation which the statute, or whatever the superior norm in question may be, permits" (Friedman 1967, 282). Dworkin develops this common notion, however, in a significant manner by placing moral constraints upon the creation. As Dworkin puts it, "propositions of law are not simply descriptive of legal history, in a straightforward way, nor are they simply evaluative in some way divorced from legal history. They are interpretive of legal history, which combines elements of both description and evaluation but is different from both" (Dworkin 1983a, 251). And subsequently, "it is the nerve of my argument that the flat distinction between description and evaluation on which . . . skepticism relies—the distinction between finding the law just 'there' in history and making it up wholesale—is misplaced here because interpretation is different from both" (266).

Dworkin's notion of interpretation by principle is certainly disputable. (Indeed, as I have already indicated, my own agreements with Dworkin are very limited.) But it would seem relatively uncontroversial that there is something akin to concretization that takes place in legal interpretation— or, at the very least, that there is, in Dworkin's words, a "difference between interpreting and changing a work" (Dworkin 1983a, 253). However, Stanley Fish has argued against precisely these points.

Fish begins by criticizing Dworkin's analogy of the serial novel. As it turns out, the analogy is weak in many of the ways Fish indicates. However, this only goes to show that the sort of interpretation and creation relevant to the composition of a novel is not the sort relevant to legal judgment. As we discussed earlier in this chapter, interpretation of a statute involves the delimitation of a set of nonsatisfaction-conditions and the judgment of their fulfillment or nonfulfillment in the particular behavior, act, or state of affairs in question. The interpretation of precedents, on the other hand, involves something akin to induction and generalization within the legal system as a whole, as well as something like statutory interpretation with respect to the statements of the judges. In addition, both involve judgments concerning what statutes or precedents are germane to the particular behavior, act, or state of affairs in question. Neither sort of interpretation is to be found directly in the composition of a serial novel. This is not to say that it is a bad analogy but that it is merely illustrative. Thus no conclusions about Dworkin's theory of law—either in support of that theory or in opposition to that theory—can be drawn from conclusions about the serial novel.

Fish's more important arguments, however, derive from his own earlier work in literary theory and his conclusions regarding literary interpretation. Put simply, for Fish, truth is not a matter of valid argument but a matter of persuasion. Or, rather, for Fish there just is no such thing as argument that is independently valid. Validity in argumentation is, for Fish, just whatever a given community takes it to be and nothing more. For Fish, the facts themselves are what a community takes to be the facts. As Fish puts it in "What Makes an Interpretation Acceptable?" "the fact of agreement, rather than being a proof of the stability of objects, is a testimony to the power of an interpretive community to constitute the objects upon which its members (also and simultaneously constituted) can then agree" (Fish 1980, 338). For Fish, "the text is always a function of interpretation" and "the text cannot be the location" of any "core of agreement." The text does not constrain our interpretations; rather our "literary institution" or other community defines for us "ways of *producing* the text" (342).

I myself am in complete agreement with Fish on the question of the degree to which institutional factors govern the practice of interpretation and the degree to which persuasion is a matter of communal recognition and not valid argument. Indeed, I have argued elsewhere that there are concrete economic and political reasons for this situation (see Hogan 1990a, chapter 5; 1993). However, whereas Fish finds this situation unobjectionable and inevitable, I find it deplorable and avoidable, at least in part. A full discussion of this issue would take us far from our main topic. Therefore, I shall confine my comments to two major points. First of all, I should like to reconsider the notion of argumentative validity in light of Fish's arguments (or persuasions) against the independence of the former from institutional conventions. Second, I should like to discuss why Fish's thesis appears to many people more plausible in literary and, as we shall discuss, legal interpretation, than elsewhere.

As to the first, I really only wish to make an obvious point. An argument is valid if it follows fundamental principles of logic and the Principle of Minimal Interpretation and is in accord with the available data. In other words, an argument is valid if it is not self-contradictory and so on, if it does not involve excessive or overly complex hypotheses (relative to alternatives), if it does not predict the occurrence of phenomena at variance with systematic observation—in short, if it is the product of rational inference.

I should emphasize that this does not assume data to be independent of theories. As we discussed earlier, data are not independent of theories. This is, I think, indisputable. However, I believe it is also indisputable that data are, or can and should be, independent of the theories being defended by reference to those data. Without going into the details, we must keep in mind, as noted in chapter 1, that any single theory is in effect a complex of theories, or subtheories, if you like. For example, contemporary physics encompasses a theory of atoms, a theory of atomic constituents, a theory of quarks, and so on. Moreover, these theories or subtheories develop in a hierarchy. The data supporting any given subtheory are, indeed, relative. However, they are not relative to the subtheory they are being used to support. Rather, they are relative to a *precedent* subtheory. For example, the data used in arguments in support of positing, say, protons and neutrons are not data relative to a theory and neutrons; rather, they are data relative to the theory of atoms or atom nuclei. We do not say that we should posit protons and neutrons in order to account for the behavior of protons and neutrons; rather, we say that we should posit protons and neutrons in order to account for the behavior of atoms or of nuclei. (Proton and neutron behavior would be accounted for by the positing of proton and neutron properties, subsequently quarks, and so on.) Certainly, things are messier in literary and legal interpretation, and this is not an insignificant fact. The point, however, is just that the theory-relativity of data does not pose any problem of principle for a definition of valid argument independent of persuasion.

Note also that this does not imply that valid arguments are compelling or true. Indeed, valid arguments—as we all know—need not persuade anyone, just as persuasions need not be argumentatively valid. More important, a valid argument, in our sense, does not necessarily lead to a true conclusion. Related to this, an argument that is valid at one time may become invalid at another, because of the discovery of contravening data, the formulation of simpler explanatory principles governing several subtheories, and so forth. Moreover, as data are not unequivocal, relative simplicity is frequently difficult to determine, practical reasoning is often necessarily elliptical and probabilistic, and so on, it may be impossible to ascertain even at a particular time which of several competing and contradictory hypotheses is the most plausible, which relies on the most nearly valid argument—in which case, all such arguments must be considered equally valid, or invalid.

Fish defends his community-relativist conclusions by reference to two phenomena that he feels others are unable to explain. The first is evidently unresolvable difference of opinion. The second is the potential defensibility of any thesis whatsoever.[2] According to Fish, for those who believe that truth is not relative to a community and that there can be such a thing as valid argument distinct from persuasion, "disagreement can only be a theological error." For such theorists, Fish tells us, "truth lies plainly in view, available to anyone who has eyes to see." Thus such theorists cannot present "a coherent account of *dis*agreement" and their only "explanation of . . . waywardness" can be "original sin" (Fish 1980, 338). For Fish, the true, the valid, and the "self-evident" (338) are necessarily one and the same. Thus the absence of self-evidence proves the absence of nonrelative truth and of argumentative validity. But this is a *non sequitur.* Far from entailing self-evidence, our preceding analysis of rational inference (which, in this regard, is pretty standard) indicates that self-evidence will literally never occur. All our claims and all our arguments are necessarily tentative, because of the uncertain nature of empirical study, with its heavy reliance on simplicity evaluations. Indeed, prima facie it would seem harder for Fish to account for disagreement. Indeed, strictly speaking, he cannot claim that there really is disagreement (between, say, his view and that of Toulmin), but only that his interpretive community has constituted such disagreement, along with the disputants and so forth. Another interpretive community might constitute the two positions as agreeing; it might even go so far as to constitute Fish and Toulmin as one person (perhaps on the model of Superman and Clark Kent).

As to Fish's further point—that any thesis whatsoever is defensible—much the same is true. Fish's (Duhemian) premise is, in my view, entirely correct. His conclusions, however, do not follow. Any thesis whatsoever is, in principle, defensible. Indeed, just as we can never quite certainly know one thesis to be true, we can never quite certainly know another thesis to be false; just as we can never know that a presently valid argument will not become invalid, we can never know that a presently invalid argument will not at some time be open to valid reconstrual. To take Fish's example, right now no one would accept a reading of "A Rose for Emily" that claimed the story concerns Eskimos. No such argument would be persuasive; I would add that it is extremely unlikely that any such argument would be valid. However, imagine "the discovery of a letter in which Faulkner confides that he has always believed himself to be an Eskimo changeling" (Fish 1980, 346). Persuasions would follow, fast and thick. Valid arguments might also follow. This is, after all, in complete accord with our preceding claims. It is an ordinary case of the discovery of new data, data that necessarily alter the criteria for argumentative validity in Faulkner interpretation, at least to some degree.

Thus Fish is entirely correct in viewing argument as necessarily open-ended, as in some sense always inconclusive. However, his inference from this—that it is "wrong" to say that "the unacceptability" of any given interpretation is "a function of the text" (346)—does not at all follow. Or, rather, this claim does not follow if we take it to mean that there is no such thing as valid, rather than persuasive, argument based upon the text, or, more broadly, the available data. Indeed, Fish's own example indicates precisely that valid argument based upon the data is quite possible. The reason that the situation is different after the discovery of Faulkner's Eskimo letter is, again, just that the data are different. Fish can conclude

from this case that no set of data can be considered complete, unequivocal, and determinative—and this is certainly true, whether we are speaking
of "A Rose for Emily," or quarks, or legal statutes, or whether or not the
cat is on the mat. However, he cannot conclude that the data are in principle irrelevant, or a mere "function of interpretation," or that it makes no
sense to speak of valid argument guided by or coherent with a set of data
conceived of as independent of that argument.

And yet, many people have the sense that there is something to Fish's
claims regarding literary and other linguistic interpretation, even if his
more general conclusions are faulty. Much of our daily conversation involves sentences such as 'It is raining' or 'The cat is on the mat' or 'Maybe
Reagan didn't know about the spare parts sales, but he certainly knew
about and sought to support Salvadoran terror bombing'. It seems intuitively implausible that sentences such as these should be true or false only
by way of communal agreement or disagreement. Moreover, it seems both
wrong and dangerous to claim that there is no valid argument, but only
persuasion, concerning the proper aerodynamic design for airplane wings
or the precise number of legal votes cast for each candidate in an election. However, much literary criticism involves sentences like 'Macbeth is
about ambition' or 'Hamlet is about incest' or 'Juliet is the sun means that
Juliet is the source of life', and most of us are far less uncomfortable with
the idea that sentences such as these are true or false only by way of communal agreement or disagreement, that there is no strictly valid argument
concerning such theses, but only persuasion. Why is this so?

The problem with these cases, I believe, is that we just have no clear idea
as to what the truth-conditions for these sentences might be; thus we have
no clear idea as to what sort of argument would support the claim that
these conditions do or do not obtain. In the case of rain, presidents, cats
on mats, elections, bombing sorties, and successful airplane flights, in contrast, we have a fairly firm idea of truth-conditions, and hence of evidence.
But why are we uncertain as to the truth-conditions of interpretive claims?
This returns us to the problem we first addressed in the opening chapter.
When we interpret, we seek 'the meaning' of the text, but we fail to define
our notion of meaning. Rather, we argue about its 'true nature' and employ the term in an ambiguous and inconsistent manner—thus giving our
claims ambiguous and inconsistent truth-conditions.

But, again, the solution to this is not to argue about the meaning of
'meaning'. Once more, questions about the meaning of 'meaning' concern
not facts but definitions or extensions. And definitions and extensions are

stipulative, not empirical or logical or intuitive. They are things we decide upon, not things we discover. Thus, as we have stressed, it follows that we should give up arguing about the nature of meaning and start talking instead about the various ways in which we might *define* 'meaning'. Hence we might speak of authorial intentional meaning or authorial expressive intentional meaning and authorial aesthetical intentional meaning, unconscious authorial meaning, such-and-such an individual reader's responsive meaning, the conventional meaning implicitly adopted by such-and-such a community, and so on. As soon as such a stipulative and non-normative enterprise is undertaken and applied, the truth-condition problems that are peculiar to interpretive claims evaporate. We have a fairly clear idea of what it means to claim that in *Macbeth* Shakespeare set out (or intended, or meant) to teach his audience a lesson about ambition or that most readers of *Hamlet* tend to imagine Horatio to be a woman. It may be no easy task to gather appropriate contravening or supportive evidence for some theses, to decide upon their likely truth or falsity, but we do have a fairly clear idea of what such evidence would look like and, more important, what it would mean for such theses to be true or false. Such claims are of the same sort as claims about rain, cats, and airplane wings. They are not of the same sort as those that concern 'the meaning of the work per se' and other mysterious entities.

Returning to legal interpretation, we find exactly the same situation. As I remarked above, in his reply to Dworkin, Fish extends to legal interpretation his arguments concerning literary interpretation. Ultimately, Fish concludes that the distinction between interpreting the law and just making up a new law is "nothing more than a distinction between a persuasive interpretation and one that has failed to convince" (Fish 1983, 278). In law as in literature, Fish tells us, there is no such thing as valid or invalid argument, only persuasive or unpersuasive argument. Dworkin replies to this in a rather peculiar manner by saying that making up a new law is a matter of "acting deceitfully" (Dworkin 1983b, 306), and thus that it is sincerity that distinguishes interpretation from creation. This does not seem to be consistent with Dworkin's notion that "a theory of interpretation must contain a subtheory about identity of a work of art in order to be able to tell the difference between interpreting and changing a work" (Dworkin 1983a, 253); presumably the same should hold of statutes. In any event, whether we view interpreters' sincerity as important or not, the crucial issue here is clearly not one of sincerity or insincerity, but one of the in-principle possibility of validity in argument with regard to legal interpretation.

Here, Fish's arguments concerning literary interpretation recur. First, there is widespread disagreement over correct legal interpretations. Second, in principle any interpretive thesis whatsoever may be defended with regard to any law whatsoever. For example, it may seem impossible to interpret the "unreasonable searches and seizures" clause of the Fourth Amendment as establishing that police officers who have epileptic seizures while in someone's house are thereby acting in violation of that person's constitutional rights. However, we can imagine evidence surfacing in support of this thesis—polemical antiepileptic writings penned by irate delegates to the constitutional convention, a history of bizarre cases involving British tax collectors frightening people out of their houses by having seizures, then recovering in time to abscond with their wealth, and so on. But in each case, the appropriate response to Fish is the same as in the case of literary interpretation. The concept of argumentative validity in no way entails the concept of the self-evidence of truth. In legal interpretation as elsewhere, the nature of data, of generalization, of simplicity, and so on, as we have discussed, almost guarantee disagreement among rational parties on questions of any complexity, and they certainly guarantee the impossibility of establishing absolutely the truth or falsity of any particular (noncontradictory/nontautological) thesis.

However, much as in literary interpretation, legal interpretation involves judgments—for example, the judgment that the due process clause of the Fifth Amendment forbids, or permits, minimum-wage legislation—which many people feel to be merely conventional in a way that they do not feel judgments as to whether or not it is raining to be merely conventional. Here too, such a feeling is no doubt primarily the result of an ambiguous and inconsistent notion of meaning giving rise to ambiguous and inconsistent truth-conditions for interpretive claims. The appropriate response to such a feeling in any area is, again, the stipulation, categorization, and clarification of the varieties of meaning germane to the specific purposes and practices of the interpretive discipline under consideration— in this case, law.[3]

VARIETIES OF LEGAL MEANING/VARIETIES OF LEGAL INTERPRETATION

Though for the most part, it seems, not reflectively aware of their shifting notions of meaning, lawyers and judges engage in many different varieties of interpretation and thus aim at many different varieties of meaning in their everyday professional work. As A. J. Greimas has pointed out in "The Semiotic Analysis of Legal Discourse," practitioners of law seek to establish an explicit lexicon of legal terms through legislation and legal judgment. Unfortunately, the success of this undertaking will be very limited until the legally germane meanings of 'meaning' have been adequately clarified—and this task of clarification has not been pursued systematically, either by the practitioners or by theorists of interpretation, such as Greimas. Though I do not necessarily hope to define all varieties of meaning germane to legal interpretation, I should like in this section to indicate what I take to be at least the most important. In the final section of this chapter, I shall say something about how, in my view, these various sorts of meaning and interpretation might best be organized and how conflicts arising between them might be adjudicated.

Following the arguments of chapter 2, I shall assume that all varieties of meaning are intentional, that meanings exist in persons and not anywhere else. Thus, I shall be concerned with two variables: 1) types of intent and 2) types of intending subject. The varieties of meaning, and thus the varieties of interpretation, will result from the pairing of each type of intent with each type of intending subject. Within this general framework, I should like to distinguish two general sorts of intent and two subcategories of each type. I should then like to distinguish two general categories of intending subject, with three specific divisions under each.

As to the intent per se, I should like first of all to distinguish what I shall call 'referential intent' from 'aim'. In the case of statutes, the former would involve a definitional part and an extensional part. In the case of precedents, it would involve a categorial part and what might be called a 'coextensional' part. In the case of both statutes and precedents, aim would involve a moral part and a part concerned with policy. (See figure 2.) By 'reference' in this context, I intend anything that connects statements with nonsatisfaction-conditions and nonsatisfaction-conditions with particular events or states of affairs. In statutes, reference proceeds from statements to nonsatisfaction-conditions to particulars. In precedents, however, reference proceeds in the reverse direction (with the qualifications indicated

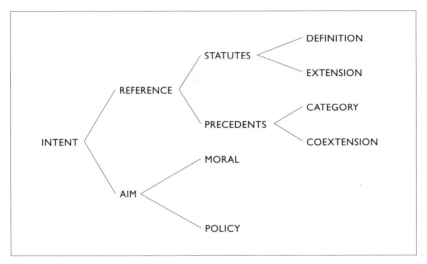

Figure 2

above). Whenever we wish to determine which sorts of acts a particular statute forbids, enjoins, or limits, or what general legal principle is instantiated in a precedent, we are attending to reference in this sense.

By distinguishing between definitional reference, on the one hand, and extension on the other, I intend to distinguish between definitional considerations alone and definitional considerations particularized in some way, usually by empirical beliefs, though sometimes by a more direct enumeration of instances (for instance, what cases the legislators 'had in mind'). As I discussed earlier, there are serious problems of principle with the distinction between definitions and empirical beliefs when applied to single words. In the case of legal interpretation, these problems usually are not relevant because we are most often dealing not with isolated words but rather with sentences as built up out of such words and with empirical beliefs that apply not to the words but to the sentences. For example, suppose those who drafted the Fifth Amendment to the Constitution believed that the only way one could be "compelled . . . to be a witness against himself" would be through physical torture. Thus, *extensionally,* the forbidden acts would be torture and torture alone. However, presumably none of these legislators would *define* 'compelled' as 'tortured'. The relevant empirical belief here concerns compulsion *to be a witness against oneself,* not compulsion *in general.* Thus *definitionally* the forbidden acts would encompass torture but would not be confined to torture—because, again, the meaning of 'compulsion' would never have been narrowed to 'torture', as there was no relevant empirical belief at the level of word meaning.

Of course, sometimes single words are indeed at issue in legal interpretation. In these cases, the distinction between definition and empirical beliefs is relative, in the manner discussed above. However, the fact that this is a distinction of degree rather than one of kind has significant practical consequences only rarely. This is true, first, because in many cases the distinction is clear anyway and, second, because problems with unclear cases are often resolved by reference to other aspects of the legal system, other varieties of legal interpretation, and so on, before they even arise.

Suppose, for example, that a judge used the word 'landowner' in a ruling at a time when no women could own land. Clearly, the extension of this term would, for him, include no women. Would 'male' then be part of his definition of 'landowner', or would he have an empirical belief about landowners being men? In fact, we could probably resolve this difficulty by taking 'landowner' to be compound, equivalent to 'one who owns land', and recognizing that 'male' cannot be part of the definition of 'one'— along the lines just indicated in the example from the Fifth Amendment. But the problem does not arise because if we are to make use of this decision in any case today, we have no choice but to take 'landowner' to refer to women as well as men, because, if we do not, we violate the coherence of the current legal system (in which 'landowner' elsewhere refers to both men and women).

Turning to precedents, the difference between categorial reference and coextension in the case of precedents is directly parallel to that between definitions and extensions in the case of statutes. By 'categorial reference', I intend the general category under which the act or state of affairs of the precedent is conceived to fall. This category may be implicit or explicit, but, insofar as it is purely categorial, it is broadly definitional rather than narrowly empirical. By 'coextension', I intend all the other cases—real or possible—that are intended to combine with the precedent in constituting the extension of the category. For example, in *Riggs v. Palmer* (115 NY 506, 22 NE 188 [1889]), the court decided that a man could not inherit according to his grandfather's will as that man had murdered that grandfather. The judge writing the opinion supported this conclusion by arguing that "no one shall be permitted to profit by his own fraud" (115 NY at 511, 22 NE at 190). Thus the judge provides us with an explicit statement of the principle he intends instantiated in his decision. This statement construed definitionally is, in our terms, the categorial reference of the precedent (for this intending subject). The coextension here is merely this statement specified empirically so as to indicate all cases that the judge did or would have conceived to be of the same type and to fall under the category (including, for example, any cases cited as precedents on this point).

As to aim, I use the terms 'moral' and 'policy' in their ordinary senses. Thus, by 'moral aims' I intend aims concerning the protection of general rights and the fostering of the fulfillment of general duties. Aims of policy, on the other hand, involve prudential considerations of the citizenry or government. Thus, as we have already noted, the moral aim of a national speed limit might be to reduce highway fatalities, thereby protecting the fundamental extralegal right to life. The policy aim might be to reduce the import of foreign oil—a prudential consideration bearing on the national economy.

Turning, then, to the intending subjects, I should first like to distinguish between subjects of the present time and those of the time of the legislation or precedent decision. Among the latter, I should like to isolate the individual judge or judges in precedent decisions, the body of legislators responsible for statutes, and the relevant national community as a whole. I leave aside the individual legislator who drafted a particular piece of legislation as I believe any intents idiosyncratic to such an individual are—and should be—irrelevant to legal interpretation, at least in a representative democracy. Obviously, individual intent enters in certain sorts of interpretation practiced by lawyers—for example, in the interpretation of wills. (Indeed, wills, along with contracts, require distinct treatment for they involve distinct sets of meanings.) The point is just that individual intent does not enter into the interpretation of laws governing wills (that is, in representative democracies; the situation would no doubt be different in, say, an absolute monarchy). Turning to contemporaries, I should like to distinguish the legal community, the various scientific or other specialized communities, and, once again, the national community, at the present time. I should emphasize that when I speak of the intent of a community or of a body of legislators, I do not imagine some sort of mysterious communal mind operating upon statutes. In speaking of, for example, the referential intent of a body of legislators, I wish only to refer to the descriptive reference and extension of a statute as commonly intended within that body of legislators, which is to say, as shared across their idiolects (or, in cases of disagreement, as shared across idiolects within the various subgroups of legislators). The same holds, of course, for aims. (See figure 3.)

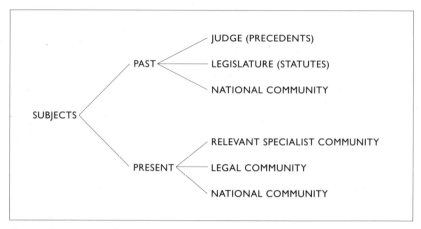

Figure 3

Thus in legal interpretation, we may look to the intents of the individual judge (in precedent rulings), the body of legislators (in statutes), the legal community at the present time, various specialized communities at the present time, and the national community, either at the present time or at the time of the statute/precedent. It appears that in actual legal interpretation, the definitional/categorial and extensional/coextensional referential intents, as well as the moral and politic aims of judges and legislators are *all* invoked in some (imprecise) way. The intents of the contemporary legal community are similarly invoked in the last three cases—extension/coextension, moral aim, and policy aim—but not, for the most part, in the first, definition/category. (Though, since more recent precedents are generally taken to supersede earlier precedents, the relevant category as understood by the contemporary legal community will often in effect supersede the category intended by a judge in an early precedent anyway.) The intents of various specialized communities are of concern principally with regard to extension/coextension. The intents of the national communities enter almost only with respect to moral aims. (We might tabulate the actual occurrence of the various sorts of legal interpretation as in table 1.)

Thus, in actual legal practice, the following types of meaning play a role in legal interpretation (the order is not intended to indicate relative importance): 1) The category a given judge takes his/her decision to instantiate. 2) The other cases or sorts of case the judge would consider to fall under the general category, given his/her general beliefs. 3) Any moral aims that the judge takes to justify the principle given in the category. 4) Any policy

Table I   Varieties of Intent

		Reference			Aim	
		Category/ Definition	Coextension/ Extension		Moral	Policy
Varieties of Intending Subject	Judge (past)	X	X		X	X
	Legislator (past)	X	X		X	X
	Community (past and present)				X	
	Legal Profession (present)		X		X	X
	Specialized Group (present)		X			

aims that the judge takes to justify the principle given in the category. 5) The definitional nonsatisfaction-conditions of a statute as these would have been generally understood by the legislators. 6) The specific extension of the statute insofar as this is given by the definitions and common empirical beliefs of the legislators or simply by an enumeration of those cases the legislators had in mind. 7) The moral aim of the legislators in passing the legislation. 8) The policy aim of the legislators in passing the legislation. 9) The relevant moral aims of the community at the time of the legislation. 10) The relevant moral aims of the community at present. (As we shall see, 9 and 10 are most often considered jointly.) 11) The extension of a given statute as that would derive from the empirical beliefs and standard practices of the legal community at present. 12) The relevant moral aims of the legal community at present. 13) The relevant policy aims of the legal community at present. 14) The extension of a given statute or coextension of a given precedent as that would derive from the common empirical beliefs of a relevant group of specialists at present.

Other categories might perhaps be included and other sorts of meaning and interpretation isolated from legal practice. However, these appear to be at least the principal varieties. The degree to which legal interpretation can end in misunderstanding and confusion when these varieties are not distinguished but classed together as 'meaning' should be evident.

For the most part, the nature of these varieties should be clear. We have already indicated the nature of referential and telic interpretation of the intents of judges and legislators. In *Riggs v. Palmer,* mentioned above, the *category* of the judge's intent is that one should not profit by his/her fraud (and thus that no heir can inherit under a person's will when that heir murdered that person in order to inherit under that will). The *coextension* would involve, for example, considerations of the judge's empirical beliefs about responsibility for murder (for instance, empirical beliefs about the nature of mental illness and its effects upon freedom of choice), the nature of motivation, and so on, and thus the circumstances under which killing could be considered fraud. The moral aim is to prevent fraud. (There appears to be no policy aim.) A clearer example of the difference between coextension and category might be found in an hypothetical case involving the labor of some white person, during a time and in a state where all blacks were slaves, but no whites, or other nonblacks, were slaves. Suppose the judge makes reference to 'all and only free persons of this state' in his/her judgment concerning the propriety of certain labor practices under consideration in this case. Categorially, the phrase refers to all free persons of the given state as such, independent of race. Thus, once slavery has been abolished, we may interpret the phrase as referring to *all* persons of that state. However, as the judge's empirical beliefs involve the identification of free persons with nonblacks, the *coextension* of the judgment, by his/her intent, concerns nonblacks only. Coextensionally interpreted by reference to judge's intent, the phrase refers only to nonblacks even after the abolition of slavery.

The statutory divisions, those relating to the common intent of the body of legislators, run parallel to the divisions of precedent. Unfortunately, judges (and legal theorists) rarely distinguish clearly between description and extension in examining legislative intent. For example, Dworkin seems to refer to definitional intent when he says that "most of the literature assumes that interpretation of a particular document is a matter of discovering what its authors (the legislators, or delegates to the constitutional convention) meant to say in using the words they did" (Dworkin 1983a, 251). But his phrasing is general enough to encompass extensional as well as definitional intent. On the other hand, there are some clear cases of definitional intent, for example, in the writings of Justice Holmes, and in Justice Douglas's decision in *Harper v. Virginia State Board of Elections,* quoting Holmes: "the Due Process Clause of the Fourteenth Amendment 'does not enact Mr. Herbert Spencer's Social Statics' " (383 US 663 [1966] at 1082). Here the empirical beliefs of the legislators, influenced by Herbert Spencer, are explicitly dismissed, and definition is chosen over extension. Most often, interpretation of definitional intent is implicit in judgments attending to other subjects. Thus in *Roe v. Wade,* Justice Blackmun invokes contemporary medical science in establishing the limits for human life—or, rather, the limits for state interest in "potential" human life—as we shall discuss below. In this case, Justice Blackmun and other concurring justices are to some degree implicitly interpreting the constitution definitionally and allowing contemporary medicine to provide the empirical beliefs necessary for determining the extension. For a more straightforward example, we could slightly alter our preceding hypothetical case concerning the precedent judgment employing the phrase 'all and only free persons of this state'. Now suppose the phrase appears in a statute rather than a precedent decision, all other conditions remaining the same. Again, the definitional interpretation of legislators' intent, following the abolition of slavery, would make the phrase refer to all persons of the state. The extensional interpretation of legislators' intent would, in contrast, make it refer to all nonblacks.

There are also some straightforward cases in which interpretation of legislators' *extensional* intent supersedes interpretation of definitional intent alone. An interesting case along these lines is *Cabell v. Markham* (148 F 2d 737 [2d Cir 1945]), in which considerations of legislators' extension and of legislators' politic aim combine in determining the decision. Judge Learned Hand wrote:

> Of course it is true that the words used, even in their literal sense [definition], are the primary, and ordinarily the most reliable, source of interpreting the meaning of any writing: be it a statute, a contract, or anything else. But it is one of the surest indexes of a mature and developed jurisprudence not to make a fortress out of the dictionary [thus definition]; but to remember that statutes always have some purpose or object to accomplish [aim], whose sympathetic and imaginative discovery is the surest guide to their meaning. Since it is utterly apparent that the words of this proviso were intended to be limited [in extension] to seizures made during the last war, and could not conceivably have been intended to apply [in extension] to seizures made when another war revived the Act as a whole from its suspension, it does no undue violence to the language [definitions] to assume that it was implicitly subject to that condition which alone made the act as a whole practicable of administration.

This case, then, provides us not only with an example of interpreting to legislators' extension but also with an example of interpreting to legislators' aims of policy. (Note, by the way, that the extension here is not fixed by legislators' empirical beliefs, but by what instances the legislators 'had in mind'.)

Another case of a policy aim—in this instance, a policy aim interwoven with a moral aim—may be found in a decision of the English court by Lord Wright, *Sumners v. Salford City Council* (59 TLR at 80 [1942]), referring to the Housing Act of 1936: "The section must, I think, be construed with due regard to its apparent object, and to the character of the legislation to which it belongs. The provision was to reduce the evils of bad housing accommodation and to protect working people by a compulsory provision. It is a measure aimed at social amelioration, no doubt in a small and limited way. It must be construed so as to give proper effect to that object." A more narrowly politic example may be found in *Wickard v. Filburn* (317 US 111, 63 S. Ct. 82, 87 L. Ed. 122 [1942]). Here, Justice Jackson, speaking of the Agricultural Adjustment Act of 1938, relies in his opinion on the view that "one of the primary purposes of the Act in question was to increase the market price of wheat and to that end to limit the volume thereof that could affect the market."

An interpretation more narrowly concerned with moral aims may be found in Justice Goldberg's concurring opinion in *Griswold v. Connecticut* (381 US 479, 85 S. CT. 1678, 14 L. Ed. 2d 510 [1965]). In this opinion, Justice Goldberg maintains that "to hold a right so basic and fundamental and so deep-rooted in our society as the right of privacy in marriage may be infringed because that right is not guaranteed in so many words by the first eight amendments to the Constitution is to ignore the Ninth Amendment." The Ninth Amendment states that "the enumeration in the Constitution, of certain rights, shall not be construed to deny or disparage others retained by the people." Justice Goldberg clearly takes this to indicate, amongst other things, that the moral aims of the constitution are not confined to the moral aims stated therein. He continues, more explicitly, in this vein: "The entire fabric of the Constitution and the purposes that clearly underlie its specific guarantees demonstrate that the rights to marital privacy and to marry and raise a family are of similar order and magnitude as the fundamental rights specifically protected."

This decision makes reference not only to the moral aims of legislators but also, by way of the Ninth Amendment, to the moral aims of the national community, past and present. In interpretations relating to the moral aims of the national community, the interpreter is most often concerned with establishing the presence of some powerfully felt and strongly maintained moral belief, usually of long standing, which is directly germane to the case at issue. As the belief is most often thought to have legal weight only if it is long-standing, it is rare for judges to concern themselves with the moral attitudes of past or present national communities in isolation. Rather, they are concerned with the two conjunctively and with the history that relates them. Thus, for example, Justice Blackmun, delivering the opinion of the court in *Roe v. Wade* (410 US 113, 93 S.Ct. 705, 35 L. Ed. 2d 147 [1973]), remarks that in seeking "to resolve the issue" of legislative restriction on abortion "by constitutional measurement," one must take into account, amongst other things, "what . . . history reveals about man's attitudes toward the abortive procedure over the centuries."

By interpretation of extension in the intention of the contemporary legal community, I intend only the interpretation of referential terms in such a way as to make their extensions coherent with the extensions of the same (definitionally identical) or relevantly similar terms in the body of law as currently interpreted, enforced, and so forth. A good example may be found in our preceding hypothetical case containing the phrase 'all and only free persons of this state'. Following the abolition of slavery, the extensional intent of the legal community no longer identifies *free persons* and *nonblacks*. It may seem that, at this point, a definitional interpretation of this phrase would necessarily make it refer to all people of this state whatever their race. However, this is not quite correct. In order for us to determine the phrase as making reference to anyone at all, we have to link it to some beliefs, practices, and so forth—some further intentions—which fix its extension. Thus, in order for us to determine the phrase as making reference to all persons of the state we must interpret the phrase as definitionally intended by the legislators *in the extensional context of the contemporary legal community*. This is, of course, an extremely ordinary sort of interpretation, though it is difficult to isolate particular and explicit cases precisely because it is so banal, and thus immediate or unreflective also. Some of the most interesting cases of this variety of interpretation are to be found in the various extensions of the equal protection clause of the Fourteenth Amendment, originally intended to have a racial extension governing blacks in relation to whites. The very same considerations apply to the determination of coextension—for example, in judging a precedent involving explicit or implicit reference to 'free persons' (from a time when blacks were enslaved), 'landowners' (from a time when women could not own land), and so on.

Interpretive reference to aims of the contemporary legal community is quite common also. For example, in cases such as those surrounding the extension of the equal protection clause and in the development of the doctrine of reasonable classification, reference is inevitably made to aims, both moral and politic. Often these aims are general and of long standing, and, in such cases, current aims are indistinguishable from those of past legislators. However, such aims are at times more narrowly contemporary, relating to recent legislation or what the court views as pressing moral issues. Thus a court might uphold preferential hiring practices benefiting women or minorities not as a constitutional practice in general but as a constitutionally permissible practice in the context of certain pressing moral concerns—which were not the concerns of past legislators—along with strictly contemporary considerations of policy. Numerous examples could be found along these lines. Though it primarily focuses on the extension and aims of particular precedents, the Per Curiam opinion in *Califano v. Webster* (430 US 313 [1977]), provides a good illustration. The case concerns gender-based disparities in Social Security benefits operating to the advantage of women. The opinion begins, "To withstand scrutiny under the equal protection component of the Fifth Amendment's Due Process Clause, 'classifications by gender must serve important governmental objectives [contemporary legal aims, moral or politic] and must be substantially related to achievement of those objectives.' Craig v. Boren, 429 US 190, 197 (1976). Reduction of the disparity in economic condition between men and women caused by the long history of discrimination against women has been recognized as such an important governmental objective. Schlesinger v. Ballard 419 US 498 (1975); Kahn v. Shevin, 416 US 351 (1974)."

Finally, we have extension (or coextension) as determined by the intention of some scientific or other specialized community. Here we take a term in the definitional intent of the legislators (or precedent judge) and seek the expertise of representatives from some relevant group in order to determine the relevant empirical beliefs and thereby determine the extension (or coextension) of the term. This too is quite common. Indeed, François Geny, in his 1899 *Méthode d'interprétation et sources en droit privé positif* names scientific research as one of the four sources of law—along with statutes, customs, and precedents. We have already given one example of this from *Roe v. Wade,* where a criterion for state interest in "potential" human life—specifically, viability—is derived in part from contemporary medical practice and opinion. Justice Blackmun writes that, when isolating the most important stages of embryonic/fetal development, "physicians and their scientific colleagues . . . have tended to focus either upon conception or upon live birth or upon the interim point at which the fetus becomes 'viable,' that is, potentially able to live outside the mother's womb, albeit with artificial aid" (410 US 113, 93 S.Ct. 705, 35 L.Ed. 2d 147 [1973]). The importance of such expertise is not confined to the biological sciences. For example, as Friedman points out, "such notions as 'monopoly,' 'competitive regime,' 'fair and reasonable price,' which are essential for legal interpretations of the Sherman Anti-Trust Act, must be ascertained by reference to the results of economic science" (Friedman 1967, 299). Other relevant varieties of expertise could be cited also.

These, then, appear to be the principal varieties of interpretation employed—most often implicitly and unreflectively—in legal interpretation today. It should be evident at once that when one is discussing 'the meaning' of a statute, interpreting for that 'meaning', urging others to attend to that 'meaning', and so on, a lack of clarity about precisely what meaning one has in mind can result only in confusion and misunderstanding. In debates over legal interpretation, the disputants rarely go beyond a distinction between the meaning of the language itself and the meaning intended by the legislators (sometimes adding undifferentiated 'purpose' as well; see, for example, Brest 1988, 69; or Levi 1979, 225–26).[4] As I have argued, the former does not appear to exist, and the latter is both too broad and too narrow—too broad in that it includes a variety of intents that it is important to distinguish; too narrow in that it excludes a variety of intents that it is important to recognize.

There are many examples of the problems that arise when the terms of debate on legal interpretation are thus grossly marked out. One striking example may be found in the important dispute between Justice William J. Brennan and Attorney General Edwin Meese, amongst others. Meese follows Robert Bork in claiming that, in constitutional interpretation, "framers' intent" should be the sole object of inquiry and should provide the sole criterion of validity (see Levinson and Mailloux 1988, 5). Brennan argues that it is both wrong and "arrogant" to seek framers' intent or to pretend that we can isolate it and thus use it as a criterion (Brennan 1988, 15f). Prima facie, the positions seem perfectly clear. But obscurities quickly arise. As Levinson and Mailloux explain, Meese goes on to restrict various aspects of constitutional interpretation by reference to quite particular beliefs, values, and so on, derived from his "specific reconstruction of late eighteenth-century attitudes" (Levinson and Mailloux 1988, 9). Brennan disputes this by insisting that we remain "faithful to the content of the Constitution" (Brennan 1988, 17), which "was not *intended* to preserve a preexisting society" (18; emphasis added), but "to declare certain values transcendent, beyond the reach of temporary political majorities" (16). Thus Meese can invoke intention (in some undefined sense) to oppose the Miranda decision and support school prayer, while Brennan can deny intention (in some undefined sense, perhaps the same) by invoking intention (in some other undefined sense) and thereby support the Miranda decision and oppose school prayer.

This is obviously a muddle. And it is a muddle because neither disputant has been clear about meaning. Meese appears to have legislators' extension in mind when he refers to intent and establishes it as the goal of interpretation. Brennan appears to have legislators' extension in mind when he denounces intent. But when he invokes intent against writers such as Meese, Bork, and others, he appears to be thinking of legislators' moral aim. In this way, there is not really a debate at all, but only a feeling of disagreement between people who have not yet succeeded in adequately clarifying their own positions, for themselves or for one another.

Unfortunately, even when one is clear about the varieties of meaning and interpretation and even when one is explicit about the sort of interpretation one is undertaking, difficulties arise from two sources. The first concerns the equivocal nature of data, the indeterminacy of simplicity evaluations, and so forth. It concerns, in other words, the uncertainty of rational inference on any empirical issue (for instance, on the issue of legislators' moral aim for a given statute). This sort of uncertainty is inevitable. One can only seek to construct and reconstruct valid arguments in the hope of making one's interpretations as accurate as possible. The second source of difficulty does not concern the facts about varieties of meaning but the relations between these varieties. Contemporary legal extensional intent may conflict with legislators' extension; legislators' politic aims may not obviously cohere with legislators' moral aims, and so on. This is the problem that Brennan and Meese are seeking to debate. It is the problem they would no doubt debate directly, were they more adequately to articulate their views on meaning and intent. It is the problem that raises the question as to whether Brennan or Meese is right, not only about the

Miranda decision or about school prayer but about the manner in which these issues might appropriately be evaluated.

I believe that the hierarchical wholism and interpretive conservatism defended at the outset of this essay provide a basis for limiting and hier-archizing the varieties of legal interpretation. If widely followed—which is, I must admit, pretty unlikely—a scheme such as this could help resolve some (though not all) interpretive difficulties of the second type. Thus I should like to turn, very briefly and in conclusion, to this hierarchization.

A HIERARCHY OF LEGAL INTERPRETATION

Our opening discussion of legal evaluation indicates that the most general moral principles enshrined in a virtuous legal system are the most crucial elements of that legal system. It is the operation of these principles that serves to justify the system as a whole and thereby, most often, serves to justify its contributory parts. Thus, I would maintain that legislators' moral aims are the most critical to any legal interpretation. Because of this, all interpretive conflicts—between legislators' moral aim and legislators' politic aim, between legislators' moral aim and precedent judge's category, between legislators' moral aim and extensions intended by the legal com-munity, between legislators' moral aim and any other variety of interpre-tation—should be resolved in favor of legislators' moral aim, precisely as Justice Brennan implied. (Of course, here as elsewhere, complications may arise that will make this hierarchy debatable. For example, it may happen that definitional intent is fairly clear while moral aim is muddy, or policy aim was agreed upon by all the legislators, while there was disagreement about moral aim. Issues such as these have to be thought out, debated, and decided case by case. My view is that moral aim should prevail ceteris paribus, not that it should overwhelm all other considerations in all cases.)

The interpretive conservatism implied by our wholism (which, needless to say, should not be confused with *political* 'conservatism,' such as that of Meese)[5] indicates that legislators' definitional intent is of an importance second only to that of legislators' moral aims. In conflicts with precedents, with the moral aims of national communities, and so on, legislators' defi-nitional intent should be favored. I should note that there are hierarchies within both moral aims and definitional reference. First of all, the aims and definitional references of the Constitution should be favored over aims and definitional references of other, subsequent legislation. We may wish, in addition, to hierarchize aims or definitional references within the constitution itself, privileging, for example, those which are necessary conditions for preserving constitutional government at all.

After legislator's moral aims and definition, our general evaluative principles seem to indicate that precedent judges' moral aims should follow, with precedent judges' categorial reference next. Internal hierarchies here usually function to favor later over earlier precedents; the preceding analysis is neutral on this topic but certainly provides no reason that common practice should not be followed. It is not, however, neutral on the determination of extensions and coextensions. To preserve the coherence of the legal system and to achieve the highest degree of factual accuracy, extensions and coextensions should be determined according to the contemporary, common intents of the legal community and, in relevant cases, other specialized communities.

While I have emphasized the conservative and historical aspect of legal interpretation (excepting in the determination of extensions and coextensions), I cannot disagree with Dworkin and others when they point out that judicial adjudication is quite often and necessarily a creative process. Most obviously, each type of meaning we have just treated necessarily serves to guide the specification of meanings at lower levels in the hierarchy (for instance, moral aim serves to guide our determination of vague definitions). I would maintain that the remaining sorts of interpretation are not in keeping with our conservative and wholistic view of legal interpretation—some might say that they are just not sorts of interpretation at all, in our ordinary sense of the term. However, many of these remain important in guiding judicial creation in cases where the other sorts of interpretation are inadequate. Thus policies and, above policies, moral aims that are and have been widely held in the legal and national communities, but that are not legally established in statutes or precedents, may function to help guide creative judicial decisions in novel cases undecided by legislators' moral aims, legislators' definitional intents, and so on. Finally, legislators' extensions and precedent judges' coextensions—the meanings most valued by Meese—seem to me of only rare and peripheral relevance, interpretively or creatively.

A hierarchy such as the preceding will not solve all or even most difficulties of legal interpretation. However, clarity about the varieties of meaning implicit in legal interpretation, combined with reflection on their relative importance, should help to eliminate ambiguous and inconsistent legal hypotheses and limit the degree to which dialogues are conducted at cross-purposes. A serious undertaking of categorization, clarification, and evaluation, of the sort we have here sought to begin, should at the very least foster greater precision in the formulation of interpretations, greater lucidity in their explication and defense, more pointed and productive dialectic in their disputation. And this, one imagines, can only redound to the benefit of everyone concerned with, or seeking, legal justice.

4 PSYCHOANALYTIC INTERPRETATION

Ambiguity, Association, and Unconscious Intent

METHOD AND OBJECT IN PSYCHOANALYSIS

In legal interpretation, as we have seen, there are two main problems. The first concerns the variety of intents germane to such interpretation. The second concerns the proper ordering of these intents. The first answers the question, 'What sorts of things might we look for in legal interpretation?' The second answers the question, 'Which of these is most important, and if there is a conflict between types of interpretation, in what way should we resolve it?' For psychoanalysis, in contrast, there is just one relevant intent—the unconscious intent of the analysand. The entire point of psychoanalysis is to produce a salutary therapeutic effect through a technically astute discovery and working-through of this unconscious intent. Thus in psychoanalysis there can be no question of relevant varieties of intent, or of a hierarchy of such varieties.

But psychoanalytic interpretation poses a different problem. Though it may be difficult to ascertain, say, legislators' moral aim in any given case of legal interpretation, we do at least know, in general terms, how to go about trying to ascertain that intent. We do in general know what sorts of things we should take into account, not only what aspects of the text but also what sorts of context (records of debates,[1] concurrent legislation, and so forth). Indeed, at a very general level, we discover intents relevant to legal interpretation in much the same way we discover intents relevant to everyday conversation and reading. But quotidian and legislative intents are conscious, whereas, again, those of psychoanalysis are, by definition, unconscious. For this reason, in psychoanalysis, the methodological question—how to interpret for unconscious intent—becomes central. Moreover, this methodological issue is necessarily bound up with our theory of the nature and operation of the unconscious, such that the two cannot be examined separately.

More exactly, one might interpret to the unconscious meaning or intent of an utterance, an action, or a symptom, only to the degree that the unconscious may be understood to be expressed in that utterance, action, or symptom. Psychoanalytic interpretation is, in this sense, a particular type of causal analysis. Suppose we claim that when Ernst Lanzer, Freud's "rat man," mislays his pince-nez, he is repudiating or seeking to avoid the exciting memory of the prohibited and destructive desire he had, as a boy, for his governess. In making this interpretation, we are claiming that such a memory, excitation, or desire, along with the wish to repudiate or avoid it, *caused* the parapraxis in the first place. To determine systematically valid principles of psychoanalytic interpretation, then, we must first of all determine the manner in which the unconscious may be causally inferred from observable phenomena—principally speech, actions, and symptoms—and thus the way in which mental, and specifically unconscious causation operates. (For a cogent critique of the a-causal, 'hermeneutic' view of psychoanalytic interpretation, see Grunbaum 1984, 1–95).

MIND, INTENT, AND MECHANISM

I have already argued, in connection with Chomskyan representationalism, that there is no such thing as 'mind' conceived of as an object or *res cogitans*. Rather, there is body (brain and so forth) and there is experiential subjectivity. There is no mentalistic thing, complexly mechanical, operating through the interplay of force and substance. Rather there is only our continuing, momentary, reflective, acting, feeling 'self'—everyone, as he/she is for him/herself, "what it is like to be" him/her, in the phrase Thomas Nagel uses to indicate the "subjective character of experience" (see Nagel 1979, 166 and throughout; see also Nagel 1986, 6–8; a similar distinction is drawn by 'qualia' theorists such as Frank Jackson, who stress the difference between the [physiological] stimulation of nerve endings and [correlate] experiential 'raw feels'). This is not to say that, for example, human behavior—including reports of subjective states—is not open to physiological or other objectal explanation. Of course it is. However, an explanation of this sort must seek coherence with other sorts of physiological/objectal explanation, not with subjective intent. In other words, a physical explanation of 'mind' must be an explanation of *correlates* of subjective feelings (usually brain correlates), and not of subjective feelings per se. Moreover, the explanation of these correlates must make sense in connection with the usual sorts of physical explanation.

This idea of distinct causal sequences or accounts is central to my view of the mind and of the mind/body problem. In the second chapter, I presented a brief argument that no physicalist account of the world can be complete, for it necessarily leaves out the meaningful speech in which the account is expressed, and thus the intent that defines that meaning. I take it that Ludwig Wittgenstein was getting at something along these lines when he wrote in the *Tractatus* that "the subject does not belong to the world: rather, it is a limit of the world" (5.632). The conclusion I draw from this argument is that mental construals are not causally continuous with physical construals. Rather, the two are radically disjunct. The mind and the body are not two substances that mutually interact ('interactionism'), or two substances that do not interact ('psychophysical parallelism'), or two substances that have a unidirectional causal relation (from body to mind in 'epiphenomenalism', from mind to body in 'subjective idealism') or one (physical) substance mistaken for two ('physicalism' or 'physicalist reductionism'; for a detailed, though tendentious overview of the various traditional views of the mind/body problem, see Popper and Eccles 1977). They are, rather, parts of distinct and irreconcilable (as well as incomplete and necessarily complementary) causal accounts. Thus a physical explanation of 'mind', which is to say, of mental correlates, must be good neurophysiology (full stop). A mentalistic account of mind (an account of mind per se) must in contrast preserve its subjective character, not turning mind into a pseudo-object, like a ghostly second brain. (Note that this is not a version of 'neutral monism'. My claim is not that these are two different ways of describing the same thing [or substance]. Indeed, the notion of some underlying 'same thing' [or 'same substance'] makes no sense on this conception.)

Again, linguistic representationalism does not satisfy these criteria. It seeks to explain language by way of a theory that neither concerns subjectivity nor strictly coheres with neurophysiology (or other physicalist systems of explanation) in the sense of becoming part of its causal sequences. Instead, it posits an intermediate realm, a pseudo-objective mind related in some unexplained way to both subjectivity and materiality. While not developed with the same rigor as Chomsky's theories, Freud's analyses of mind in terms of libido, energy, drive, instinct, cathexis, and so on are of the same general type and thus open to the same objections. Despite the debate among psychoanalysts as to whether psychoanalysis is a science or a phenomenology or both (see Grunbaum 1984, 1–95, for discussion and citations), psychoanalysis, in its (representational) metapsychology, is neither good physical science nor good phenomenology (understood in the very broad, non-Husserlian sense, of the systematic study of subjectivity).

But this is not to say that psychoanalysis cannot be reconciled with a subjectivist view of mind. The structure of psychoanalytic theory, like the structure of any other theory, is hierarchical (a point made by Freud himself; see Grunbaum 1984, 5 for references and discussion). We may accept the (clinical) data, the basic methodological principles (for instance, analysis through free association), low-level theoretical posits (such as the unconscious itself or the transference), and still reject unrelated or 'higher level' theoretical and other principles (for instance, the instinct theory). Indeed, it is, in my view, crucial to rethink these principles and develop alternatives not only to advance the theory and practice as a whole but to clarify and refine those lower-level principles that we have already accepted. Our methods of interpretation will remain immature to the degree that we cannot conceptualize the structures that permit rational inference to unconscious phenomena. Our understanding of the unconscious will be impoverished to the degree to which we cannot adequately specify the functioning of repression or the organization and status of unconscious thoughts.

If we are to proceed in this retheorization, and if we are to hew to the 'noetic' line, it seems that we have no choice but to begin with so-called "folk psychology," the ordinary, everyday psychology of belief, desire, and reason—what Aristotle calls "final causality" (see *Physics,* II, iii)—though folk psychology enhanced by empirically ascertained cognitive principles (for discussion and defense of folk psychology as a starting point for systematic psychology, see, for example, Brand 1984 and Horgan and Woodward 1990). Ordinarily, in explaining a person's actions, we have recourse to talk of beliefs, aims, and principles of reasoning (fundamentally, the basic principles of logic, such as the Principle of Non-Contradiction and Modus Ponens and the Principle of Minimal Interpretation). Thus we explain someone's driving down the highway by saying that he/she wants to go to the store; we explain his/her going to the store by reference to his/her belief that there is a sale on; we explain his/her belief by reference to his/her inference from reading an advertisement, and so on. It is by way of this very ordinary sort of mentalistic explanation—extended and further articulated through experimental psychology and cognitive science—that I should like to approach the unconscious.[2]

ON INTERPRETATION

AIMS, DESIRES, AND THE VARIETIES OF PLEASURE

As I am using the terms, 'aims' differ from 'desires' only in that the satisfaction of desires involves 'organ pleasure'. I am inclined to follow classical psychoanalysis in taking all aims to lead to or derive from desires in this sense. In other words, I am inclined to believe that all aims are either a) directly motivated by desires, their fulfillment serving as a step on the way to the fulfillment of desires, or b) developmentally derived from desires ('anaclitically', as classical analysts would say). In any event, both aims and desires are directed toward fantasized or imagined pleasures, and it is important to reflect for a moment on the nature and varieties of these pleasures, for they are clearly crucial to any understanding of motivation, conscious or unconscious.

In her excellent essay, "On the Grammar of 'Enjoy,'" Elizabeth Anscombe distinguishes between two types of enjoyment, or, we might say, pleasure. The first is "enjoyment of substance" (Anscombe 1981, 98). One enjoys the substance of an experience when one directly and immediately feels pleasure in the experience itself, without reference to anything beyond the experience. The second sort of enjoyment is "enjoyment of fact" (98). One enjoys the fact of an experience when one feels pleasure not necessarily in the event or state itself but rather in the thought that the event occurred or that the state obtains. Thus someone wishing to diet may enjoy the substance of eating a bowl of ice cream but then in turn deplore the fact. Conversely, someone more successfully dieting may enjoy the fact of eating nothing but lettuce while in turn deploring the substance of that act.

Upon the basis of this, I should like to draw a further distinction—between enjoyment of a substance per se and enjoyment of a substance qua. By enjoyment of a substance per se, I mean organ pleasure, a pleasure independent of any ideation, a, so to speak, pure pleasure or a pleasure 'in itself' (something like the Lacanian notion of *jouissance*). By enjoyment of a substance qua, I mean the enjoyment of a substance only insofar as it is construed in a particular way. Thus one enjoys the substance of an orgasm per se. But one does not necessarily enjoy the substance of a kiss or embrace per se. A heterosexual male who kisses what he takes to be a woman will enjoy the substance of the experience only insofar as he construes it as 'kissing a woman' (or 'kissing a woman with such-and-such characteristics'). His enjoyment will presumably be lost if he discovers he is kissing a transvestite.

130

The various enjoyments we have just mentioned do not operate in isolation but are inseparable from *norms, ideals,* and *fantasies*. Specifically, norms are principles that define ethical rectitude, principles that determine, for example, obligation. Ideals are principles that define ethical perfection, principles that determine, for example, benevolence. Fantasies, finally, are the imaginative constructions that we develop around persons, events, and so forth to 'fill them out' or render them more complete. Norms and ideals clearly contribute to the enjoyment of facts. Specifically, that part of our enjoyment of facts that is moral (as opposed to the parts which are vindictive, narcissistic, and so forth) is governed by norms and ideals. (N.B. I am speaking only of *subjective* morality here, what an individual *takes* to be ethical—correctly or not.) And, enjoyment qua is always enjoyment of an experience as embedded in some fantasy, in our very broad sense of the term.

Of course, not all fantasies are pleasurable—some are painful and some are neither. Similarly, not all norms and ideals contribute to the enjoyment of facts. There are many norms and ideals—again, subjective norms and ideals—that people accept abstractly but that do not please them in practice, even as facts. In other words, someone may accept a certain principle as just—admit its justice, accept its moral force—and still be indifferent to or unhappy about even the *fact* that it is followed in particular instances, or that he/she has followed it him/herself. For example, a department head might abstractly view preferential hiring of women and minorities as just but then follow affirmative action hiring only because of university pressure, in the end being unhappy about the fact that women or minorities were chosen over white men. Similarly, a voter might tell a pollster that he/she finds contra funding immoral but then vote for Ronald Reagan and be entirely indifferent to Reagan's procontra policies. Thus, amongst pleasures in facts, I would distinguish those governed by norms and ideals from those not governed by norms and ideals. Similarly, amongst norms and ideals, I would distinguish those that govern pleasures in facts from those that do not.

The beliefs and aims that animate any intentional action are closely interrelated in that the beliefs invoked in that action are invoked by reference to the aim and the aim itself is focused and evaluated in terms of the beliefs. As the aim is always itself a function of imagined enjoyment, any action—and, indeed, any belief—is itself necessarily formulated and 'deployed' in the context of such imagined enjoyment. One acts, then, when and because one's beliefs cohere appropriately with imagined pleasures,

131

when and because one sees that these pleasures can be achieved and how they can be achieved.

All of this concerns what is classically termed "the pleasure principle." My assumption thus far has been that all actions conform to the pleasure principle. But there are some apparent exceptions to this. The most important of these, and the one that proved crucial for Freud, is the 'repetition compulsion', the compulsion to repeat, in thought or action, a painful or traumatic event. In part, this can be explained in common-sensical, non-psychoanalytic terms. A trauma surprises and hurts us and is beyond our control. This is surely painful—not only in the hurt itself but in the surprise and the feeling of helplessness also. Our dwelling upon traumas in thought is partially adaptive (cf. Hartmann 1958, 39); in part, it involves an examination of the circumstances of the trauma and an effort to see how the trauma might have been prevented. Adaptive practices, practices in accord with the "reality principle," are not themselves strictly pleasurable, but they are a necessary prerequisite to pleasure generally. Acting adaptively is acting in rational accord with the pleasure principle. Beyond this, reflection on traumas also frequently involves an effort to see if the trauma had been exaggerated, an effort to see if it—and thus its pain—can be reduced or diminished. This also is in accord with the pleasure principle.

Reenacting a trauma, re-creating the situations in which the trauma will occur, multiplying the trauma and its pains, however, is not adaptive or pleasurable. Someone who was painfully rejected by a parent and who continually creates situations in which he/she will be painfully rejected by others is not behaving in a way conducive to pleasure. There may be a degree of moral, factual enjoyment in the suffering, but there is often something else going on also. Which leads us to the notion of repression.

REPRESSION, ACTING OUT, AND TRANSFERENCE

Repression is, first of all, an effort to preserve pleasure. Specifically, it is an attempt to preserve pleasure by eliminating pain per se or by undermining conflicts between pleasures. Thus there are two sorts of things upon which repression operates. The first is (thoughts of) pains, specifically traumas. A repressed trauma is a forgotten trauma, a trauma that, in one sense at least, no longer causes pain. I follow classical analysis once again in assuming that only infantile traumas are repressed. Or, rather, I follow Freud in assuming that only infantile traumas are repressed in isolation, in 'primary repression'. Events of later life may be repressed only insofar as they are assimilated to the infantile or primary repression. I take this to be the case for the usual reasons—that the child is incapable of working through traumas in the manner of the adult, that the relevant traumas (parental seductions, the 'primal scene', and so on) are part of the oedipal development that leads to the critical change in the child's psychosexual life, including his/her recognition of sexual difference, first 'internalization' of norms and ideals (first experiences of normative pleasure in facts, itself developed in the usual, conditioned manner—*not,* in my view, through the castration complex), and so on.

Beyond pain, repression operates on pleasures and imagined pleasures also. Enjoyments of facts, moral or not, can conflict with enjoyments of substances, per se or qua, real or imagined. For example, a sexual desire may conflict with a norm and thus the (imagined) factual pleasure of the latter would exclude the (imagined) substantial pleasure of the former. Should a person suffering such conflicts *choose* the factual pleasure over the substantial pleasure, he/she would be doing something like what is called 'sublimating'.[3] But the person suffering conflicts of aim and pleasure might not reflectively choose between the alternatives. Indeed, he/she may find that one of the wishes itself is, even as a wish, repugnant to his/her moral sensibilities. In this case, he/she may, so to speak, choose not to wish for the forbidden pleasure. Indeed, he/she may come to believe that he/she does not wish for and has never wished for the pleasure. In other words, the aim or desire and the related fantasy, through conflict with pleasure-governing norms and ideals, may come to be repressed. Much like traumas, aims or desires and related fantasies are repressed in isolation only in early childhood. Subsequent repressions function by assimilation only.

Thus traumas, aims or desires, and associated fantasies (current or recollected), as well as memories of substantially pleasurable experiences, may be repressed. Traumas are repressed because of the pain caused directly by their recollection.[4] The others—and traumas also under certain circumstances—are repressed because of the pain caused indirectly by their incoherence with pleasure-governing norms and ideals. Both involve 'primary' repressions of the oedipal period and subsequent 'secondary' assimilations.

We may think of repression as operating in roughly the following way. As already mentioned, we appear to have only a sort of perceptual experience of ourselves. In other words, we do not have direct introspective access to patterns in our thought processes, to the principles that guide our actions, and so forth. We must *infer* such patterns, principles, and so on, much in the way we infer them about others. We do of course have some direct experiences of ourselves (our thoughts and such), just as we have perceptions of the external world. But these too are partially inferential in that our perceptions of ourselves (no less than our perceptions of the world) are guided by expectations, filled in by strongly held beliefs, and so forth. Put simply, our knowledge of ourselves is theoretical and highly fallible. Researchers in cognitive science have demonstrated that our self-theory (or theories)—roughly what Lacan calls the "ego"—are often radically mistaken because of cognitive errors. As Nisbett and Ross summarize their overview of findings:

> Knowledge of one's own emotions and attitudes, though commonly believed by the layperson (and many philosophers) to be "direct" and certain, has been shown to be indirect and prone to serious error. Such knowledge is based in large part on inferences about the causes of behavior. People's causal accounts explaining their own behavior have been shown in a wide variety of settings to be: (1) often empirically wrong, (2) little different from the accounts of observers working from impoverished information and without benefit of the introspective clues available to the actor, and (3) based more heavily on causal theories than on the observation of mental events. (Nisbett and Ross 1980, 227; see also Nisbett and Wilson 1977, and Gopnik 1993)

Repression may be understood as a specific type of error in self-theorization: First of all, it is not merely cognitive but highly motivational (it results from the pleasure principle). Secondly, it concerns a memory or desire that itself has strong motivational force (often connected with a complex of affects, such as fear, anger, and so forth). Finally, both the repressed memory/desire and the relevant aspect of the self-theory (or ego, in Lacan's sense) derive from almost the earliest period of one's self-theorization. This last point is important because a great deal of experimental work indicates that early beliefs—especially sets of beliefs structured into schemas—can be extremely difficult to eradicate and may remain in place even when faced with massive disconfirmatory evidence (see chapter 8 of Nisbett and Ross 1980). This gives us reason to expect that repressed infantile traumas and fantasies would have enormous importance for subsequent cognition (for self-understanding or understanding of others). This would seem all the more likely as they involve strong motivational components in addition to the cognitive bias.

Indeed, in the context of this comparison with cognitive science, it is important to stress the centrality of motivational force to a psychoanalytic account of repression. Again, in repression, there is a double motivational force comprising the force of the repressed memory/desire and, in opposition to this, the force of the repressing theory. Note that, in removing memories, desires, and so on from reflective evaluation, repression does not thereby remove or 'neutralize' this prior motivational force. It merely removes the motive from conscious evaluation and decision. For example, a repression might prevent a child from considering his patricidal wishes, but it does not render those wishes innocuous or irrelevant to his motivations. A repressed wish is a wish that one cannot consider, but it is still a wish; a repressed trauma is a trauma that one cannot analyze, but it is still a trauma. In this way, one may have no choice but in some manner to act on a repressed wish rather than rejecting it. And one may have no choice but to repeat in action — to act out — a repressed trauma rather than reflecting upon it and analyzing it adaptively. In psychoanalytic theory, then, repression is servitude and repetition — and therefore suffering.

But analysis is or should be liberation, for it seeks to reveal, within certain technical constraints, what repression has concealed. Insofar as repressed traumas and wishes surface in speech, thought, feeling, or action, they must surface indirectly. Usually, a death wish for one's father cannot have undergone repression if it surfaces directly in the thought, 'I wish my father would die'. The problem of method in psychoanalytic interpretation is, then, a problem of understanding the indirect manifestation of unconscious traumas and wishes, and perhaps most importantly of understanding their *transference* onto contemporary situations or persons.

The notion of *assimilation,* already mentioned in connection with primary and secondary repression, provides some idea as to how indirection functions in the transferential expression of the unconscious. Assimilation is the relating of later traumas, wishes, and so forth to earlier, repressed traumas, wishes, and so forth, such that these later traumas, wishes, and so forth become repressed also. Transference is the relating of the present events, persons, and so on back to unconscious prototypes in such a way that the subject acts or reacts toward the present events or whatever in a manner partially governed by his/her relation to the prototypes. Assimilation and transference are, in effect, the same process, a process that can be clarified by further articulating the structure of belief, on the basis of research in experimental psychology and cognitive science.

What we refer to as 'belief' is better thought of as a complex of interrelated procedural and referential structures. The procedural structures would include skills and implicit rules that guide action, as well as more self-conscious schemas. The referential structures would include concepts, empirical beliefs, memories, and so forth. More exactly, we can think of the mind as including a sort of lexicon, a structured memory that includes morphemes (as well as larger semantic units) along with a wide range of associated material—definitions, empirical beliefs, personal memories, relevant procedural schemas, and so forth.[5] For example, the entry for 'bicycle' would include a definition of 'bicycle', personal memories about bicycles, and procedural schemas for riding a bicycle. The self-schema or 'ego' is, in effect, one of these entries. More exactly, entries include 1) broad structures or schemas, both procedural and referential (a schema of how to ride a bicycle and a schema of what a bicycle is); 2) prototypes, which is to say, a standard instance of the type in question (the prototypical bicycle has two wheels of equal radius, though different radii are in principle possible); 3) exempla or instances of the type (my bicycle when I was ten—a purple Schwinn with a banana seat). These entries are cross-indexed in various ways—by definitional relations such as subsumption (for instance, 'weekday' and 'Monday') or opposition (for instance, 'black' and 'white'), by sound pattern (for instance, homophony), and by contingent, biographical relations (such as that between the entry for a city and the entry for a friend who lives in that city).

It appears that we have several degrees of possible awareness of our various lexical entries. Obviously, we can be directly aware of a word or meaning or memory; we can have it in mind when speaking or understanding or recollecting. Also we can be entirely unaware of a word or meaning or memory, even though it is available to us in 'long-term memory'. But there are other possibilities as well. Research in cognition indicates that, when we first come upon a word (for instance, when reading), we recall a large part of the entry initially, then quickly eliminate irrelevant information (see, for example, Johnson-Laird 1993, 566). (Johnson-Laird argues that we are more selective than is usually believed and that access is guided by contextual relevance. Either construal will fit the following analyses. All that is important here is that we do not access only a single, 'correct', definitionally shallow item, which then necessarily remains in awareness.) We also tend to 'prime' a range of related or cross-indexed entries, making them more readily or directly accessible (see Garman 1990, 494, and Holland et al. 1986, 57). Researchers are able to isolate these different degrees of awareness because they have effects. Even though we do not remember accessing contextually irrelevant material from a lexical entry, that material affects our immediately subsequent understanding, behavior, and so forth.

Even though we are not aware of priming cross-indexed entries, these entries alter our responses to subsequent words, and so forth.

We can conceive of repressed memories/desires as included in one or more entries and either not accessible or immediately suppressed when accessed. When primed or when accessed and eliminated, they would have effects, which could be quite powerful, given their motivational force. But what sort of effects would they have? Given our current knowledge of how lexical entries operate in cognition and action, it seems most plausible that they would take up the modeling function of salient exempla. Specifically, it is fairly well-established that we tend to use salient or 'vivid' exempla as models for understanding and responding to current or new situations (see, for example, chapter 3 of Nisbett and Ross 1980). For example, I tend to interpret the behavior of dogs and respond to them, not on the basis of, say, statistical knowledge about dogs or even on my implicit schema of a dog, but on the basis of such salient exempla as a neighbor's sociopathic monster that almost unmanned a friend of mine in grammar school. It is easy to see how this sort of model could operate even if I did not or could not call the exemplum to mind. Indeed, transference can be understood as precisely this sort of unconscious modeling: understanding and responding to someone in one's current environment by tacit reference to the exemplum (accessed and suppressed or primed but inaccessible) of some salient fantasy object from one's childhood, usually a parent. Note that this modeling would be likely to include a series of stereotyped behaviors based on the transferential exemplum and deriving from the repressed trauma or fantasy. It would, in other words, typically entail a sort of schematic repetition.

Before going on, there are a couple of implications of this analysis that it is important to draw out. Again, both assimilation and transference result from the association of something in the current environment with some repressed memory or desire. There are three possible results of this association: 1) The repression is lifted. 2) The new event itself is repressed because of assimilation. 3) The connection is repressed, the now-unconscious relation between memory and event surfacing in transference. In order to achieve the first result, we must come to understand the motivations that are leading to the repression and the cognitive structures through which this occurs. The most obvious way of doing this is by tracing the path that led to the association, a path that necessarily proceeded through lexical entries. Thus, to understand paths of association, we would do well to begin by considering the structural connections between lexical entries. As I have already indicated, these connections are a matter of a sort of cross-indexing. And this 'cross-indexing' typically proceeds by idiosyncratic biographical links or by more socially available meaning and sound connections. The classical method of analysis in effect focuses on biographical links, which it seeks to uncover through free association. It pays only sporadic attention to those connections that are isolable through semantic analysis or attention to sound (especially full and partial homophony). Finally, as transference manifests itself in a repetitive structure based on the crucial lexical exempla, an analysis of structural repetition in transference provides yet a third body of evidence for our inference concerning repressed memories, etc. In this case, the connection is not between lexical items but between the repressed, schematic elements of an item and the complex actions and reactions derived from these schematic elements. Thus we have (at least) three ways of gathering data in order to construct and evaluate interpretive hypotheses regarding the unconscious, which is to say, the repressions, of a particular analysand: 1) free association, seeking contingent, biographical links between lexical entries, 2) analysis of meaning or sound, seeking semantic or phonetic links between entries, 3) analysis of structural repetition in transference, seeking inaccessible schemas in lexical entries.[6]

ASSOCIATIONS, AMBIGUITIES, AND STRUCTURES

Let us take a simple example. Suppose I encounter a man who has gray, rounded glasses, silvered hair, and a mustache, all of which calls to mind my father's appearance at a certain time. Recollections of this time might include certain memories of traumas or wishes long repressed and still painful. In the transference, I repress these connections and, instead of reflecting upon and dismissing them as inconsequential, I act upon them, behaving toward this man in effect as if he were my father at the period of the repressed memory or wish. I may act with unmotivated fear or aggression, incomprehensible affection or solicitousness. In severely pathological cases, the assimilation may be less abstract and more debilitating, involving quite particular fantasies and acts.

In a similar manner, a random phrase used by this gentleman may call to mind a phrase of my father's associated with some further repressed trauma or wish. In this case, I might again react transferentially, or I might merely repress the comment—and ultimately be entirely unable to recall its recent use. Needless to say, as regards the expression of the unconscious, I need not encounter a man like my father by accident. I may, unconsciously, seek him out. Similarly, I may unconsciously seek to provoke the comment that I then repress—acting, again, on the wish or repeating the trauma.

In these rather simplistic examples, assimilations and transferences are triggered—or, alternatively, expressed—by contingent and idiosyncratic properties such as hair color or speech. Again, the use of free association to examine these properties, reactions, and so forth has been the prime focus of (classical) psychoanalysis. In contrast, the analysis of structural repetitions in transference and of semantic and phonetic connections— 'ambiguities', in a broad sense—have been almost ignored, despite their considerable value.

As to structural analysis, this is hinted at in Lacanian work (see, for example, Lacan 1975, 53; 1978, 410) but is not well developed, even in that context. Indeed, structural analysis has been developed almost entirely outside of psychoanalysis, most rigorously in works of structural anthropology, such as Claude Lévi-Strauss's *Mythologiques*. By definition, this sort of analysis focuses not upon properties but upon relations. For example, rather than comparing all tales about, say, birds, a structural analysis might instead compare a story about a bird living in the water with a story about a fish living in a tree as both would exhibit a similar inverse relation between natural and mythical habitats. As Lévi-Strauss explains, a structural analysis is not "carried out according to the Cartesian principle of breaking down the difficulty into . . . many parts" (1969b, 5), but rather by examining the "transformations" that define "isomorphic links between sequences" (2). In psychoanalytic interpretation, the structural analyses of which I am aware primarily concern obvious and even conscious isomorphisms—which is to say, isomorphisms that are not even transferential. For example, one of the most famous instances is to be found in the case of the rat man. Ernst Lanzer (the rat man) was in love with a poor woman but was under pressure from his family to marry a wealthy cousin and thereby secure his financial position. In this way, Ernst's situation exactly recapitulated the structure of his father's youthful dilemma in deciding whether to marry Ernst's mother. Certainly, this is a structural repetition. However, it is far from a transference. Ernst was aware not only of the two structures but of their relation as well. No psychological or structural analysis was required to unearth this connection—which is, consequently, of very limited psychoanalytic interest.

In contrast, a genuine example of structural repetition—indeed, struc-

tural repetition ignored by the analyst—may be found in a case of Masud
Khan (Khan 1979; I have discussed this case, very briefly, in Hogan 1990b).
In this case, a young woman actually recalls a traumatic event but claims
that it was not traumatic, thereby repressing it *as* trauma. In consequence,
she reenacts its structure in a transmuted form. The traumatic event—in
this case an ethically, factually painful event—is the following: In her late
teens, this woman had genital intercourse and became pregnant. She had
the child and abandoned it on the subway. She had "little guilt or remorse,"
Khan tells us (1979, 178), evidently repeating the woman's own assertion
to this effect. Years later, she began having oral intercourse in the WC at
work with boys in their late teens. She developed a phobia about "encountering a vomit in subways" (178), which, in turn, inhibited her ability to go
to work—and thereby inhibited her ability to meet the boys and have oral
intercourse with them.

Khan interprets that this is a case of perversion, in which "the mouth
and the hand play a cognitive role in the transitional area of sensual foreplay" and "foreplay" becomes, not "the facilitating ambience for true genital sexuality" but, rather, "the whole of its experiential terrain" (184). An
attention to structure and transformation, however, suggests something
rather different. It seems that, despite Khan's claim, this woman felt very
guilty about abandoning her child. Indeed, the unconscious significance
of the pregnancy and abandonment is so important that she repeated the
entire event with a single, consistent transformation—what is genital in
the trauma becomes oral in the transference. Thus initially we find genital
intercourse in the late teens leading to the abandonment of a child on the
subway. It appears that this was accompanied by disgust at the abandonment and at the intercourse itself, as well as fear for the child, quite possibly even a fantasy of finding the child dead and decayed on the subway.
Because of the repression of these feelings (and of the associated moral
precepts that gave rise to guilt over these facts), along with the repression
of her prior enjoyment of genital intercourse, this woman began to avoid
genital intercourse, shifting to fellatio, which is to say, intercourse that
could not result in pregnancy (and that could not give her direct orgas-
mic pleasure). Moreover, she engaged in oral intercourse with men in their
late teens—men of approximately her age at the time of the pregnancy.
The mouth replaces the vagina in the intercourse itself; consequently, in
the phobia, the stomach replaces the uterus, and the issue of the stomach,
vomit, replaces the issue of the uterus, the child. Thus, the young woman,
having repressed her fear and disgust over the abandonment of the child in

the subway, expresses this fear and disgust by way of a phobia of encountering, also on the subway, a disgusting vomit, a pool of rot and decay reminiscent, perhaps, of the dead child as she imagined him/her.

The interpretation of sound and meaning connections—the analysis of what Lacan called "the constitutive ambiguity" of language (see Lacan 1966, 83)—is also occasionally found in classical psychoanalysis. However, it is of central importance only in the work of Lacan and his followers. Like all lexical components, meanings are multiply accessible. We recall words by sound, by meaning, by rhyme, by their place in idioms, by rhythm, by synonymy, by antonymy, and so on. Like the networks of memory, the networks of verbal association lead to transference, secondary repression, or cure. Of particular importance for our purposes, of course, is the ambiguity that surfaces in the *expression* of the unconscious. This sort of ambiguity allows, for example, an analysand to express conscious anxiety over her bill and thereby, unaware, express her unconscious anxiety over someone named *Bill,* in a case reported by James Gorney (see Gorney 1990). Or, to take a well-known case, it allows an analysand to report (in French) a dream of *"six roses"* and thereby communicate an unmentioned and unacknowledged concern over someone with *"cirrhose"* (cirrhosis; a homophone of *'six roses'* in French). In this way, the expression of the unconscious can operate through accidental features of an utterance. There are many different ways in which the preceding analysand could have reported this dream—'a bunch of roses', 'several roses', 'some flowers', 'roses—maybe six of them', and so on. My inference is that the phrasing 'six roses' was determined by the primed but inaccessible (or accessed and suppressed) 'cirrhose'. The same holds for a range of phenomena from word choice ('bill' rather than 'fee', for example), to image, metaphor, idiom, and the like (for instance, when an analysand whose father was a medical doctor chooses a metaphor of 'doctoring' from a set of possible idiomatic descriptions for an illicit act). Beyond this cognitive explanation, the only thing I would add to the usual Lacanian approach here is that 'constitutive ambiguities' should be analyzed not only in isolation but also and more importantly in the patterns they form across an analysand's speech. For the most part, Lacan and his followers have concentrated on single, 'key' signifiers ('bill/Bill'). By unreflectively constraining their interpretations in this way, they risk missing a great deal of important material. Analyzing only 'key' signifiers is rather like analyzing a patient's associations with only one image in a dream. However central that image might be, such an analysis would clearly be too limited. (An at least partial exception to this usual confinement to key signifiers may be found in the Quebec school of Willy Apollon; however Apollon's approach differs from that discussed here and below in that it focuses upon phonetic or phonemic repetitions that often do not involve meaningful units. This is an interesting approach that is neither supported nor controverted by the lexical principles I have been advocating.)

EVIDENCE AND ANALYSIS

Before going on to illustrate these interpretive principles in a discussion of Freud's rat man, however, I should say a few words about the (highly controversial) data of psychoanalysis and, related to this, the (highly controversial) status of psychoanalysis as a theory. The standard method of supporting psychoanalytic theory is through clinical analysis. Initially, Freud believed that psychoanalytic cure provides cogent evidence for the veracity of psychoanalytic theories and most particularly the theory of repression. In brief, repression causes neurosis, which is in turn manifest in symptoms; the lifting of repression cures neurosis, thereby alleviating symptoms. Therefore successful analytic cure—as manifest in the alleviation of symptoms—verifies psychoanalytic hypotheses.

But, analytic cures did not come—or they did not come as easily and as universally as was required for them to count as validating psychoanalytic theory. In order to account for the unexpectedly poor therapeutic results, Freud introduced several qualifications to the earlier theory—including the notion that a symptom could initially be caused by a certain repression but then subsequently become tied to others as well, thus rendering it impervious to the analytic discovery of the initial cause. However plausible these qualifications might be, they introduced a complexity into the relation between theoretical verification and clinical cure that made the possibility of inference from one to the other obscure.

Adolf Grunbaum refers to Freud's initial belief in the probative value of psychoanalytic cure as the "Tally Argument" and maintains that, after the collapse of the Tally Argument as just recounted, Freud had no reason to accept data from clinical psychoanalyses as having any evidential weight whatsoever. Specifically, Grunbaum has two objections to the use of clinical material as evidence for psychoanalytic hypotheses. The first concerns the status of the clinical material itself, the degree to which, for example, the associations of the analysand are in fact spontaneous and the degree to which they are, intentionally or unintentionally, elicited and guided by the analyst. His argument here is that the structure of the analytic situation virtually determines that the analysand's judgments, and even his/her memories, wishes, and so on, will be to some degree shaped by the analyst's expectations, wishes, and so on. Grunbaum cites convincing evidence that this is not only possible but extremely likely. The constraints on the following examination should considerably weaken the force of this objection. By confining my study to the first two weeks of the analysis, and, more important, concentrating upon aspects of the analysand's speech to which Freud was virtually oblivious, I hope to avoid making any crucial use of those memories, wishes, and so forth shaped by Freud's beliefs and desires. Though he attended occasionally to structures (as mentioned above) and to key signifiers (such as 'Ratten'), Freud paid little attention to unconscious or transferential isomorphisms and seems to have been entirely unaware of systematic ambiguities. Moreover, my interpretation of the case is very different from Freud's; indeed, Freud virtually ignores several factors that I see as absolutely crucial to the etiology of Ernst's neurosis (such as the death of his elder sister). Both of these factors, as well as the brief, early period under consideration, should greatly reduce problems of suggestion in the present reanalysis. Indeed, Grunbaum himself recently acknowledged that it is possible to separate out valid from invalid data through the use of transcripts (Grunbaum 1993, 111–12).

Grunbaum's second, and in some ways more important objection concerns the value of even uncontaminated clinical material. Grunbaum's view is that we have no warrant to infer from an associative connection to a causal connection, even when the associatively related events, objects, situations bear some resemblance to one another, even when they have what he calls "thematic affinity." Thus, according to Grunbaum, only large-scale epidemiological studies can test psychoanalytic hypotheses. For example, one might test the hypothesis that repressed homosexuality is causally relevant to the genesis of paranoia by studying the degree to which changing social attitudes toward homosexuality (and thus, presumably, varying degrees of the repression of homosexuality) affect the incidence of paranoia.

On this second objection, let me first say that I wholeheartedly believe that psychoanalytic hypotheses should be integrated into a systematic research program (in roughly the sense of Lakatos 1970, with the preceding adjudicative criteria replacing his—not entirely dissimilar—"sophisticated methodological falsificationism").[7] To my dismay, I have spoken with many analysts for whom any empirical study of psychoanalysis is anathema—analysts who are not merely indifferent to such research but vehemently opposed to it. For them, psychoanalysis is not a field of human knowledge, subject to rational evaluation, but some sort of religion to which one is or is not converted (or, more cynically, a business through which one can support a wealthy lifestyle if one keeps others converted). Such an attitude is extremely harmful to psychoanalysis both as an intellectual discipline and as a therapeutic practice. Indeed, in the latter case it is highly unethical as well. (Though, one must add immediately that psychoanalysis is not necessarily worse in this regard than medical psychiatry, despite the fact that the latter is part of a systematic research program— a research program that is itself, unsurprisingly, mixed up with business interests and religious feeling.)

That said, however, I cannot claim to be as sanguine as Grunbaum about the possibility of testing psychoanalytic hypotheses epidemiologically. The problem is that epidemiological research can bear only upon etiological generalizations—such as that connecting paranoia with repressed homosexuality. But these generalizations are, I think, peripheral to psychoanalysis. The important causal inferences in psychoanalysis are individual, involving very particular beliefs, desires, memories, and so on. In principle, they are no doubt open to generalization, but the number of variables involved render epidemiological research on precisely formulated generalizations extremely difficult, to say the least. For example, there is no obvious way of testing epidemiologically the connection between the abandonment of a child on the subway and a phobia about a vomit on the subway, or even the connections between structural repetitions in general. And it is these sorts of connections—not those between paranoia and repressed homosexuality—that are central to psychoanalysis.

On the other hand, I am not at all as pessimistic as Grunbaum about the possibility of using clinical evidence in support of psychoanalytic theory. Certainly, it would be desirable for psychoanalytic hypotheses to be supported by experimental studies that directly address causal issues. However, the most general criteria for the evaluation of explanatory hypotheses are, again, empirical adequacy, logical coherence, and simplicity. The absence of experimental or epidemiological studies does not in any way indicate that psychoanalytic hypotheses cannot be evaluated rationally by these criteria.

Of course, this alone does not respond to Grunbaum, for his objections may be rewritten in terms of these criteria. Take simplicity. In some circumstances, simplicity considerations may lead us to attribute certain patterns to chance. If on a given day I sneeze only when standing beside red objects, it is simpler to assume that this is mere coincidence than to claim that there is a causal connection between the color and the sneezing. It is simpler, because the assumption of a causal connection would require me extensively to revise my understanding of causality and of what sorts of things may stand in causal relations. On the other hand, sometimes it is simpler to assume that a certain pattern does manifest a causal connection. Suppose over a period of weeks, I sneeze when and only when a certain cat enters the room. It is simplest to assume that the cat, rather than some unknown further object, caused the sneezing. Finally, we sometimes have no good reason to assume or not to assume a causal connection. If a cat enters the room once and I sneeze, we just do not know. We need further evidence. Grunbaum's point about "thematic affinities" or "meaning connections" is that they are either of the first or third sort. They are either unlikely or ill-supported (see Grunbaum 1984, 55–6; 1989).

In order to decide if Grunbaum is correct, we need to consider more fully the conditions in which we are justified in inferring causal relations. As a general principle, we may say that we have reason to posit a causal connection when a covariation (that between sneezing and the presence of a certain cat) is statistically unlikely and consistent with general causal principles. Thus, the single co-occurrence of a sneeze and a cat's entrance lacks adequate statistical unlikelihood to lend significant evidential support to an hypothesis of causal connection between the two. Even multiple co-occurrences of sneezes and red objects involves objects too inconsistent with our general causal principles to allow an hypothesis of causal connection. However, multiple co-occurrences of sneezing and a certain cat entering the room are adequately unlikely and adequately consistent with our general causal principles to lend evidential support to the positing of a causal connection.

As this last example indicates, repetition—especially, though not necessarily, repetition in controlled experimental studies—is the best way to establish statistical unlikelihood. But in certain cases—and these are crucial for our present concerns—detail and extent of correspondence in a single case may suffice. To take a stereotypical example, a woman may infer that her husband has been unfaithful if he repeatedly comes home late and is not at the office. But she may also infer that he has been unfaithful if he once comes home late, was not at the office, smells of perfume, has lipstick on his collar, etc. Or consider a hypothetical case from linguistics. Suppose we are investigating two languages in the hope of discovering whether or not they are related. We are unlikely to feel compelled to explain the presence in each of a single unusual species-identification, expressed by evidently unrelated words. On the other hand, the presence of unusual syntactic or morphological structures in the two languages, even given different vocabularies, would count as a fact requiring explanation. We would not demand that the linguist provide further, experimental confirmation before we would be willing to accept that the 'thematic affinity' here should not be attributed to chance but rather requires a positive explanatory account.

Returning to psychoanalysis, the "thematic affinity" between forgetting the word *aliquis* and worrying about a possible pregnancy—the well-known case of Freud cited by Grunbaum—does indeed seem extremely tenuous. But the connections between the various events in the life of Masud Khan's patient appear, in contrast, rather striking. Grunbaum is, I think, too ready to dismiss "thematic affinity" on the basis of examples such as the former and without really considering or even acknowledging cases such as the latter.

Indeed, Grunbaum tends to dismiss thematic affinity out of hand, simply assuming its probative irrelevance even in cases where thematic connections are entirely plausible. Consider, for example, a case cited by Grunbaum as evidence against relying on thematic affinity for inferring causal connections: "Thomas Jefferson and John Adams, who had been friends, died within a few hours of each other on the 50th anniversary of the Declaration of Independence, written by Jefferson with the aid of a draft to which Adams had contributed" (Grunbaum 1993, 134). It seems that a reasonable view of this situation would be the following: It is possible that the correlations were accidental or that they were not. Holidays, birthdays, and such affect people's emotional states and their health. The same is true of news concerning a friend's illness and impending death. It is far from implausible (though also far from certain) that the two deaths and the anniversary are connected. But Grunbaum does not adopt this view. Rather, he insists that the deaths "call for *separate* causal explanations" (135), evidently without even considering the possibility of a causal connection. This is not, it seems, a rational argument against the probative value of thematic affinity but rather an a priori dismissal of a range of possible accounts—a dismissal that does not appear to be at all consistent with the principles of rational inference.

Of course, one apparent difference between psychoanalytic hypotheses and the cases we have been citing is the prior plausibility of the type of causal connection under consideration. It is uncontroversial that having an affair is one type of thing that causes late hours, lipstick stains, and so on; a historical connection between two languages is the sort of thing that causes common syntactic and morphological structures; emotional changes are the sorts of things that affect health, including morbidity. We certainly need more serious study of the sorts of causal connection posited by psychoanalysis. On the other hand, it is important to recognize that a great deal of psychoanalysis is coherent with well-supported hypotheses in cognitive science, as we saw in the preceding section. Recall the connections between transference and modeling by salient exempla, association and cross-indexing, repression and priming (or, alternatively, access and suppression), and so on. In this way, many (though not all) of the sorts of causal links posited by psychoanalysis appear quite plausible in light of experimental studies, even though the psychoanalytic specification of these sorts of connection has not itself been tested. In other words, it is hardly as if the theory relies primarily on types of causal connection unheard of elsewhere in psychological theory—quite the contrary, in fact. Certainly, it could turn out that psychoanalytic causal hypotheses are invalid at precisely those points where they diverge from hypotheses in cognitive science (primarily, in the treatment of motivational factors). But it is not the case that these hypotheses posit types of causal connections that are implausible by the lights of currently well-supported theories.

Indeed, some of what Grunbaum takes as evidence against the validity of using of thematic affinities appears to have just the opposite implication, for it indicates the broad plausibility of causally connecting mental events by such affinity. For example, Grunbaum cites Paracelsus's advice— "To cure the liver, treat with a herb that is shaped like a liver" (1993, 136)—as a good example of the problems with causal inferences based on thematic affinity. But note the difference between Paracelsus and Freud. Paracelsus is claiming something about physical objects, that they are often causally linked if they are similar in certain ways. Freud is claiming something about the human mind, that thoughts are often causally linked by some sort of similarity in their objects. In fact, Paracelsus's advice—like a wide range of similar hypotheses that can be found in the history of all disciplines—is an instance of precisely the sort of causal connection Freud is positing. Many people in many places and at many times have drawn such 'Paracelsian' connections despite their fairly evident invalidity. It seems clear that, if anything, this counts in favor of the general type of connection Freud posits, not against it.

In sum, I am in complete agreement with Grunbaum that psychoanalytic hypotheses should be subjected to rigorous examination and evaluation in the context of a systematic research program. However, in terms of the plausibility of the type of causal hypotheses it invokes, its consilience with related psychological theories that are experimentally well-supported, its logical consistency, its explanatory scope, and its empirical basis in thematically related mental phenomena, psychoanalysis does not appear to be worse off than most of its companion 'soft' sciences. Finally, there seems to be no reason we could not rationally evaluate, develop, revise, and apply psychoanalytic hypotheses in the absence of experimental and epidemiological studies.

THE RAT MAN

On Tuesday, the first of October 1907, Ernst Lanzer came to Freud for a preliminary interview. He told Freud about several compulsions—to slit his throat, to harm his "honored lady," and so on. All earlier treatments, he explained, had failed, excepting a hydrotherapy, a *Wasserkur* (literally, water cure); this was successful because he met someone at the clinic with whom he had regular, *regelmaessig,* sexual relations, which were otherwise rare and irregular, *unregelmaessig.* He expressed feelings of disgust before prostitutes. He explained that he masturbated between the ages of sixteen and seventeen and first had sexual intercourse at twenty-six. Freud proposed terms for treatment. Ernst checked with his mother and returned the following day to accept Freud's terms and start the analysis.

Ernst began the first session (on 2 October) with two recollections that appear fully transferential, even though it should be too early for a transference to have established itself. The first concerns his friend, his *Freund,* Dr. Palatzer. Whenever he feels that he is suffering from a criminal, *verbrechericher,* impulse, Ernst goes to Dr. Palatzer and asks if Dr. Palatzer despises, *verachte,* him as a criminal, *Verbrecher.* Dr. Palatzer, then, always reassures Ernst. Evidently, Ernst saw himself as now telling *Dr. Freud* (rather than his *Freund,* the *doctor*) of his criminal impulses, perhaps seeking reassurance from him also.

Immediately following this reflection, Ernst recalls a young medical student who deceived and cheated him as a child. Unlike Freud, Palatzer was not a medical doctor. This medical student then has some relevance to Freud in contrast to Palatzer. This student was very kind and complimentary to Ernst, making Ernst feel himself to be almost a genius. But then he became Ernst's tutor—paid, presumably, by Mrs. Lanzer—and his attitude changed completely. Certainly Freud must have been kind and complimentary in the preliminary interview—in the notes, he refers to Ernst as having a sharp, clear mind, just before mentioning his fees and Mrs. Lanzer (Freud 1974, 2). Evidently, Ernst is concerned that this physician might repeat the behavior of the medical student (hence the need for reassurance).

Ernst then recounts a peculiar incident. The medical student and a friend tell him some wild medical stories. As Ernst believes these tales, they mock him. This too has bearing on the analysis—the wild medical stories perhaps recalling Freud's tales to Ernst concerning the psychoanalytic cure. In any event, the expression Ernst uses here is important—"[*jemandem*] *Baeren aufzubinden*," to tell tall tales, but literally to strap a bear onto someone. This leads to the sexual themes that are central to the patient's obsession—and, ultimately, to the transferential distrust we have been considering as well. After recounting this incident, Ernst goes on to say that the medical student was initially nice only in order to gain access to the Lanzer household, because of his interest in one of Ernst's sisters. Again, the relation to Freud is evident; though its particular nature is at this point unclear, the connection with Ernst's sisters is suggestive of a familial schema of the sort we would expect in the transference.

Indeed, Ernst's next memory is fully in keeping with this connection. Specifically, from this memory of age fourteen to fifteen, just before the period of masturbation (sixteen to seventeen), Ernst continues, not to the adolescent masturbation itself but rather to his introduction to sexuality, during the oedipal period ten years earlier. This conjunction is significant, primarily because it suggests a connection between Ernst's infantile sexuality and his sister, the object of the medical student's interest (though it may also hint at a connection between the doctor, the medical student, and Ernst's father, the oedipal rival). Specifically, Ernst thinks of his governess, Miss Rudolf. (For the names of the figures in Ernst's story, see Mahony 1986). She allowed the young Ernst to crawl under her skirt and touch her genitals, on the condition that he tell no one. He recalls, in particular, waiting for her to come naked into the bath, with his sisters. This suggests an incestuous desire for the sisters—already hinted at in the shift from the medical student's desire to his own—and associates this with the desire for Rudolf. More significantly, it indicates the importance of Ernst's desire for Rudolf and the importance of these early experiences for his later sexual development. Specifically, it directly links Ernst's brief cure, owing to regular coitus during the 'water cure' at the *baths,* to his *baths* with Rudolf and his delight at seeing her "enter naked into the water," "*ausgekleidet ins Wasser stieg*" (3).

At this point, Ernst shifts to his sixth year and another governess—Miss Paula. One might wonder what happened to Rudolf, or how young Ernst reacted to the change, taking place at the end of the oedipal period. Paula was also an object of Ernst's desire. As with Rudolf, he eagerly awaited the bath. But even more important than the bath per se was Paula's nightly ritual of squeezing out the abscesses on her seat—"*die Abscesse am Gesaess hatt, welche sie abends auszudrucken pflegte*" (4). In response to a question, Ernst says that he did not sleep regularly with Paula. The phrasing here— "*nicht regelmaessig*" (4)—recalls his earlier statement that he did not have regular, *regelmassig,* sexual intercourse, except during the watercure at Munich. Thus we begin to see a complex of associated ideas—cure, regularity of sexual contact, the bath; the woman in Munich, his sister, Rudolf, Paula; viewing the buttocks, touching the genitalia. Significantly, when Ernst did not sleep with Paula, he slept with his parents.

Here, Ernst recalls an obscure event involving Paula, two other young women, Ernst, and his brother Robert, younger by one and one-half years. Paula says, "One could do it with the younger, but Ernst is too uncoordinated; he would certainly miss the mark," "*mit dem Kleinen koennte man das schon machen, aber der Ernst sei zu ungeschickt, er werde gewiss daneben fahren*" (4). As this upsets Ernst, Paula explains that a girl was locked up when she did 'that' with the children of whom she was in charge. Precisely what was in question is unclear. What is clear, however, is that Ernst was spoken of as the sort of child who would get a governess into trouble. One might recall here Rudolf's disappearance and her insistence to Ernst that he not tell anyone about his sexual contact with her. Interestingly, Ernst claims here that he was seven at the time. Later it turns out that he was eight, *acht.* In light of the preceding analysis, and in light of the fact that Ernst has already said that he considers himself a felon, it seems relevant that *die Acht* means *outlawry.* (Indeed, when he first mentioned his idea of being a felon, a *Verbrecher,* he did so in the context of asking his friend, Dr. Palatzer, if "*er ihn als Verbrecher verachte,*" if "he despised him as a criminal" [2]). In changing the age, Ernst is, perhaps, evading this suggestion of guilt.

In any event, Ernst continues along the same lines, saying that he believes Paula did not abuse him sexually—an ambiguous comment, further complicated by the immediately following statement that he played with her genitalia, and thus, perhaps, (from his point of view) abused her. Moreover, she was an unmarried mother at twenty-three and in this sense abused by her lover—though they were later married, *geheiratet,* and she became *Frau Hofrat.*

From these reflections relating to men or boys getting women 'into trouble', Ernst turns to his own infantile erections, concerning which he sought relief from his mother, in an oedipal gesture too obvious to require interpretation. He recognized that these erections were related to his fantasies and his "curiosity" (5)—what he felt when touching Rudolf's genitalia (3). Keeping in mind that Ernst had just been speaking of how male desire can harm women and that sexual relations with boys can get governesses incarcerated, and keeping in mind also that Rudolf had insisted that Ernst not let anyone know about their relations, Ernst's next statement is extremely suggestive. He was getting erections because of the fantasies and memories related to Rudolf, *and he came to believe that his parents could read his mind, that they could hear his thoughts. And this,* he says, *was the beginning of his illness.* Evidently, there is a connection here between Ernst's sexual thoughts and something bad happening—most obviously to Rudolf. Indeed, given that his parents could (he imagined) read his thoughts, he did not even need to tell anyone about his contact with Rudolf. His mere recollection of their encounters was enough to reveal this secret and lead to her dismissal, in (as he may well have imagined it) a punishment much like that of the governess mentioned later by Paula. (*Hoeren,* to hear, is nearly homophonous with *Huren,* whores or prostitutes. Thus his disgust at prostitutes [2] may also be a result of this early fear that his parents would hear his thoughts about the unchaste or prostitutelike governesses and that something might therefore happen to them.)

Ernst then continues, just as we might expect, saying that whenever he thought of naked women, he had a great fear that something awful would happen. But his example does not concern a woman undergoing punishment. Rather, it concerns his father dying (5). This is, of course, not surprising, as it explicitly brings the relation with the governesses into an oedipal context. We have already seen how Ernst linked his mother with his erections. It is hardly surprising then that the imagined/desired/feared death of the father should be part of the associated sexual fantasy.

But what of the fear for the mother/governess that is implied by the preceding analysis but not stated by Ernst? This comes out in the second session. Here, Ernst finally tells the story of the incident that made him decide upon analysis—the famous rat story. It was August. He was on military exercises. On break, he listened to a cruel captain tell about a horrible rat torture in which a pot (*Topf*) full of hungry rats is strapped (*angebunden*) to the seat (*Gesaess*) of the condemned person—and the rats bore in. He then imagines—in a *Vorstellung* (8), just as he imagined naked women in *Vorstellungen* that gave him erections (5)—that this is being done to the lady he loves. Some connections are immediately clear. Particularly evident is that between the infantile sexual *Vorstellungen* that aroused him, which his parents could hear, which caused harm to his father and, by our analysis, Rudolf, and the later *Vorstellung* of his beloved Gisela Adler (and, we find out later, his father as well) being harmed. But, if Gisela is being harmed, our analysis indicates that Ernst must have had a sexual thought before this particular *Vorstellung*. This is hinted at in the mention of the *Gesaess* that is eaten away by rats, like the seat of Paula, Frau Hof*rat,* which was eaten away by abscesses, which she had to squeeze or *pinch* out. In a parapraxis that is almost a confirmation of this, Ernst, during this same break, loses his pince nez, his *Zwicker,* literally his *pincher*—a name that could equally be applied to a pince nez or to Paula/Frau Hofrat as she pinched her seat in the bath, thereby arousing Ernst as he *watched* (watching being, of course, just what he cannot do without the *Zwicker*).

The other interesting and obvious connection here is between the pot that is *strapped onto* (*anbinden*) the lady and the idiomatic medical bear that got tied (*aufbinden*) when Ernst's tutor humiliated him with tall tales. This again connects the sexual theme with Ernst's sister—recall that the tutor was interested in the Lanzer girls, and not in Ernst—and also reintroduces the interfering paternal figure, here in the form of the tutor. As Mahony points out, one of Ernst's older sisters, Camilla, died during August; the military exercises on which the *Zwicker* was lost took place, years later, in August also. Evidently, Camilla died at the age of nine—though Ernst reported her age to be eight, *acht.* Ernst was three at this time. Later, Ernst recalls that it was only when he saw Camilla on the pot (the *Topf,* such as that in which the rats were placed) that he first glimpsed female genitalia. In context, it seems plausible to conjecture, on the basis of this, a feeling of responsibility for Camilla's death. Indeed, such a feeling is, I believe, a particularly crucial factor underlying the more general fears that wishing to see a woman's genitalia will bring harm to that woman.

Continuing to the next evening, Ernst tells of how he received from the captain a new pince-nez, sent from Vienna. The captain said that Ernst must reimburse Lt. David for the COD payment on the package. He then reports having had the contradictory thoughts that he would not pay and that he must pay Lt. David the *3 Kronen 80*. He says this to himself *halblaut,* half aloud. Here, in a compulsion that derives from a parapraxis concerning *seeing* and *pinching* and *punishment* involving a *pot* and is thus related to Paula/Frau Hofrat in the bath and to Camilla on the pot, Ernst is compelled to pay *3* Kronen *80*, a sum with its own significant associations to this complex. Once again, three was Ernst's age at the time of Camilla's death; and eight, *acht,* was the age he took her to be at the time of her death, as well as part of the idiom Ernst used initially to introduce the theme of his criminality—*Verbrecher verachte*—and a word meaning 'outlawry,' as we have already seen. Moreover, he says that he muttered this compulsion half aloud, *halblaut,* just as he had earlier felt that his parents could read his thoughts—and thus punish the women he desired, such as Rudolf—as if he spoke them aloud, *lautaussprach* (5).

Here, Ernst returns to the theme of doctors, already hinted at in the reference to binding on the pot of rats—like the "medical bear" of the earlier idiom—but also indicated perhaps in the *drei Kronen achtzig,* for Freud's regular fee at this time was *dreizig Kronen* (see Eissler 1965, 545n.; needless to say, this could have been one of Ernst's associations during the analysis, but not during the original dilemma). Ernst refers specifically to Dr. Wagner von Jauregg, mentioning that he used to smile when Ernst spoke of his obsessions—possibly like the young medical student who laughed at Ernst's gullibility—and who thought at least one of Ernst's obsessions was positively salutary.

From here, Ernst continues with the story of the payment, telling how he gave the money to a subordinate to pay Lt. David. The subordinate, however, was unsuccessful. Finally, Ernst met Lt. David, but David would not accept the money. He then thought again of his father and Gisela Adler (his beloved lady) suffering the torture.

As his father was already deceased, Ernst goes on to explain that, in his obsessions, torture is not confined to this world. He discusses his religious devotion before the age of fourteen or fifteen and his subsequent development into a free thinker. He ends with a plan he had devised for fulfilling his compulsion despite David's refusal of the money.

The third session opens with the dating of his father's death and the information that the unsuccessful officer was a medical assistant. (Ernst's reference to a medical assistant's failure, like his earlier reference to Wagner von Jauregg, may indicate again his skepticism toward Freud, or even a transferential mistrust of Freud.) He then tells the now famous story of his efforts, or nonefforts, to give David the money—the doubts on the train to Vienna, the repeated decisions (ultimately not followed through) to get off and return to David, the meeting with Palatzer, the further doubts, and the decision to see a doctor. Of all the details of the tale, the one that may be most important is one commonly ignored. He decided to see Freud, he says, because a friend came by and demanded the return of some books Ernst had borrowed. One of these books is *The Psychopathology of Everyday Life,* which Ernst looked at again before returning. In looking at the volume, he was reminded of his own trains of thought and thus decided to see Freud.

First of all, this is interesting because the compulsion that had precipitated his decision to see a doctor concerned an unsuccessful repayment, and the decision to see Freud in particular derived from a successful return of items borrowed. This is particularly relevant in light of the relation between Freud's fee and the *3 Kronen 80,* already mentioned. Indeed, we later discover that from the first mention of the fee, Ernst had explicitly brought it into relation with this complex by thinking of the Kronen as *rats* (168). Secondly, this is significant because the entire conflict about the payment derived from the initial parapraxis with the pince nez—thus, what book would be more appropriate to Ernst's condition than *The Psychopathology of Everyday Life?* Turning to the relevant section, on mislaying objects, we find that two of Freud's three examples in this section refer directly to some form of repayment. One focuses on the return of books; the other attends to the payment of fees—once again, the two concerns of Ernst that precipitated his decision to enter analysis with Freud. These connections, then, reinforce one important implication of Ernst's tale—that his entry into analysis crucially involves a concern over what he owes and an attempt to repay a debt of some sort. At the end of the notes for the preceding session, Freud remarks that at one point Ernst referred to Freud by the title of the captain, "Herr Hauptmann" (12). In this context, that seems to indicate not only a fear of cruelty on Freud's part (like the cruelty of the medical student) but also a desire to find out from Freud to whom and how he should pay off his debt.

The fourth session, taking place on a Saturday, precedes the first Sunday break in the analysis. Having ended the previous session with a discussion of his choosing a doctor, Ernst begins this session with the story of his father's death—including, of course, his medical treatment by the family doctor. When his father had an attack of emphysema, Ernst asked the doctor when the danger would pass. The doctor said the following evening. Not suspecting that his father would not live that long, Ernst explains, he decided to take a one-hour nap, between 11:30 and 12:30. He slept a half hour longer than he anticipated and was asleep when his father died. He was told by a medical friend of the family when he awoke. This furthers and complicates our understanding of Ernst's relation to doctors—especially as it indirectly leads us back to Ernst's sisters, specifically to Camilla's death. Here again we find a triangular structure: Ernst/the doctor/the patient—first Camilla, then Ernst's father (cf. the related triangle, Ernst/the medical student/Ernst's sister). Indeed, the structure is elaborated in the rat obsession itself, for it is in effect these two patients who are subjected to the rat torture—with Gisela substituted for Camilla. Moreover, this is related to Ernst not paying some debt to a lender, a lender of whom Freud and David are only two secondary representatives.

Because of his absence when his father died, Ernst continues, he suffered guilt, especially when he was told by a nurse—*"eine Pflegerin"* (18)—that his father had asked for him. The use of the word *"Pflegerin"* is significant. First of all, when he first mentioned Paula's habit of squeezing her abscesses, he used the verb from which *"Pflegerin"* derives, saying she *"auszudrucken pflegte,"* took care to squeeze out, the abscesses (36). In this way, just as Paula was a *Zwicker,* a pincher, she is also one who takes care (to pinch), a *"Pflegerin."* Here the *"Pflegerin,"* and thereby Paula, is related to the death of the father. One might infer from this to an underlying oedipal scenario in which Ernst, in desiring his mother or governess, desires the death of the father. We have already glimpsed this complex in connection with the rat fantasy. Indeed, the relation between the rat torture and the use of the term *'pflegen'* in this context is reinforced when one realizes that one older and now chiefly poetical idiom for taking someone's counsel—what Ernst does with Palatzer in the story of the rat obsession, and what he does with Freud by going to analysis (because of the rat obsession)—is *seiner Rats pflegen.*

Ernst's feelings of remorse became acute, and he began to consider himself a criminal, only later, when an aunt died and he went to the funeral home. Though Ernst subsequently gives another explanation, it seems that at least one crucial reason for the intensification of his guilt was the fact that the aunt was in Baden (literally, *bath*) and thus her death, conjoined with the memory of his father's death, 'activated' the complex involving the bath, the infantile desire for Rudolf and Paula, the death wish for the father, and so on—the complex that was later to surface in the rat torture. It was from this time that Ernst began to conceive of tortures extending into "the beyond" (19).

After the break, the bulk of the Monday session is given over to re-assurances by Freud and explanations of psychoanalysis. (Though I do not pretend to know anything about technique, this does not seem to me a bad thing, given the severe anxiety Ernst expressed, indirectly, with regard to Freud and the treatment, as we have seen.) Toward the end, Ernst tells how formerly, in 1903, his obsessions would attack, and he would suffer from eight to ten days. (We need hardly remark on the recurrence of *acht* here.) Now, however, he is resigned, for he feels he has already committed the crime and can do no more evil—perhaps this is related to the fact that his first coitus was in 1904 (see Mahony 1986).

The sixth session begins with a childhood memory. At the age of eight (yet again, *acht*), he felt his parents could read—here, *erraten*—his thoughts. In part, this seems to indicate that he sees his outlawry (*Acht*) and the rat tortures for which he was responsible (in not paying a debt re-lated to looking and to a pincher), as somehow related to his parents read-ing (*erraten*) his thoughts. Again, a feeling of responsibility for Rudolf's disappearance seems plausible. In addition, the mention of eight here re-calls Camilla's death at eight and perhaps implies that he felt his parents could read his thought when Camilla was eight—implying his respon-sibility in her death as well. Ernst's immediately following recollection seems almost to confirm this: at the age of twelve—he loved the *sister* of a friend and thought that she would love him if only *his father would die*. It seems that this tale of the love for a friend's sister and of the indirect death wish for his father substitutes for a repressed tale of desire for his own sister, Camilla, and of a direct death wish for his father in that connection.

Summarizing our analysis thus far, we might reconstruct the etiology of Ernst's neurosis along roughly the following lines: Ernst desires Camilla and Rudolf and Paula/Frau Hofrat, in a series of transferences presum-ably leading back to his mother, whom he broached to seek help with his infantile erections, as we have seen. But his desirous thoughts, which his parents can *erraten,* are dangerous to his beloved, causing her harm—death in Camilla's case, some other sort of disappearance in the case of Rudolf, perhaps the abscesses in Paula's case, the imaginary rat torture in the case of Gisela (with the bites recalling Paula's abscesses). In contrast, he desires the death of his father, first of all for the standard oedipal reasons, but also perhaps as he may connect his father with the death of Camilla and the dis-appearance of Rudolf, on the implicit assumption that his father read his thoughts (both his sexual thoughts and his initial, oedipal death wish).

After an intervention by Freud, pointing to the desire behind the thought of the father's death, Ernst thinks of other, similar instances. About six months before his father's death, he thought that, if his father were to die, he would become rich enough to marry Gisela. The structural identification of Camilla and Gisela—and Rudolf, and Ernst's mother, and so on—is expected. What is perhaps less expected is the introduction of the monetary theme, already introduced, through inversion as debt, in connection with the *Zwicker* and Freud, but not previously related in a clear way to Ernst's feared sexual fantasies per se. After having this patricidal thought, Ernst then wishes that his father would leave him nothing. Debt, with which, as we have repeatedly remarked, Ernst is deeply concerned, is only a continuation of the sequence that runs from receiving inheritance to receiving nothing to owing something. Clearly, this debt is bound up with Ernst's sexual desires and his death wish for his father. It seems plausible to infer that it is a form of recompense for the harm that he feels his desires have caused.

Ernst begins the seventh session by saying that he cannot believe he wished for his father's death. He then shifts immediately to the recollection of Suderman's *Die Wunsch,* a novel about two sisters, in which one sister wishes for the death of the other in order to marry her husband but then commits suicide when the second sister does in fact die. Ernst then says that it seems to him quite fair that one should die for one's thoughts. In this context, the crucial importance of the death of the sister (Camilla) is again emphasized, as is his (differently motivated) role in causing that death—and, more broadly, the very deep guilt he feels for his thoughts. Ernst next reports that he would like to kill his brother Robert's fiancée. This may at first seem to go in the opposite direction, perhaps indicating a homosexual component in his feelings and a death wish for the sister (mother, and so on). In context however, it seems more likely that he in fact wishes for the death of his brother/rival (not his future sister-in-law); he is, in other words, in the position of the unwed sister in the novel, wishing for the sibling's demise. All this seems to be a fairly straightforward transferential repetition of the structure we have been considering.

These themes are broached again in another variation during the eighth session. Here, Ernst speaks of various odd compulsions (such as counting between thunder and lightning) before going on to tell of his resentment at Gisela's departure when her grandmother was ill. In this regard, he first thinks of killing himself—like the jealous sister discussed in the preceding session, the sister who, in Ernst's view, deserved to die for her thoughts. He then thinks that the only proper thing to do is to go and kill

157

the old woman. This is all that Freud reports for the session. This seems to indicate again that the most critical unconscious structure functioning in Ernst's case involves first of all a heterosexual incestuous desire for the mother/sister/governess, now transferred to Gisela, and a death wish for the interfering parent/father.

Up until this point in the analysis, Ernst has refused to discuss or even name Gisela. Freud, in an attempt to free Ernst from this resistance, which is clearly inhibiting his following the fundamental rule of entirely uncensored association, suggests that Ernst bring in a picture of his beloved lady. The next session begins with some predictable unpleasantness over this suggestion, which fits in perfectly with Ernst's transferential suspicions about Freud's motives. Afterwards, Ernst speaks of his unsuccessful counterobsessional prayers and of the formula that he substituted for lengthier prayers, in order to oppose the obsessions. (Freud is unsure precisely what this is—"something like Gigellsamen," he writes; in the published case history, however, he points out that it involves a conjunction of *'samen'* [German, semen] with a transformed version of the name of his beloved lady [Freud 1982, 60–61].)

Ernst goes on from here to discuss the harmful effects of his thoughts, this time in such a way as almost to confirm the critically oedipal nature of his desire for his sister and death wish for his father. He cites as a prime example of his telepathic powers the hydrotherapy at Munich. We have already seen that the woman with whom he had sexual relations in Munich was unconsciously linked, by way of the bath, with Rudolf, Paula, and his sisters—and thereby, presumably, with his mother as well. During his first visit to Munich, he and this woman had rooms next door to one another. During his second visit, he could not stay next door to the woman because that room was occupied by "the Professor" (34). Ernst hoped that the professor would die of a stroke—*Schlag.* Fourteen days later, Ernst awoke with the thought of a corpse. That night, he later discovered, the Professor suffered a stroke. The death wish itself, the infantile belief in its efficacy, the paternal position of the Professor, the sexual associations of the bath, and so on all suggest again that Ernst felt precisely this sort of death wish toward his father in connection with the string of structurally identified women and girls he desired—his mother, Camilla, Rudolf, Paula. It may also indicate a transferential hostility toward professors or doctors, such as Freud.[8]

The following session falls on a Saturday, and thus before the second break in the analysis. Judging from Freud's notes, it was a particularly productive hour. Ernst begins by explaining how he attacked his maid after returning from the theater. He then goes on to discuss his masturbation. Having on the first day said that he masturbated only between sixteen and seventeen, Ernst now says that he began to masturbate at twenty-one, after his father's death. (As his father died in July, this may place the beginning of masturbation in August—the month of Camilla's death and of the military exercises.) He describes how he feared that his masturbation may have endangered his mother's spiritual well-being. Superficially, this is owing to a chance similarity between one of his compulsions and an utterance of his mother's. More significantly, however, it appears to confirm and extend the oedipal generalization, mentioned above, of his fear that his desire and fantasy will harm the object of that desire.

Ernst goes on to discuss the several occasions when he did, subsequently, masturbate, telling of the "beautiful moments" that drove him to onanism. The first concerns a postillion playing—*blasen*—in the street. The second concerns a story in *Dichtung und Wahrheit* wherein Goethe breaks the bonds—*zerriss . . . die Fessel*—of a curse and kisses his beloved. What is interesting for our purposes is that *Blasen*—which caused his first masturbation—as a noun, means *blisters,* like those on Paula's buttocks. As to the second, the German *Fessel* is almost homophonous with the French *fesses, buttocks.* We know that Ernst knew French (see Mahony 1986, 8), and, given his interests, it is difficult to imagine that he did not know this word. Thus '*zerriss . . . die Fessel/fesses*' might be translated, 'rupture the buttocks'—what Paula in effect did in expressing her *Blasen*. The two instances of masturbation thus lead back to Paula and her abscesses, as we might have expected. (There is a third example, where no details are reported, except that a maid excited him, which fits in an obvious, literal way—as does his actual attack on his maid, mentioned at the beginning of the session.) The second example is also interesting because the curse from which Goethe broke free was closely related to that from which Ernst unconsciously felt he suffered. Specifically, because of a conflict between two sisters, Goethe was cursed so that he came to believe any woman he might kiss would suffer in some "unheard-of spiritual manner" (533)—like the entire series of women Ernst desired, but especially like Ernst's mother, as mentioned earlier in this session. (It is evidently important that the sister conflict recurs here. One wonders if there might not have been, perhaps, a conflict between two of Ernst's sisters, or even between Ernst's mother and one of his sisters. Unfortunately, there is just no information on this topic.)

Ernst then returns to prostitutes. He was with a prostitute and she told him that there would be an extra one-half added to the fee if she had to undress. Ernst leaves in disgust. This may have a transferential relation to Freud's fee. In this case, talk of a prostitute's fee tends to put Freud in the place of the prostitute—creating the comic and humiliating picture of Freud refusing to analyze in the buff for any less than 45 Kronen. More importantly, the extra one-half is reminiscent of Ernst's extra one-half hour's sleep when his father died. The disgust, in this case, derives at least in part from the recapitulation of the crucial connection between his father's death and his own sexual desire—prominently, his desire to see his governess (and presumably his mother) naked, which is to say, undressed. This connection is further reinforced, and the transference relation is simultaneously emphasized, by the term Ernst uses to express the *increase* in fee—*Aufschlag.* Containing, as it does, the word *schlag,* stroke, it connects directly with the death of the *Professor* whose presence in Munich inhibited his sexual relations with the young woman.

Not surprisingly, the young woman in Munich is mentioned in the very next sentence. Ernst then tells how he lost sexual interest in her—much as he lost interest in the prostitute. Though the reasons are superficially very different, they ultimately appear to be closely related. Specifically, Ernst explains how this woman told him of the death of her first love and of how she had been called to his deathbed. It was immediately upon hearing this that Ernst lost sexual interest in her. He claims that this was because he has a need to separate love and desire. But it was more likely because the death of the (earlier, unknown) rival (unconsciously) reminded Ernst of his father's(/rival's) death and the mention of someone being called to the deathbed (unconsciously) reminded him of his having been called to his father's deathbed—all of which recalled his earlier death wish for his father, his related feelings of guilt, and so on.

Toward the end of his entry for this session, Freud records, uncertainly, three memories reported earlier but not previously recorded. 1) Ernst is three. Camilla is taken to bed. 2) He asks his weeping father, "Where is Camilla?" 3) His father leans over his weeping mother. It is interesting that Freud reports these memories late and uncertainly. Up until this point he has almost entirely ignored Camilla—despite the fact, evidenced by these memories, that Ernst had spoken of her.

Monday, the fourteenth of October, ends the second fortnight of Ernst's meetings with Freud—Ernst having come to Freud first on 1 October, the same day he joined the army in the year of his father's death. The fourteenth of October is the day before Gisela's birthday, and his sister Olga's wedding anniversary. And it is the last day on which Freud took daily notes for the case. The day begins with Camilla. Ernst recalls that Camilla had said to him, "My soul, if you die, I do myself in" (38) — "*Meiner Seel, wenn du stirbst, bring ich mich um.*" This sentence relates to the structure we have been considering in a number of ways. Most obviously, it makes Camilla's death literally contingent on Ernst. Secondly, it inverts Ernst's sense that he — like the sister in *Die Wunsch* — should kill himself for (the death/s caused by) his thoughts. Finally, it connects Camilla with Ernst's mother at the very moment when he began to fear that his masturbation might harm her, as he reported in the preceding session. Specifically, this fear was triggered when his mother urged him not to visit Gisela after the death of her grandmother — whom he had earlier wanted to kill, *umbringen* (the same word used by Camilla). More important, the particular wording used by Ernst's mother was associated with Camilla's statement by way of its opening phrase: "*Meiner Seel, du wirst nicht fahren.*" Thus the fear that Ernst expresses for his mother, deriving at least in part from his earlier sexual desire, comes to indicate again and more strongly the correlate guilt for his sister's death, related also to his sexual desire. Evidently Ernst's fear that his infantile masturbation killed his sister has been extended to the idea that it might now harm his mother's soul — that is, the soul to which she referred in the sentence just quoted, in the phrase repeated from Camilla (who died after referring to her soul in this manner).[9]

As if the connection between Camilla's statement on suicide and Ernst's masturbation fears were not already clear, Ernst turns at this point to a discussion of masturbation and from there returns to the theme of patricidal wishes associated with sexual pleasure. Specifically Ernst twice had the thought, during coitus, that such an experience is so exquisite that one could even kill one's father for it. The first time he had this thought is during his first coitus in Trieste — the city in which his oldest sister lives. The second time is with the young woman at the baths in Munich. Thus the first was connected with a sister, and thereby indirectly with Camilla; the second is connected, by way of the baths, with Rudolf, Paula, and Ernst's sisters, in a relationship already associated with the near death of an interfering older man, the Professor.

By the end of this twelfth meeting, the main outlines of the structure of Ernst's obsession, centering about a death wish for his father and a fear that his desire is harmful to the desired woman (protypically Camilla), appear relatively clear. Further complications enter subsequently. But the basic concerns—the basic desires and conflicts—have all been introduced, remaining only to be reworked and elaborated. Moreover, they have been introduced not only through Ernst's contingent associations, the standard objects of psychoanalytic concern, but equally through his transferential repetition of structures, and through the "constitutive ambiguity" of his speech.

5 LITERARY INTERPRETATION

Suggestion, Relevance, and Structure
in Aesthetical Intent

CAUSALITY, ASSOCIATION, AND THE EXPERIENCE OF ART

In some ways, the theory of literary interpretation is much simpler than those of legal or psychoanalytic interpretation. In literary interpretation there are no special evidentiary or methodological problems, such as are to be found in psychoanalytic interpretation. Neither is there any need for hierarchization of varieties of interpretation, as there is in legal interpretation. Despite the debates of literary critics, there is no need to privilege author's final evaluative intent (his/her final judgment concerning the rectitude of a certain character's actions), or expressive autobiographical intent (in, for example, the autobiographical prototypes of characters or events), or even authorial intentional word-meaning. Moreover, there is no logical or empirical basis for any such hierarchization. One need only make one's claims explicit with regard to the sort of intent under consideration—from authorial moral evaluations to readers' associations.

On the other hand, one needs to know what sorts of intent one might specify, what characterizes these, and so on. For the most part, literary interpretation involves reference to common types of intent—for example, utterer's word-meaning—which there is no need to explicate. But we might nonetheless ask if, in addition to the garden varieties of intent, there are varieties of intent peculiar to literary study, or of particular importance in literary study. Now, what is peculiar to literature—in contrast with ordinary conversation, statutes, an analysand's speech, and so on—is its aesthetic function. Any variety of intention particularly germane to literature would, then, presumably be related to this aesthetic function. One such variety of intent would be that by which an author synthesizes and evaluates his/her work aesthetically, as beautiful, as the cause of aesthetical pleasure. I shall refer to this as 'authorial aesthetical intent'. (Other relevant varieties would include the parallel aesthetic response of an individual reader, the features common to the aesthetic responses within a particular group and so on. I take it that all these, insofar as they are forms of aesthetical intent, follow the same general principles as authorial aesthetical intent and thus do not require separate treatment. This is not to say that they are less important than authorial aesthetical intent or less worthy of study.)

More exactly, no author of value simply 'expresses what he/she feels'. By definition, a literary work is aesthetically good, a good work of literature, if and only if it is aesthetically effective. Now, when we adopt the 'aesthetical attitude' towards a work, this means that we are allowing the work to affect us in a certain way. We are allowing the sounds, the events portrayed, the relations between characters, and so on to produce in us aesthetical pleasure. As Wittgenstein put it, "A poet's words can pierce us. And that is . . . connected with the way in which . . . we let our thoughts roam up and down in the familiar surroundings of the words" (Wittgenstein 1967, 28e). Needless to say, authors are aware of this and strive in their work for this sort of aesthetical efficacy, efficacy in pleasing a reader who has adopted the aesthetical attitude. (This is not, of course, to say that authors do not do other things as well, or that the aesthetic aspect of a literary work is or should be the most important for an author or reader.)

What this means, then, is that authors write and, at once or subsequently in revision, themselves adopt—to the degree they are able—a generalized aesthetical attitude, an attitude assimilable to that which readers, or viewers, or auditors, will or might adopt. In other words, the artist, or the aesthetically successful artist, in reconsidering and reworking a piece of literature adopts an attitude anyone (or anyone in a certain educational, cultural, or other group) might adopt, an attitude that leads to aesthetical pleasure independent of that artist's purely personal associations. Thus the more capable the artist is in generalizing his/her aesthetical attitude— which, I should stress, need *not* involve making the work 'impersonal'— the more successful his/her art will be.

Descriptions of the 'artistic process' tend to fit this general scheme well. For example, S. H. Butcher derives from Aristotle the idea that "if the artist shares at all in the distinctive pleasure that belongs to his art, he does so not as an artist but as one of the public" (Butcher 1951, 207). Anand Amaladass makes a closely parallel point, drawing on the writings of the ninth-century Indian aesthetician, Ānandavardhana (see Amaladass 1984, 108), and parallel ideas can be found in the Arabic theorists as well (see Cantarino 1975, 119 and 155). Arnold Hauser writes similarly that "artistic creation . . . consists in a whole series of more or less independent functions—conscious and unconscious, rational and irrational—and their various products have to be thoroughly sifted and edited by the artist's critical intellect [therefore in the aesthetical attitude adopted in revision] in much the same way as the manager of the lodge tested, corrected, and harmonized the products of the individual workmen" (Hauser 1957, 1:248). Subsequently, Hauser cites Friedrich Nietzsche in a related vein, writing, "The imagination of the artist continually produces good, middling and bad things . . . it is his discernment that first rejects, selects and organizes the material to be used" (Hauser 1957, 4:182–83). And, from yet another perspective, Philip Johnson-Laird argues for a view along these lines based on researches in cognitive science (Johnson-Laird 1988, 258). A particularly acute description of this process may be found in Barbara Herrnstein Smith's discussion of "*Artistic Creation as a Paradigm of Evaluative Activity*":

> [a] thousand individual acts of approval and rejection, preference and assessment, trial and revision . . . constitute the . . . process of literary composition . . . selecting this word, adjusting that turn of phrase, preferring this rhyme to that . . . all the while testing the local and global effectiveness of each decision by impersonating in advance . . . various presumptive audiences . . . . Every literary work—and, more generally, artwork—is thus the product of a complex evaluative feedback loop that embraces not only the ever-shifting economy of the artist's own interests and resources as they evolve during and in reaction to the process of composition, but also all the shifting economies of her assumed and imagined audiences, including those who do not yet exist but whose emergent interests, variable conditions of encounter, and rival sources of gratification she will attempt to predict—or will intuitively surmise—and to which, among other things, her own sense of the fittingness of each decision will be responsive. (Smith 1988, 44–45)

Not only critics and theorists but artists too have represented creative work in the same general terms. For example, in a recent interview with Lalita Pandit, Anita Desai explained that though anything she writes is initially expressive, her work is ultimately formed through a receptive and critical approach, adopted and acted upon subsequently. More strikingly, in her portrait of Lily Briscoe, Virginia Woolf not only describes but illustrates this process. Lily paints, then scrutinizes, then paints, experiencing and reexperiencing her work in the aesthetical attitude. When dissatisfied, she thinks, "There was something perhaps wrong with the design? Was it, she wondered, that the line of the wall wanted breaking, was it that the mass of the trees was too heavy?" (Woolf 1955, 287). Lily is seeking the right effect, an aesthetic completion. Finally, "with a sudden intensity, as if she saw it clear for a second, she drew a line there, in the centre. It was done; it was finished," she judges. "Yes, she thought, laying down her brush in extreme fatigue, I have had my vision" (310)—and that vision is the painting itself as an aesthetic experience.

Clearly, in each of these cases, the artist is understood not to express the immediacy of his/her internality (or to imitate the reality of the external world and so on); rather he/she is understood to, in a sense, rethink and evaluate his/her work through the aesthetical attitude of prospective readers or viewers.

But what is the aesthetical attitude, what is it that such readers or viewers do, what is it that *we* do when approaching an object (for instance, a poem) specifically as an object of aesthetical pleasure? What is involved in adopting the aesthetical attitude? The two most common characteristics used to define the aesthetical attitude in Western writings on the topic have been appropriate 'distance'—neither too much nor too little—and 'disinterestedness' (see, for example, Dickie 1989, 100). But there are serious problems with a definition along these lines. Indeed, George Dickie has argued at length that there is no such thing as an aesthetical attitude involving these properties. Specifically, Dickie argues that the terms are ultimately vacuous. To have appropriate distance from a work of art or to consider it disinterestedly is merely to pay attention to that work of art. For example, consider someone who, in watching *Othello*, begins to wonder about his/her spouse's fidelity. Many theorists of the aesthetical attitude would say that this person does not have appropriate distance from the work. Or consider someone who has invested money in a concert and is delighted by the concert—not because of the music but because of the large crowd. This is a classic case of aesthetic experience being distorted by 'interest'. But Dickie argues that each is simply a case of the person in question not paying attention to the work of art at all. The jealous person is considering his/her spouse, not *Othello;* the entrepreneur is considering attendance, not music. It is not that the jealous person or the entrepreneur lacks a particular ('aesthetic') attitude toward the work of art, but that he/she is not really concerned with that work of art at all.

Dickie is certainly right that these criteria are inadequate to define an aesthetical attitude. And, considered as strict criteria, they are problematic in precisely the way Dickie indicates. On the other hand, the writers who invoke distance and disinterest seem to be getting at something in aesthetic experience, if in an overly vague manner. As to distance, it seems right to say that aesthetic experience engages us personally (we 'relate to the characters' in a novel and so on) without leading us to dwell explicitly on those personal elements. And, as to disinterest, it seems that we could pay careful attention to a work, line by line, word by word, while focusing on its likely impact on an audience; imagine, for example, reading a play in order to decide if it should be performed before a monarch whom you know to enjoy flattery and mystery but to have no interest in sound or rhythm patterns, word choice, or depth of characterization. Though this sort of reading need not preclude reading the same work with aesthetic interest, the two are clearly different. I can read a work to judge its impact on the monarch without in any way opening myself to an aesthetic experience—and I can open myself to an aesthetic experience of a work, without in any way concerning myself with its likely impact on the monarch. Indeed, Dickie acknowledges as much when he says that a reader may "concentrate his attention (when he does read a poem) on certain 'informational' aspects of a poem and . . . ignore remaining aspects" (348). But if one can attend to or ignore aesthetically important aspects of a work, then one can adopt or not adopt an aesthetical attitude. For this is the basic point about the aesthetic attitude: that we sometimes attend to a work of art (or a natural object) as an aesthetic object, whereas sometimes we don't. (See Beardsley 1987 for a discussion of some related points.) On the other hand, the nature of this attitude is only hinted at, obscurely, by the standard definitions in terms of distance and disinterest.

Perhaps a better way of approaching the aesthetical attitude may be found in the preceding quote from Wittgenstein, which indicates that the aesthetical attitude allows or even evokes a broader range of association than would be common in nonaesthetical understanding or response. Psychoanalytic writers have made a similar point in connecting literary art with unconscious fantasy and with highly associative "primary process" thinking (see, for example, Holland 1968 and Lyotard 1979, 143 and citations). The obvious problem here, however, is that aesthetic associations cannot be unlimited or unstructured. As many writers have emphasized, reading a literary work is a process of synthesis or constitution based on an assumption of coherence or unity. Obviously, European and North American literary critics and theorists since Aristotle have emphasized the unity of the literary work. Indian theorists have expressed the same attitude. For example, Vāmana, a ninth-century Indian theorist, speaks of the unifying *ātman* or soul of poetry (see Gerow 1977, 236) and the very early *Nāṭyaśāstra* explicitly emphasizes the importance of establishing the integrity of the literary work (see Gerow 1977, 248, 250). Chinese theorists too pressed this point, as may be seen in the seventeenth-century writings of Wang Fu-chih (see Rickett 1978, 132–33 and 136–37) and Chin Sheng-T'an (see Wang 1972, 48–49 and 97).

Unfortunately, few of these writers make clear precisely what they mean by 'unity'. They often seem to have in mind causal or logical coherence, but these seem inadequate for a broad range of cases. For example, postmodern works may lack causal and logical consistency but nonetheless maintain, and require us to assume that they maintain, some type of coherence—as, for example, Bordwell has noted (see Bordwell 1989, 134). Here and below, I will use the terms 'unity', 'integrity', and so forth somewhat differently to refer to *mutual relevance between parts or elements of a work*. Note that a work can be unified in this sense without being, for example, logically or causally consistent. Consider a conversation. If Buffy makes a claim and Jody disagrees, Jody is nonetheless saying something relevant, and the conversation has unity (in my sense), despite the logical contradiction between the two positions. In contrast, if Jody changes the topic, the conversation will be logically consistent but will lose a certain sort of unity.

Though this is, I believe, the appropriate way to define unity—in literature, ordinary conversation, and elsewhere—it does not yet solve our problem, for it does not tell us anything about the precise nature of unity in literature. For this, I believe, we must return to the aesthetical attitude—for we are concerned with literary unity precisely insofar as it is part of or germane to aesthetical experience. As we have already seen, the standard results of Western studies of the aesthetical attitude—primarily the isolation of appropriate distance and disinterestedness—are of little help. However, treatments of related topics in the Indian and, to a lesser extent, Chinese traditions are, in my view, extremely valuable for understanding this psychologically and interpretively important phenomenon. I should like, then, to approach the aesthetical attitude again, this time from the perspective of the great Sanskrit theorists, especially the eleventh-century Kashmiri aesthetician, Abhinavagupta.

Roughly in line with the Western notion of disinterestedness, but perhaps more suggestively, Abhinavagupta begins his analysis by drawing an analogy between aesthetic experience and savoring the taste of food. Different from the satiation of hunger (see Abhinavagupta 1968, xxxiii and 59–60), this savoring involves "the squeezing out of the poetical word. Persons aesthetically sensitive, indeed, read and taste many times over the same poem" (xxxii). Thus, for Abhinavagupta, aesthetical experience involves something like the sort of play mentioned by Wittgenstein, a sort of dallying with the meanings, contexts, associations of the words and phrases. Specifically—and this is what is crucial—it involves the delectation of their *dhvani,* their *suggestions* or *evocations* (in Amaladass's translation; Amaladass 1984, 79), which suggestions, Abhinavagupta insists, are linked to a particular *rasa,* a particular flavor or *sentiment.*

Dhvani and *rasa* are the central terms of Sanskrit poetics. As already indicated, *dhvani* means suggestion or evocation. Sanskrit theorists, such as Mammaṭa (twelfth century) are at pains to distinguish dhvani from mere 'indication', which is to say secondary or directly implied meaning. Taking up a famous example, Mammaṭa explains that "a hamlet on the Ganga" *indicates* or *implies* that the hamlet is on the bank of the Ganga, as it could hardly be on the Ganga itself. In contrast, it *suggests* sanctity (Mammaṭa 1970, 16, 25), as well as peace, purity, and so forth (see Amaladass 1984, 82). Dhvani is thus a certain sort of association (in this case triggered by the common view that the Ganga is sacred). Moreover, like associative chains of other sorts, and unlike straightforward implications, it is, the Sanskrit writers emphasize, not fully paraphraseable. This is in part owing to the extent of the associative chains. But it is equally owing to the fact that dhvani is emotive as well as cognitive. As Amaladass points out, "dhvani proper" cannot be expressed but only evoked, because dhvani proper is precisely *rasadhvani,* sentiment evocation (see 92–93), a set of associations along with the complex of feelings they call forth. Moreover, according to virtually every theorist of rasa from Bharata-Muni to Abhinavagupta (see, for example, Gerow 1977, 248), this complex must be dominated by a single *rasa,* a single sentiment or feeling, if the work of art is to be successful.

Thus we have our first real indication of what sort of unity we might find in the aesthetical attitude—a unity of rasadhvani, a unity of emotionally evocative association. In fact, Amaladass goes so far as to refer to a "*dhvani*-attitude" of aesthetic consciousness (117). Though he develops the notion rather differently, this—or perhaps 'rasadhvani-attitude'—would be a perfectly appropriate name for what we have been calling the "aesthetical attitude," and 'rasadhvani intent' could appropriately define what we have called "aesthetical intent."

Concerning rasadhvani, Abhinavagupta argues that associations evoke sentiments by connection with "latent traces left by corresponding preceding causes" (79). More exactly, when a spectator in the theater sees acts of love or hate, sadness or joy on a stage, these acts trigger his/her associations, which in turn evoke emotions. As Abhinavagupta puts it:

> Acts of horripilation, etc., which have repeatedly been seen by the spectator in the course of everyday life as indexes of delight, etc., serve, in this case, to make known a delight, etc., uncircumscribed by either time or space. In this delight, just because he possesses the latent traces of it in himself, the Self of the spectator also actively participates. For this very reason, this delight is perceived neither with indifference, from the outside, nor as if it were linked with a particular cause—for in this case, intrusion by pragmatic requirements, interests of gain, etc., would occur—, nor again as if it exclusively belonged to a defined third person—for, in this case sensations of pleasure, hatred, etc. would occur in the spectator. (Abhinavagupta 1968, 87)

Later, linking the notion of aesthetic savoring or relishing to rasadhvani, Abhinavagupta writes, "Everybody's mind is indeed characterized by the most various latent impressions; for as it has been said . . . 'On the ground that the remembrances and the impressions are homogeneous there is an uninterrupted succession of latent impressions . . . .' Therefore, it is established that Rasa is perceived. This perception, in its turn, presents [itself] in the form of a relishing" (112). Thus, Abhinavagupta maintains that the personal aspect of aesthetical experience is crucial and is built up out of memories ("latent traces" or "latent impressions") or rather feelings associated with memories, but in some way isolated from their specific, original context. Moreover, in each case, these memories are evoked and unified in a rasa. Abhinavagupta argues that latent impressions can enter into or define a rasa *only* when they have been isolated from their pragmatic context and thus "generalized." In other words, for, say, personal sorrow to become an aesthetic rasa, it must be in some way generalized from specific memories of personal loss, which is to say that it must be in some way removed from those specific memories, while at the same time remaining in some way connected with them (as the continuing source of the feeling). As we have already indicated, this is a topic of particular importance to an understanding of aesthetical intent, for it is necessarily this generalized associative response that the author or artist seeks to evoke in his/her audience or reader and thus it is this response that he/she seeks to experience and evaluate in aesthetical intent.

The generalized character of aesthetical experience is emphasized by a wide range of Indian aestheticians, especially through the concept of "the sahṛdaya [connoisseur, literally someone 'with heart'], who is skilled in appreciating *rasa*" (Amaladass 1984, 107). Ānandavardhana, the ninth-century theorist of dhvani, was explicit about the associative function of the words of poetry for the sahṛdaya (see Amaladass 1984, 107). Amaladass explains Ānandavardhana's view of the sahṛdaya as a person "of sensibility to the particular chain of associations which the poet could arouse in the minds of people from his own tradition" (113).

Adding to these views the results of more recent research in cognitive science, we can, I think, get a fairly good idea of what is involved in aesthetical experience. When we adopt the aesthetical attitude or rasadhvani attitude, part of what we do is allow ourselves to 'savor' the emotionally evocative associations that we have to the different aspects of a certain work—its sounds, words, images, characters, events, and so on. But these associations are not all of one sort. Like all other aspects of our semantic cognition, they are hierarchized. Again, our internal lexicons encompass not only what we would normally consider 'meanings' but general empirical beliefs, as well as specific memories, fantasies, and so on, and they are organized into hierarchies, both within and across lexical entries. In other words, some entries and some elements within entries are more readily accessible than others. To a degree, these hierarchies are context-sensitive. When speaking of shoes, we have ready access to 'laces' and one meaning of 'foot' is uppermost in our entry for that term. When speaking of poetic form, we have ready access to 'spondee' and a different meaning of 'foot' takes the top spot in that entry. Outside of the aesthetical attitude, our accessing of lexical entries may be relatively shallow. Moving through a piece of argument with an eye on its logic and an eye on its conclusion, we invoke only those meanings germane to the argument—perhaps by briefly accessing the whole entry, then eliminating what we judge irrelevant, perhaps by accessing only part of the entry while keeping the rest primed. When reading in the aesthetical attitude, however, we do not move swiftly, but 'savor' each word, image, and so on, and thus go deeper into our lexical entries, accessing more meanings and priming more associations (more cross-indexed entries), or eliminating less after initial access, and doing so less quickly. Of course, our access to these entries is still hierarchical and thus, so to speak, 'weighted', but even here the hierarchization is somewhat different from that in purely informational or other nonaesthetic sorts of reading. One especially important aspect of this rehierarchization of lexical entries in the aesthetical attitude is that we should expect literary and aesthetic associations in particular to be elevated or primed or otherwise rendered more readily accessible—in keeping with the aesthetic principles of the Sanskrit theorists as well as the general principles of lexical structure (if medical texts to some degree prime medical elements of lexical entries, then literary texts should prime literary aspects).[1]

Clearly, aesthetical intent may be understood in precisely the same terms, for it seeks both to anticipate and to guide aesthetical response. (As Edwin Gerow has pointed out, dhvani is a function of "non-literal [authorial] intention" [Gerow 1977, 252].) Following from this, interpretation to aesthetical intent may be understood as in the first place the determination of rasadhvani through complexes of association—especially literary association—in accordance with a presumption of unity or relevance.

How, then, does this occur? We may conceive of the process—both that of the author and that of the reader—in the following way: Our lexical entries, again, involve 'memory traces', as Abhinavagupta said. These memories, when recalled, evoke certain feelings—'sad' memories make us sad and so forth. In the aesthetical attitude, we more fully prime or more deeply access these entries than would ordinarily be the case. Thus we are affected by the associated feelings. However, we do not dwell on the memories themselves. Rather, our attention remains on the work. There are several ways of conceiving of this. One, which seems plausible, is that in ordinary reading we access entries only at a definitional level, not accessing memories at all. In the aesthetical attitude, we access these memories (and are thus affected by the associated feelings), but suppress them, just as we suppress irrelevant meanings. (There is, in fact, some empirical evidence that aesthetic and ordinary reading are different in just this way—see Halasz 1991; Larsen, Laszlo, and Seilman 1991, citations; unfortunately, each of these studies fails adequately to control for some relevant variables and thus none is entirely trustworthy.) Rasa is then built up from the patterned *dhvani* or evocation of one type of memory (sad memories, romantic memories, and so on). It is important to stress that the memories at issue here are not merely personal but are, crucially, literary and aesthetic as well. One's emotional response to literature derives not only from one's life but from one's past experience of literature also (see Ānandavardhana 1990, 473).

Now, in the case of, for example, joy, it is plausible to assume that the mere evocation of the feeling would produce pleasure. But the rasas include the pathetic, the furious, the terrible, and the odious (see Bharata-

Muni 1967, 102). In these cases, it would seem that such evocation alone is not enough to account for aesthetical pleasure. But the Indian theorists more or less leave the problem there. In this connection, I think it is valuable to turn to Aristotle, for while Aristotle has little to say on the issues of dhvani and rasa, he has quite a bit to say about katharsis, and thus his work nicely complements that of the Sanskrit writers.

Concentrating on the painful emotions of pity and fear, Aristotle recognized that aesthetical pleasure cannot be solely a matter of experiencing a particular emotion (or sentiment). Rather, he saw it as a matter of working through a feeling in a structurally unified piece of literature that, one might say, makes sense of the pain—and thereby to a degree relieves it—by integrating it into that structure and even giving it a sort of necessity. The most obvious way of creating such a structure is through a literal causal sequence (see VII.2–6). This more or less 'mimetic' component of literary coherence is certainly relevant to aesthetical intent. But perhaps even more relevant is a second type of necessitation mentioned by Aristotle, a type that is more associative, closer to a form of dhvani—necessity "by design" (ἐπίτηδες). Aristotle gives the following example: "the statue of Mitys at Argos killed the man who caused Mitys's death by falling on him at a festival" (39; IX.12). Unfortunately, beyond this single instance, Aristotle presents no general description, typology, and so forth of design or, as we might call it, 'epitedic necessity'.

In considering the issue from our current point of view, it is valuable to note the parallel between the two sorts of literary coherence distinguished by Aristotle—causal and epitedic—and the two 'levels' of dreams as posited by Freud. In dreams, *manifest* unity (where it exists) is causal. It is a unity wherein precedent events give rise to subsequent events in a roughly rule-governed fashion. When such causal coherence is found in literature, it might reasonably be referred to as the 'manifest unity' of a literary work. A dream's latent unity, on the other hand, is associative. Again, we find the same situation in the case of the aesthetic unity of literary works, which might in turn be called 'latent.' Both sorts of unity—the manifest and the latent, the causal and the epitedic—are part of any aesthetical intent, just as they are part of any dream. On the other hand, there is a crucial difference between dreams and literary works. In dreams, the latent associative intent is entirely personal and idiosyncratic. Literary works no doubt have such an idiosyncratic or psychopathological meaning in an author's (unreflective) expressive intent. However, literary works are also unified associatively and structurally in a more or less public way in aesthetical intent—at least insofar as the author is capable of successfully adopting an aesthetical attitude toward his/her work in revision, as we have emphasized.

Design, then, may be conceived of as a noncausal, alogical, mutual relevance—or 'maximal relevance' (see Kiparsky 1987, 189, 196n.7)—of various dhvani evoked by a work. Aristotle's example fits this definition nicely. Connecting the falling of the statue with the previous murder is certainly a case of maximizing relevance in a way that does not fit our causal beliefs about the real world. On the other hand, this example is somewhat misleading in that the mutual relevance of various associations may be maximized in many ways.

More exactly, in the aesthetical attitude, we have concerns about relevance or unity at all levels. Ānandavardhana claimed that rasadhvani is manifest in letters, words, sentences, structure, and "the whole work" (Amaladass 1984, 105). As this list indicates, the unity of a work is not only a matter of narrative elements, or even meaning, but of sound and rhythm patterns as well, patterns we savor in the aesthetical attitude, but that we pass over when reading for argument, information, and so on. Sometimes these sound patterns in some way reinforce the particular rasa, the sound echoing the sense, as Pope had it. However, they frequently operate more like music, simply "displaying" (in Mary Louise Pratt's term) their nonsemantic coherence. Indeed, part of the aesthetical attitude involves the savoring of pattern and variation as such, the emergence of both semantic and nonsemantic order out of chaos. In ordinary speech, we pay little attention to rhythms and sounds or to meanings and implications other than those germane to logical and causal relations. Indeed, in ordinary speech, these are random, the accidental by-product of speech aimed, for the most part, at information, argument, and so on. But in literature, rhythms, sounds, and various aspects of meaning (or suggestion) come to be patterned. In the aesthetical attitude, stresses, pitch contours, images, complexes of metaphor, and a wide range of other ordinarily irrelevant features, come to be candidates for relevance.

Needless to say, many aestheticians have emphasized the importance of pattern and variation defining a form of relevance drawn out of the random. For example, as David Pollard points out, writers of the Chinese *Ku-wen* school, which flourished a millennium ago, named "variability," "fullness," and "connectedness"—thus the development of pattern and variation at a number of levels—as "most valued effects" of poetry (Pollard 1978, 55). Like causal connection in plot, the patterning of sound and stress is relatively clear, involving the standard musical/metrical features of repetition, inversion, augmentation, and so on. However, as the Ku-wen writers indicate, the same sort of pattern/variation development is important to all other levels of aesthetic unity or relevance as well—and here its nature is not nearly as clear. Unfortunately, Ānandavardhana's list of word, sentence, structure, and whole work (a list reminiscent of the similar but more rigorous stratification to be found in Ingarden 1973) does not tell us much. Chinese writers, however, provide more suggestive, if less systematic categories in this connection.

Perhaps the type of noncausal relevance most obvious to anyone familiar with American New Criticism is that of imagery. But the notion is neither New nor American, nor even Western. For example, the seventeenth-century Chinese critic and theorist Chin Sheng-T'an stressed the importance of image patterns, as did many eighteenth-century literary commentators (see Wang 1972, 69; 1978, 211). Another obvious technique is that of foreshadowing. This too is indicated, in a slightly different form, by Chin (see Wang 1972, 68–69). We may follow Chung-Wen Shih and add "symbolism, parallelism, and allusion" (Shih 1976, 124) to this brief list of unifying poetic techniques. Symbolism—clearly a function of a type of association—involves an indirect reference to beliefs, ideals, and so forth that are of particular intellectual and emotional importance to a community (think of 'red, white, and blue' for a U.S. patriot, for a U.S. dissident, for a Nicaraguan peasant, and so on). By evoking a complex of significant, communal ideas and feelings, it serves to draw together aspects of the rasadhvani, thereby giving the work greater unity—or, more accurately, rehierarchizing our lexicons in such a way as to encourage us to unify the work by considering diverse dhvani, specifically in their semantic and emotive relevance to the symbol. Allusion links one artwork with another to similar effect. Parallelism is primarily an internal, syntactic device. However, if conceived of more generally, and connected with broader structures, it leads directly to the notion of isomorphism, which we have already found fruitful in psychoanalytic interpretation.

Both allusion and structural connection (whether related to parallelism or not) are germane to the Chinese notions of imitation: *to-t'ai*, "evolving from the embryo," which is to say, "using the general form and even the words of a former poet's writing to express an idea that goes beyond or is different from that in the original poem" (Rickett 1978, 109, 111); and *huan-ku*, "changing the bone," which is to say, expressing "a similar meaning . . . in different words" (114). In each case, part of the effect of the later poem and part of its structure or, more broadly, its internal relevance are contingent upon its connection with the predecessor poem. Indeed, this sort of connection is no doubt part of what Indian theorists have in mind when they speak of the understanding of the sahṛdaya. For the sahṛdaya is necessarily a reader who is, self-consciously or unself-consciously, attuned to the allusions and structural parallels between later and earlier poems (see, for example, Amaladass 1984, 113; Dimock 1967, xvii).

Drawing upon all of these notions, we can now define the sahṛdaya more fully as a reader, viewer, or whoever, who, in the aesthetical attitude, is able to experience (though not necessarily formulate or reflect upon) the associative relevance or coherence of the author's publicly available evocations or suggestions (dhvani)—prominently those relating to precedent literature and art—in an emotionally sensitive and responsive way, in a way that links these to a complex of (primed or briefly accessed) personal feelings coherent in a dominant sentiment or rasa. This also allows us to define aesthetical intent. For the aesthetical intent of an author is precisely his/her aesthetical experience of his/her work not insofar as he/she is an expressive, mimetic, or other creator but insofar as he/she has taken up the position of a sahṛdaya—and, more specifically, a unique sahṛdaya, a sahṛdaya who can change the work in question and who has final say as to when it is complete. Put differently, aesthetical intent is the complex of rasadhvani that an author experiences in deciding his/her work to be aesthetically 'right', to be finished (or, at least, to be 'finished enough'). An interpretation aimed at this intent, then, involves isolating the elements of this rasadhvani and their patterns of coherence—whether or not any of this is reflectively known to the artist or to a reader.

It is worth dwelling for a moment on this last point. Artists can certainly feel that associative or other patterns are right without being able to explain them, without knowing why they are right. As Paul Kiparsky puts it, "poetic form is apprehended unconsciously" (Kiparsky 1983, 37). Or as Roman Jakobson argues, "complicated phonological and grammatical structures . . . can function without any assistance of logical judgment and patent knowledge both in the poet's creative work and its perception by the sensitive reader" (Jakobson 1979, 147). As Jakobson indicates, this is perhaps most obvious in the case of sound patterns. When Virginia Woolf wrote the phrase "nodding tufts of lilac" (Woolf 1953, 18), she must have recognized that it sounded better than 'drowsy bouquets of lilies', 'shaking bunches of roses', 'heavy groups of marigolds', and so on. Part of her choice was semantic—Clarissa, the focus of this scene, has just thought, "Yes," is turning her head, has her eyes half closed, and Woolf is making Clarissa's perception of her surroundings mimic her actions and state of mind, a sort of nodding. At this level the choice may have been self-conscious. But even at the level of sound alone, the phrase is lovely for several reasons, and it is very unlikely that Woolf was self-consciously aware of these reasons. Nonetheless, it is very likely that all these reasons contributed to her (and our) sense of the line's beauty, and thus to her choice of the line. It is the duty of the critic to point out that, for example, the consonant structure of the line is clearly patterned on alveolars, with the first and last words involving an alveolar/alveolar/velar pattern. There is absolutely no need for Woolf to have known this for the (nonsemantic, musical) pattern to have been part of her aesthetical intent.

To recapitulate, we have a number of forms of relevance that are important in the aesthetical attitude, productive or receptive, conscious or unconscious. These may be divided first of all into the semantic and the nonsemantic. The latter concern such things as rhythm and sound pattern, and are relatively straightforward. The semantic category may be subdivided into the logical/causal and the epitedic, the latter including, for example, rhetorical techniques (such as foreshadowing), patterns of imagery and symbol, allusion, and structural assimilation. Principles of both types operate to pattern the feeling-laden associations of a reader (particularly a sensitive and learned reader or sahṛdaya) into a coherent rasa. The dhvani or associative suggestiveness/evocativeness of a work derives from an author's aesthetical intent in revising a work (in the aesthetical attitude) in order to allow a reader (in the aesthetical attitude) to prime or momentarily access relevant lexical entries, prominently memories with their associated affects. Finally, these memories include not only recollections from personal life but also the more public and thus more interpretively significant memories of other literary works (including instances of their rhetorical techniques, imagery, and structure).

To illustrate the distinction between causal and epitedic coherence, we might turn briefly to some comments made by Anita Desai concerning her novel, *Baumgartner's Bombay*. The story of this novel concerns a Jew who, as a young man, flees Nazi Germany and lives the rest of his (alienated) life in India. Desai said that there were two ways in which she could have ended this novel. In either, Baumgartner would have been killed. In one scenario, he would have been murdered by an Indian street person. In the other, by a German drug addict who had been put in his care. Either ending, she said, would have worked. However, she chose the latter because it was, she explained, more *meaningful*. Given the present analysis, I think we can see what Desai was speaking about. Both endings fit causally. But only one—the ending that she eventually chose—calls to mind, through a very individual and personal horror, the mass horrors of the Holocaust (themselves already important to the history in the novel); it is only this ending that is associatively 'right'. Both endings have causal coherence. Only this one has epitedic coherence as well.

In what follows, I should like to look in more detail at associative coherence and particularly at one commonly neglected form of associative coherence, structural assimilation, in *King John* and *King Lear*. More specifically, I shall concentrate on two points in each play where the *causal* coherence of the plot falters and thus where associative considerations are forced upon us. Needless to say, an interpretation to aesthetical intent does not require or even typically involve a causal incoherence. Indeed, ideally, associative coherence should complement causal coherence, not substitute for it. However, I have chosen this particular case precisely because there is a discrepancy, which thus allows us to see the operation of associative relevance more clearly than would otherwise be the case.

Before going on to this, however, I should like briefly to indicate how the preceding analysis, most particularly the concept of aesthetical intent, could prove useful in reconsidering some problems of contemporary aesthetics. Consider, first of all, the problem of found art ('How can something be art if it is merely found, not made?'). This is a problem only when art is conceived of as defined by some sort of expressive intent. If we consider it rather in relation to the artist's aesthetical intent—an intent in which he/she adopts the position of a spectator in the aesthetical attitude, viewing the work in the context of other works of art, and so on—the problem disappears. Indeed, such an aesthetical intent (sometimes straightforward, sometimes ironic) is crucial to works of this sort. Take, for example, John Cage's *4'33"*, one of the most famous cases of this type. In this piece, Cage in effect sets out to make his auditors so broaden their aesthetical attitude as to incorporate ordinary, random sounds. In a sense, this silent composition is the most purified art, for it is nothing other than the aesthetical attitude. Of course, not all found art is or is intended to be aesthetically pleasing. Duchamp's urinal, for example, is ironic or satiric. However, even it relies on a version of aesthetical intent, insofar as the work must be experienced associatively in the context of other art and from the perspective of the sahṛdaya—even if that is done only to mock the whole enterprise, to expose its pretense, or whatever.

In a related dilemma, many people wish to say that interpretation of
the work of art is normatively bounded by intent—thus *The Canterbury
Tales,* for example, just are not about Richard Nixon. But they also wish
to say that an author's/artist's explicit statements about a work are not
definitive—or even necessarily very illuminating. This appears to be a
contradiction but need not be, if we take (stipulate) interpretation to be
bounded by aesthetical intent and recognize that explicit authorial commentary most often concerns some form of expressive intent. As we have
seen, aesthetical intent is not self-reflective, or not primarily self-reflective,
but broadly associative. Again, an artist decides that a work is aesthetically
complete when he/she observes it, in the aesthetical attitude, and has the
feeling that the aesthetic effect of the work—viewed in the context of other
works, human experiences, and so on, but removed from individual idiosyncracy[2]—is 'right'. The range of associations, patterns, and principles
that give rise to this feeling, however, are by no means fully or unerringly
articulable through introspection. Indeed, as our previous discussion of
introspection indicates, any such articulation is necessarily highly inferential and highly fallible. In this way, the common view of literature—
simultaneously intentionalist and anti-intentionalist—is perfectly consistent and unproblematic.

Another long-standing aesthetic problem that is at least simplified, if
not fully solved, is that of 'creation'. As, for example, Mikel Dufrenne has
discussed, artistic creation is widely conceived of as a "mystery" akin to
that of divine creation (see Dufrenne 1979, 204–5). However, this sense of
mystery begins to fade once artistic making is understood not as divine
creation ex nihilo but rather as the careful arranging of an object toward
the end of producing aesthetic pleasure. This, of course, does not explain
why some people are so good at such arranging and others are so poor.
But it does make such discrepancies unsurprising—akin to discrepancies in
athletic abilities, logical skills, and so forth and not akin to discrepancies
between the human and the divine.

The notion of aesthetical intent could also be put to use in connection
with the "physical object problem" discussed by Wollheim, the "When is
Art?" problem discussed by Goodman, and other dilemmas.

It is also worth mentioning, what is perhaps obvious, that the stipulative understanding of meaning, set out in chapter 1, has direct consequences for aesthetic and literary problems as well. For example, there has
been a long debate on what the novel 'really is'. Predictably, this debate
has been fruitless. Recently, writers such as Tony Bennett have drawn de-

constructive conclusions from the irresolutions of this debate (see Bennett 1990, chapter 4). The correct conclusion, however, is that the entire debate rests upon a mistaken, essentialist presupposition, and should be replaced by other, better founded debates. In the cases discussed by Bennett, for example, the disputants are concerned with determining sociological conditions for the rise of the novel. This would be a valuable undertaking, if the disputants were not so concerned with what the novel 'really is'. If they wish to advance the sociology of literature (rather than debating a nonissue), they should, rather, set out to discover correlations between recurrent social conditions and recurrent literary types, with the types defined (as in the physical sciences) *solely* by the properties that define the correlations. For example, if we discover that extended, written, prose narratives arise only in specific social circumstances (for instance, urban money economies), we have discovered a principle of literary sociology. Trying to decide whether or not the novel really is or essentially is precisely an extended, written, prose narrative (full stop), and thus whether or not it is really the novel that arises in those circumstances—this is a pointless and confused endeavor that effectively condemns the sociology of literature to failure. The same point holds for many similar sorts of literary theoretical debate.

INTERPRETING AESTHETICAL INTENT: ANOMALY AND STRUCTURE IN *KING JOHN* AND *KING LEAR*

Though rarely considered as a focus of critical-interpretive scrutiny, the order received by Hubert with regard to Arthur is one of the most vexing problems of *King John*. As is well known, in Act III, scene ii, the King verbally instructs Hubert to kill the young Duke. Two scenes later, Hubert claims he has been ordered to *put out the Duke's eyes,* and prepares to comply with this order. In the following scene, Hubert presents to the King what appears to be a warrant for the boy's *execution*. But the confusion does not end here. Hubert has assured Arthur—evidently sincerely—that he will be kept safe; despite this, Arthur seeks to escape and jumps from the city walls to his death on the rocks below.

Thus we have two narratively related and, as we shall later see, thematically complementary problems. The first is: where does the order for Arthur's blinding come from and what does it mean, assuming there is such an order? The second is: What does Arthur think he is doing in jumping from high up the walls of a castle onto jagged stones?

What makes these problems problematic is the absence from the plot of any clear literal explanation of the events they concern. We could interpolate some account for Arthur's flight—he feared Hubert would have a change of heart or would be unsuccessful in protecting him and thought he should flee while escape was still possible. But at best this is too sketchy. First of all, we have no evidence that Arthur mistrusts Hubert at this time. More important, Arthur indicates that his attempt at escape is prompted by the (unexplained) certainty that if he stays he will be killed; however, the attempt still verges on suicide, as indicated in Arthur's final words before the jump—"As good to die and go, as die and stay" (IV. iii. 8)—after all, it is not as if he is being chased by the executioner right at that moment and must make a split-second decision: Face the sword or jump! Finally, Arthur's notion that he will be executed is doubly unexplained, for not only is he now under Hubert's sincere protection, no one has mentioned anything to him about execution. As far as Arthur is aware the choice is to "die and go" or be blinded and stay. While the morbidity rate for blinding was no doubt high at this time, we have at least many prominent literary examples of blinding without death (in Shakespeare and elsewhere), indicating that the two cannot simply be identified. Thus, whether or not we interpolate a literal account of Arthur's act, the point remains that Shakespeare neither provides nor in any way clearly indicates even the outlines of such a fiction.

In the case of the blinding, on the other hand, we have not only an absence of explicit or implicit literal explanation, we seem to have an out and out contradiction that precludes any such explanation. In one scene we are told the King wants Arthur killed. Subsequently, we are told he wants him blinded and has explicitly ordained this in writing (see IV. i. 33ff.). Later still we are informed, in two different contexts and through two different sources, that the King's warrant is for Arthur's death (see IV. ii. 70ff. and IV. ii. 215). Moreover, it is death that Hubert announces and that John appears to have expected. Finally, John and Hubert say no more of blinding but speak only of murder (see, for example, IV. ii. 205, 223, and elsewhere). We could follow *The Troublesome Raigne of King John* (1972, 67) and account for the final reference to Arthur's supposed death by inferring that Hubert might claim he blinded Arthur, as the King demanded, and that this resulted in the death. As, for example, Matchett has indicated (1966, 153ff.), this still leaves the question: Whence came the notion of blinding initially? We might answer this by noting that blindness would presumably have rendered Arthur unfit for the kingship, and thus accomplished John's main purpose. But, on the other hand, it would have left blind Arthur as a witness, as someone who could explain that this blinding was not some accident or random crime. Moreover, if blinding was merely a means of murdering Arthur, as the references to execution might indicate, then it is obviously irrelevant that Arthur could not be king if blind—which leads us back to Matchett's question. If blinding is a subterfuge—'Pretend only to blind Arthur, but actually murder him (by blinding)'—it is still hard to understand: how, for example, would this in any way protect John from the wrath of nobles sympathetic to Arthur? It seems implausible to expect them to say, 'Well, it's all right, he only meant to blind Arthur; the death was an accident'. Thus the contradictions surrounding the blinding seem not only unresolved but unresolvable.

Given the lack of literal explanation in these two cases and the evident impossibility of plausible interpolation in at least one, we have several options. Most obviously, we can decide that the play is in some degree incoherent. From here we might seek the source of the contradictions or gaps in the social conflicts of Shakespeare's time or simply put it down to inattention; Shakespeare found the incoherence in Holinshed and just never thought to revise it, as Matchett suggests (159). But there are problems with such approaches. As to the latter, it would be incomprehensibly odd if Shakespeare, having drastically revised, condensed, synthesized, and edited Holinshed's narrative in other ways, should suddenly become absentminded or decide to adhere unthinkingly to Holinshed's details on such an obviously problematic point as the order for blinding. As to Arthur's death, on the other hand, there are several versions in Holinshed, all explicitly conjectural (see Holinshed, 1965, 286), and thus Shakespeare had no choice but to be reflective here. On this point, there is not even a possibility of slavish adherence to the source. Moreover, if *The Troublesome Raigne* is made the immediate source, even less is explained. For example, in the case of the blinding, we must take Shakespeare to have actually decided to exclude the one bit of relevant explanation available to him— Hubert's account of Arthur's death by blinding.

Explanation by reference to social conflict, in contrast, is perfectly plausible in principle. However, this functions most often as a sort of contextualization. For example, in Plautus's *Casina* one female character argues that a woman is lost if she antagonizes her husband, that divorce is the worst thing for a woman, that women cannot have their own money. Another female character has her own money, antagonizes her husband, and seems less concerned with divorce (and, in another of Plautus's plays,

Amphitryon, a woman actually leaves her husband). This certainly appears incoherent. However, the play was probably written in the early second century B.C. And it was in the second century B.C. that the rigidity of Roman patriarchy began to weaken such that women gained greater independence, greater access to wealth, and so forth. Thus, what appears to be a contradiction may be a fairly accurate portrayal of conflicting views about women held by real people at the time the play was written. Or it may be an unconscious portrayal of the contradiction between the dominant (patriarchal) ideology and the actual social conditions of the time—a common enough occurrence in the history of literature, as emphasized by writers such as Lukács. In any case, there is no obvious way of contextualizing the problematic scenes from *King John* in a similar manner.

Another evident possibility is that of a botched manuscript. Clearly, we cannot know in this case. However, as we shall see, precisely the same problems of blinding and falling recur in *King Lear.* If the problem were one of botched manuscripts, it would be very difficult to explain this parallelism.

Finally, beyond any particular approaches to explaining the play's assumed incoherence, there is a problem with assuming that the play is incoherent in the first place. This is not because Shakespeare's genius was incapable of error or because *King John* is a 'perfect' play, or because of anything particular to Shakespeare or *King John.* Rather, it is, once again, because literary coherence is not purely causal or logical. A literary work may indeed have a discontinuous and contradictory plot and yet maintain a genuine if 'latent' unity (mutual relevance) of associations or dhvani. In accordance with the principles of interpretation to aesthetical intent, then, I should like to examine the problems of Arthur's sentence and escape not in terms of manifest plot but rather in terms of the aesthetical and publicly available associations that locate these events in relation to a series of literary and religious structures. Specifically, I view these crucial and obscure events in Arthur's story as transformations and reorganizations of events in the stories of Oedipus and Antigone, Samson, Abraham and Isaac, and Jesus. Thus I should like to look at the versions of these tales available to Shakespeare and examine their structural relations to one another and to the story of Arthur. In pursuing this interpretation, I shall assume the validity of Lévi-Strauss's maxim that, "if one aspect of a particular myth seems unintelligible, it can be legitimately dealt with . . . as a transformation of the homologous aspect of another myth . . . which lends itself more readily to interpretation" (Lévi-Strauss 1969b, 13). Note that this maxim is perfectly consistent with the analysis set forth in the first section of this chapter. Indeed, it specifies one way in which epitedic necessity can operate through the dhvani of aesthetical intent. Note also that Lévi-Strauss's view is in no way reductive of the dhvani of a work. Though a transformational study may recognize one myth as the most lucid, it does not and cannot recognize any myth as the most basic. To say that the story of Arthur stands in a transformational relation with that of Jesus is not to say that it is allegorical, that the story of Arthur is reducible to, or has as its meaning, the story of Jesus. In the present context, it is merely to say that part of the aesthetic intent of *King John,* and thus part of its unity 'by design', is this isomorphism.

Before considering any of the extra-Shakespearean structures, however, I should like first to turn to *King Lear.* As I have already indicated, there appear to be two 'nodes' in this play as well, two discontinuities so closely related to those of *King John* that the four beg to be considered together. Specifically, Gloucester's attempted suicide and Edgar's staging of that attempt perennially baffle critics. Near the end of Act IV, blind Gloucester has asked Edgar, whom he does not recognize, to lead him to the edge of a cliff by the sea—so that he might jump and kill himself on the rocks below. Edgar pretends to lead him to such a cliff, allows him to jump, and tells him after he has awakened that he has fallen from a fearsome height. Here the obvious question is: 'Why does Edgar do this?' or, in keeping with the response of my students to this sequence of events, 'What in the hell is going on here?'

In *King John,* the most baffling section concerns a blinding that never should have occurred—and didn't. Related to this is the vaguely suicidal mortal jump. In *King Lear,* the most baffling section concerns a suicidal mortal jump that never should have occurred—and didn't. Predictably, the related oddity in *King Lear* is a blinding. As in *King John,* the blinding precedes and in some sense precipitates the jump. Moreover, in each case, what is baffling is the sudden introduction of blinding when execution had previously been ordained. Specifically, Gloucester informs Edmund that he has been threatened with "no less" than death for aiding the King (III. iii. 17). This prepares us for Gloucester's execution just as John's dialogue with Hubert prepared us for Arthur's execution. In both cases, blinding is substituted—though, of course, it is effected only in the case of Gloucester.

Certainly, in *King Lear* even the baffling scenes allow some sort of literal account. Gloucester had mentioned that death would be the *least* punishment. Moreover, he had previously termed his likely punishment "perpetual displeasure" (III. iii. 4). Thus we are probably meant to consider blindness and exile a worse fate than death. Clearly Gloucester thinks so— hence his attempt at suicide. But this is still not as clear as it might be. There is not any necessary contradiction between Gloucester's statements about execution and his eventual blinding; however, there is a sort of tension between the two.

The business with the jump is more difficult. Winfried Schleiner is clearly on the right track with his reading of the scene in terms of Renaissance psychiatric theory. However, Gloucester does not suffer from *melancholy*. He suffers from *despair,* as Edgar himself says (IV. ii. 41). It is rather commonplace to claim that Shakespeare concerns himself with the mind and with the body but not with the spirit (see, for example Baldwin 1944, 1:335—though Baldwin is not quite this rigid, and his concerns are different). However, this seems just false. Shakespeare is not as attentive to spiritual concerns as are many of his contemporaries, but these concerns are nonetheless present. In the case of Gloucester, moreover, they are crucial. Despair is a failing of neither the body nor the mind but of the spirit. It does not involve a "harmed imagination," including hallucinations and delusions of the sort discussed by Schleiner. It merely involves the desire to die. It does not betray a distorted relation to reality. It betrays, rather, a distorted relation to God. Thus when Edgar tells Gloucester he has fallen from a great height, he explains that Gloucester should have died and thus that his "life's a miracle" (IV. vi. 67). In this manner, Edgar undertakes to foster thoughts of divine benevolence and omnipotence in Gloucester's mind, thereby turning him toward God and rectifying his spiritual problem. This strategy is continued by Edgar's subsequent assertions that the fellow who led Gloucester to the cliff, and who thus aided and abetted him in his attempt at suicide, "was some fiend" (IV. vi. 87). Thus Edgar connects suicide with Satan and thereby with Hell, while at once opposing both to God and hence to Heaven.

Thus in these two cases, there is a plausible literal account at least implicit in the work. However, this only makes their close, if inverse, relation to the unexplained events of *King John* all the more intriguing. It indicates, just as we would expect from the notion of aesthetical intent, that even certain events that have a literal explanation will require a further sort of analysis as well—an analysis of associations or dhvani. It seems clear that there is some relation between the scenes in *King John* and those in *King Lear*. Even if we had available to us plausible, explicit, literal accounts of each scene, this relation itself would remain to be explained.[3]

The first connection I should like to consider involves one of the most pervasive, and thus most associatively insistent mythic structures in the Western world: the self-sacrifice of Jesus for the sins of others. Repeatedly, Elinor is associated with Eve and Arthur with the savior who redeems— in this case, England from a sort of original sin. For example, Constance refers to Arthur and Elinor in the following manner: "he is not only plagued for her sin, / But God hath made her sin and her the plague / On this removed issue, plagued for her / And with her plague; her sin his injury. . . . All punished in the person of this child" (II. i. 184ff.). Were it not for the context, the obvious reference here would be to Eve and Christ. Eve's sin was "made" by God in the sense that it was defined by God's proscription of the tree. But God also "made" Eve sin in the sense that he made her fallible. Moreover, God made Eve's sin "plague" her "removed issue," Jesus, and assured that "all" would be punished in the person of this one child, in an obvious sense.

The context of this particular speech concerns a breach of rules governing 'temporal authority' whereby John has succeeded to the throne over Arthur. Elinor complains that she "can produce / A will that bars the title" of Arthur to the throne (II. i. 191–92); this is Richard's will, in which he names John as his heir. However, within the universe of the play, it has already been made clear that, in hereditary matters, a will is meaningless. This, I take it, is the point of the supposedly confusing scene in which Philip and Robert debate their relative rights. King John awards the inheritance to Philip and takes Sir Robert Faulconbridge's will to be "of no force" (in younger Robert's disgruntled words—I. i. 128–29). If the will is of no force in deciding the heir in this case, it is presumably of no force in other cases also.

Thus Arthur is loosely analogized to Jesus in connection with an 'original sin' that is social or political and involves a violation of the continuity and heredity of authority, in this case monarchial authority. It is thus a sort of transformation of a spiritual into a political structure (an extremely common sort of transformation during this period, as indicated, for example, in the doctrine of the divine right of kings).

Constance's discussion of sin and punishment is not the only point at which an implicit comparison is drawn between Arthur and Christ. Constance subsequently claims of Arthur that "since the birth of Cain, the first male child, / To him that did but yesterday suspire, / There was not such a gracious creature born" (III. iii. 79–81). If we take "gracious" in the sense of "filled with grace," the phrase can apply only to Jesus. Indeed, this sense is reinforced by the immediately following allusion to resurrection in the line, "And so he'll die; and rising so again" (86). Pembroke's eulogy over Arthur's corpse is similar: "All murders past do stand excused in this: / And this . . . Shall give a holiness, a purity, / To the yet unbegotten sin of times" (IV. iii. 51ff.). Clearly, at one level, we must take Pembroke to 'intend' his words as a hyperbolic condemnation of Arthur's supposed murder as a particularly heinous crime. However, on its own the sentence could just as readily, indeed more readily, be understood to refer to the salvational death of Jesus, through which sins are not excused, but through which the possibility of such excusing is made real.

Interesting in this context is Arthur's similarity to Shakespeare's Henry VI. For example, both wish they could live quiet lives removed from the turmoil of politics. Arthur would have been happy had he "kept sheep" (IV. i. 17). Similarly, Henry VI laments in part two, "Was never subject longed to be a king / As I do long and wish to be a subject" (IV. ix. 5–6). Moreover, the plays are similar in many ways. For example, Salisbury's equivocation on oaths (also in part 2—V. i. 182–83) directly parallels that of Pandulph in *King John* (III. i. 189ff.). Likewise, Constance's alliance with the French, broken by marriage, then restored by papal intervention, follows the structure of *3 Henry VI* III, iii, in which Queen Margaret's alliance with Lewis is first broken by a proposal of marriage, then restored by the necessary withdrawal of that proposal. Most important, Henry also is compared to Christ, most strikingly when he says of the rebels, "they know not what they do" (2: IV. iv. 38) and of his murderer, "God forgive my sins and pardon thee," thus conjunctively echoing the words of Jesus, "Father [therefore God] forgive them, for they know not what they do."

The connection between Arthur and Jesus is developed further, by way of three structurally related biblical tales: the betrayal of Jesus by Judas, the betrayal of Samson by Delilah, and the sacrifice of Isaac by Abraham. Beginning with the first, there is no obvious reason that Hubert should have to signal the executioners to enter and bind Arthur. In the religious, literary, and educational context of the period, however, the generalized associations of a writer/reader such as Shakespeare could only have led from a scene of betrayal such as this to the betrayal of Jesus by Judas. Thus, it would seem, the reason, or one reason, the executioners are dramatically called in, is an associative one. The calling-in links Hubert with

Judas. (It certainly does not, however, identify him with Judas; again, this is not an *allegorical* reading but an *associative* one.) Of course, in *King John,* the kiss of Judas is replaced by a stamping of the foot—which in fact relates the betrayal of Arthur to the betrayal of Henry VI, thereby associating the Duke and the King yet again. (In *Henry VI,* part 3, Warwick, facing Henry in the Parliament, stamps his foot to call for the troops who will defend York's claim to the throne. Interestingly, Henry does not abdicate directly, but agrees to *will* his kingdom to York.)

This scene is linked with Delilah's betrayal of Samson as well, and indeed even more clearly. First of all, Samson is *the* great Biblical figure who is blinded, as Oedipus and Tiresias are the great classical figures. Moreover, Delilah calls in the Philistines precisely in order to *bind* and *blind* Samson, just as Hubert calls in the executioners to *bind* and *blind* Arthur (see Judges 16). Finally, Samson ends his life with a self-sacrifice. He pulls down the pillars on a crowd of his enemies. Samson dies in a suicide that is in a sense the inverse of Arthur's partial suicide. Rather than falling to his death on the stones, Samson dies by allowing the building stones to fall on him.

Of course, it is no accident that we should find these two biblical figures conjoined, for from the Patristic period and through scholastic and Renaissance writings, Samson was repeatedly interpreted as an allegorical figure of Christ; an early and important example of this variety of exegesis may be found in the "Sermon on Samson" attributed to Augustine, but there are many more. (Milton Scholars have done valuable research on this topic; see, for example, Krouse 1949.) Not unexpectedly, Samson's betrayal by Delilah is regularly understood as an allegorical prefiguration of Jesus' betrayal by Judas. Thus to find Hubert recapitulating both Judas and Delilah is not only unsurprising but predictable.

On the other hand, there is, of course, a difference between Hubert and Judas or Delilah. Ultimately, Hubert does not betray Arthur. In this way, Hubert is more akin to Abraham when God ordered him to sacrifice his son. Much like Samson, Isaac was recurrently presented as a Christ-figure in devotional and theological literature of the period. This connection is explicit in, for example, the mystery play versions of Abraham's abortive sacrifice of his son. In fact, it seems that Shakespeare was drawing directly upon one of the Abraham and Isaac mysteries in constructing this scene. Specifically, in the mysteries, Isaac softens Abraham's heart with his childish pleas but then resigns himself and, expressing a mature concern for his mother, accepts his fate. Indeed, in the Brome version—and, presumably, others as well—Isaac asks his father that he not be bound. His father agrees as Isaac gives his word that he will suffer the execution patiently without any such constraint. Recall that in *The Troublesome Raigne,* Arthur speaks more like a preacher than a young child, and Hubert, far from stopping his vile act due to paternal feeling, refrains because of "feare" and "conscience" (1972, 59). In *King John,* on the other hand, Arthur shows the same degree of childishness and maturity found in Isaac. And Hubert's heart softens in the same manner as Abraham's. Most strikingly, Arthur pleads with Hubert to send away the executioners and not to bind him. Hubert, like Abraham, agrees, because Arthur, in an appropriately Christlike image, promises, "I will sit as quiet as a lamb" (IV. i. 79).

Of course, there is no talk of blinding in the case of Isaac, or in that of Jesus. It is only in the case of Sampson that blinding is an issue. In this context, it is worth considering the nonallegorical, moral interpretations of Samson's life, which were current at Shakespeare's time. In these interpretations, there were two sins of which Samson was repeatedly accused (see Krouse 1949, 33ff.). The first was suicide, but this was explained and excused easily enough by reference to the will of God. It was an act of self-sacrifice in which Samson showed his renewed closeness with God, not an act of despair in which he showed his distance and alienation from God. Recall, again, that in some sense Arthur's death recapitulates Samson's death, if inversely. The second sin of which Samson accused was fornication. For this, Samson was blinded, according to such authors as Clement of Rome. Thus in the one clear case we have considered, blinding is a *punishment* for a *sexual sin.*

Interestingly, this sexual sin is linked with broader social and political issues as well. Delilah, after three attempts, wheedles out of Samson the answer to the riddle of his strength, and then betrays him to the Philistines. Samson's Philistine wife had similarly betrayed him after exacting the answer to his riddle about strength and sweetness. Clearly, Samson's problem, beyond rather limited brain capacity, was that he attached himself to women whose loyalties were to the Philistines and not to Samson and his people. In other words, Samson was guilty of miscegenation, of violating endogamy rules. Along with exogamy rules (defining and forbidding incest), these are the most important rules regulating sexuality for the coherence of society (as Lévi-Strauss has argued at length in *The Elementary Structures of Kinship*). Thus the blindness of Samson is associatively linked with the violation of marriage rules that are central to the maintenance of social structure.

How does all this relate to Arthur? In a sense, it does not. Arthur, in contrast with Samson, has committed no sexual sin. Thus the punishment of blinding is inappropriate. Indeed, its function might be argued to be entirely negative. Arthur's near blinding might serve to indicate 'diacritically' that a mortal fall, *not* a blinding, is psychologically appropriate in his case.

In the case of Gloucester, however, we find the situation reversed. His near mortal fall might indicate that, in his case, the fall, rather than the blinding, is psychologically inappropriate, though we have yet to decide on the significance of such a fall. Conversely, his blinding is effected, and thus is evidently appropriate. Interestingly, this blinding is conjoined with a sort of exile. Similarly, after he is blinded, Samson is 'exiled' amongst the Philistines. Indeed, the same holds for Oedipus, as we shall discuss below. Thus blinding and exile seem to co-occur in connection with a sexual sin, a violation of the marriage laws.

The literal explanation of Gloucester's blinding is that he violated the laws of political authority. On the other hand, he comes to be blinded because his bastard son deceives and betrays him. Our first introduction to Gloucester is by way of an introduction to his violation of the rules of marriage in his begetting of Edmund. Moreover, Edgar's final conclusion as to the true cause of Gloucester's blinding leads us directly back to this fact. "The dark and vicious place where he thee got / Cost him his eyes" (V. iii. 208–9), Edgar tells Edmund. This is clearly a metonymy and Edgar is saying that the "dark and vicious" act of adultery, the violation of the rules of marriage, was in fact the cause of his blinding. In this way, Gloucester's punishment is not, epitedically, a punishment for defying authority. Rather it is a punishment for violating the rules of marriage or, more accurately, it has a sort of associative coherence resulting from the suggestion of such a punishment (much like Aristotle's case of Mitys). These rules are, of course, founded upon the rules of exogamy and endogamy, but here include other rules, such as that of monogamy, which serve the same unifying function. Thus Gloucester fits the paradigm of Samson and others in suffering blinding and exile as punishments for sexual violation.

This becomes even more evident when the relation between the Gloucester subplot and the story of Oedipus is considered. The most obvious link is that of blinding.[4] In most versions, Oedipus blinds himself for his incestuous marriage with his mother and his related murder of his father. In some less well known versions Oedipus is blinded by the Thebans in order that he might "no longer see the light of day," as an oracle prescribed. In any event, in the main versions, Oedipus is exiled. Like Gloucester, he must rely upon his child to lead him in an unfamiliar place. The most crucial text here is, I believe, Seneca's *Thebais,* most particularly the 1581 translation of Thomas Newton.[5] The *Thebais* opens with Antigone leading Oedipus much in the manner Edgar leads Gloucester, though Oedipus is fully aware that he is being led by his daughter. Oedipus is asking Antigone to leave him (much like the King of Paphlagonia with regard to his son Leonatus when Musidorus and Pyrocles first come upon them in the "new" *Arcadia* [II. 10], an intermediate text that was an important source for this scene as well). More important, Oedipus, like Gloucester (and like the King of Paphlagonia) wishes to make his way to the edge of a cliff in order that he might leap to his death. "Let mee I pray thee headlong slyde in breaknecke tumbling plight" (100), he implores Antigone. Moreover, like Gloucester, he chooses "an huyge Promontory that elboes into Sea" at the bottom of which there is "flinty Rocke beside" (103) reminiscent of the rocks upon which Arthur fell. Finally, again like Gloucester, Oedipus is also motivated by "dispayre" (111).

Of course, it is crucial in both cases that ultimately there is no mortal fall but only the precedent blinding. And in the case of Oedipus, it is obvious that this results from the violation of marriage laws—here incest and the related patricide. Moreover, the root of the entire tragedy is Laios's abduction of the boy Chrysippos, as is clear in Sophocles and Apollodorus. This is indisputably a violation of the relevant type, and further extends our catalogue of marriage-law violations to include pederastic rape along with miscegenation, incest, and adultery.

But this leads us to the question of what to make of Gloucester's, and Oedipus's, *not falling.* I have suggested that the psychological or associative significance of the projected blinding in *King John* concerns precisely the sort of violation committed by Gloucester. Presumably, then, the question is one of the significance of both the actual fall in *King John* and the projected, but unrealized, fall in *King Lear.* Now if it is true that blinding operates associatively as a retribution for violating certain laws, an obvious first approach would be to assume that the fall relates to some comparable but distinct violation. Moreover, we might in addition infer that this latter violation is irrelevant to Gloucester in the way that the violation of marriage rules was irrelevant to Arthur.

In fact, we already have a candidate for this violation in the rules Gloucester is *literally* said to violate—not the marriage rules of sexuality and progenitorship, but the political rules of authority and duty. Rules governing sexuality and power are, in a sense, the only necessary rules of a society, the rules that make a society cohere. Moreover, authority and sexuality are the two psychologically crucial issues or structures in a child's oedipal development. Thus we have both internal and external reasons for pairing these two sets of rules with the two sorts of anomaly we have been considering.

On the other hand, it is still unclear how the mortal fall is to be understood in this connection, what its particular relation to the laws of authority and duty might be. In considering this problem, our first task is to see who, in the tales we have been examining, does in fact fall to his death, from the walls of a city or castle.[6] In the case of Samson, we have already witnessed a sort of inversion of the mortal fall. Here, Samson sacrifices himself in revenge upon his enemies and the enemies of the Jews, thereby effecting a sort of political rectification and thus performing an act that does in fact fall under the appropriate category. However, Samson's death relates to the mortal fall only by inversion. A more exactly parallel case is to be found toward the end of the Oedipus cycle, in a sacrificial death demanded by the gods, and interpreted by Tiresias, as a condition for the salvation of Thebes from the attack of the Seven. Specifically, as told by Hyginus, Statius, Euripides, and others, the gods demanded the life of the youngest descendent of the dragon's race. This was Menoeceus, the son of Creon. Though Creon, rather like Hubert, tried to protect the boy, youthful Menoeceus, upon hearing of the oracle's pronouncement, climbed the walls of the city and plunged to his death. He thereby brought stable authority and continued self-governance to Thebes for a generation.

This associative link with Menoeceus extends and clarifies the relation between Arthur and Jesus with which we began. Both structures suggest a connection between Arthur's death and salvationary self-sacrifice. And yet the death of Arthur does not bring such stability and self-government to England (still less, universal redemption). Indeed, historically it brought precisely the opposite—partial foreign domination for a generation. Whether this is made clear at the end of the play or not, it is certainly associatively germane.[7] Perhaps this is why the scene of Arthur's death feels odd to many readers, and why the play as a whole has had such a limited impact. Through its classical and Christian dhvani, it suggests that Arthur functions epitedically as a sacrificial savior. But there is no salvation in the play. There is only more suffering with no clear resolution. The associations of the event do not fit, they jar with the rest of the play.

In any case, however we evaluate this evident discrepancy (not only between the literal and the associative but between the mythic associations and the political ones), whether we find it a fascinating complexity or a regrettable inconsistency—we seem, at least, to have gained some sense of the epitedic structure of *King John* and *King Lear*. Specifically, blinding and exile appear as individual punishments for violations of the marriage laws by which society is in part organized. Moreover, they are punishments visited upon the culpable individuals themselves. The mortal fall, in contrast, is part of a social rectification or social disruption deriving from a violation of laws governing authority. Moreover, it is the voluntary act of an individual who is not one of the guilty parties. Hence Gloucester, guilty of fornication, is blinded and exiled, while Arthur, a victim of political usurpation and tyranny, jumps to his own death. Moreover, despite the lingering contradiction between Arthur's mythic associations and historical connections, these associative structures do broadly cohere with the thematic and narrative contours of the two plays—they are, in other words, unified or internally relevant.

To adopt the aesthetical attitude is, once more, to place the work in an associative matrix that gives it an epitedic coherence and allows us—as authors or readers—to experience the work's rasadhvani. The sort of interpretation we have been pursuing is, again, centrally concerned with this aesthetical attitude. Indeed, it is aimed at this attitude not only as an object of scrutiny but as a final goal as well. In other words, the point of such an interpretation is not only to gain reflective understanding of the work but also to increase the associative complexity of our response to that work—thereby, one hopes, enriching our aesthetic experience.

AFTERWORD

A Note on the Ethics of Interpretation

Those of us in literary study are in many ways isolated from the real effects of interpretation. We talk a great deal about the political power of interpretation, its importance, its ubiquity, but for the most part this is only talk—standard opinion dutifully repeated and copiously elaborated in the pages of our most prestigious journals with little relation to serious human issues. Recently I had occasion to read two Ph.D. qualifying exams dealing with the political import of literature and interpretation. One insisted that ambiguity, verbal 'play', and—I am not exaggerating here—a refusal to make clear statements are revolutionary 'gestures' that 'decenter' patriarchy. The other maintained that novels with endings are 'phallocentric' and thus contribute to the oppression of women. (No doubt certain sorts of endings are patriarchal in ideology, but that is a very different matter.) Those aware of recent trends in critical theory will recognize that such statements are far from idiosyncratic. Indeed, they are at the very center of 'political interpretation' today.[1]

In an earlier work, *The Politics of Interpretation,* I examined and criticized some of the more influential recent views on such political interpretation. I argued that when one looks at real political issues—issues relating to real human suffering, to injustice and cruelty, to the possibility of establishing a society in which women and men could lead decent, productive lives with material security and emotional well-being—when one looks outside of one's office, the absurdity of much contemporary 'political' interpretation becomes painfully obvious. Moreover, I argued that recent obscurantist principles must be replaced by their opposite—Enlightenment ideals of clarity and rationality, a concern for truth, an advocacy of intellectual freedom—and that these ideals must be accepted not halfheartedly or with qualifications, but vigorously and totally.

In the preceding pages there are few direct political references. Despite this, I consider the present volume to be continuous with *The Politics of In-*

terpretation. I do not say this because of its critiques or positive doctrines, for which I do not claim any political status, but rather because of its concern, however imperfectly realized, with clarity, rationality, and accuracy in interpretive understanding. Most critics today would agree that interpretation does not take place in a vacuum. However, in making this claim, most critics would emphasize what they see as a matrix of social determinations—primarily class, gender, and race. I, on the other hand, am concerned less with the matrix of social determinations than with that of ethical obligations. Interpretations have effects. They make a difference—and an ethical difference. For those of us involved in interpretive disciplines, interpretation is central to our behavior as ethical agents; interpretive concerns intersect continually with the obligations that we, as members of a particular profession, have toward others. For teachers of literature, problems of interpretation enter critically into obligations toward students, colleagues, and authors; for psychoanalysts, interpretative issues are inseparable from important and consequential obligations to analysands; for judges—but for teachers of literature, psychoanalysts, and others as well—interpretation is part and parcel of one's obligation to one's community, its health, its constitution, its self-understanding.

The relation between ethics and interpretation is not something to be dealt with lightly, with facile assertions about the revolutionary disruption of sense, the liberating play of ambiguity, and so on. In each of these cases, interpretation requires—ethically requires—reason, scholarship, and dialogue. Again, interpretations make a difference. That is why it is important for us to be clear about what we are interpreting for and how we are interpreting for it. As I emphasized at the outset, this sort of clarity will not solve all interpretive problems. Perhaps it will solve none directly. However, it will put us in a position from which we can begin the analysis and dialectic that are necessary conditions for the solution of any such problems; it will put us in a position from which we can begin to address these issues with the cooperative, critical rationality they demand.

NOTES

INTRODUCTION

1 Here and below, I reserve double inverted commas for direct quotes, using single inverted commas for scare quotes, metalinguistic indications, and so on.

1 STIPULATION AND RATIONAL INFERENCE

1 According to the researches of Holland et al., people do not in fact use rigorous logical principles in ordinary inductive reasoning. Rather, they employ pragmatic schemata that, in crucial cases, lead to the same results, but that may lead to false conclusions in unusual or difficult cases (see 165ff.). This is no doubt true for other forms of inference as well, including interpretation (for an extensive anatomy of schemata in interpretation, see Bordwell 1989). In the following pages, I shall assume that such pragmatic schemata can be replaced by logical principles, at least in the self-conscious forms of interpretation we shall be examining. In any event, it is the logical principles alone that provide justification for the 'outputs' of the pragmatic schemata. Thus it is the logical principles that are normatively important anyway.

2 This is not to say that all of logic and all considerations of simplicity are unitary and absolute. Logic and simplicity considerations are complex and related in complex ways. It is possible for circumstances to arise in which we may choose to revise parts of either logic or the Principle of Minimal Interpretation (a point forcefully argued by Putnam in various writings). The obvious case is that of quantum mechanics. Quine (1961, 43) points out that quantum logic revises one part of traditional logic in order to achieve "simplicity" in theory. Nonetheless, the whole set of such methodological principles is not revisable, nor are certain particular principles—most obviously, the Principle of Noncontradiction, at least in a weakened form (as Putnam argues in the article just cited).

3 It is perhaps worth pointing out in this context that, despite common stereotypes, standard logical principles and the methodological pursuit of simplicity are not somehow peculiarly Western. Principles of rational inference are as uni-

197

versal as language, as Frits Staal has argued at length (see Staal 1988). Indeed, their importance outside of the natural sciences—the point we have been stressing—has been more widely accepted outside of Europe and North America, most especially in the East, where, as Staal points out, theorists have not been "handicapped by the irrational belief in 'two cultures'—the natural sciences and the humanities" (32).

4 I must confess a certain degree of skepticism about Keenan's data here—it sounds a bit like the Malagasy were pulling the anthropologist's leg, or were being playful with one another, just as anyone else might be. But what is important is that, even here, in deciding whether they were violating the Maxim of Quantity for religious reasons, or were pulling the anthropologist's leg, or whatever, we have to interpret their speech by simplicity considerations rather than by Grice's maxims.

5 Though, in dealing with less superficial matters—for example, important individual feelings and experiences—it is not at all clear that there is any simple correlation between social similarity and ease of interpretive inference, at least once linguistic competence is established. Indeed, ease of communication with others in one's own society is often merely imaginary, the result of a reduction of dialogue to the exchange of cliches—"*gerede,*" in Heidegger's terminology (1976, 35, 167ff.). In matters of real importance, intracultural diversity—emphasized by sociolinguists such as Hudson (see Hudson 1980, 92–94)—often becomes painfully obvious.

6 Just for the record, I find Katz's own reply to Quine—his "Refutation of Indeterminacy"—completely unconvincing. It relies crucially on the existence of bilinguals. But, if there is a problem, it applies to bilinguals as much as to anyone else. Katz also seems unaware of the depth of the problems with the analytic/synthetic distinction.

2 THE LIMITS OF STIPULATION

1 Tyler Burge has also taken up Putnam's notion to defend the idea that, even though language is a matter of idiolect (Burge 1989, 175–76), nonetheless there is a social aspect to meaning in that "the individuation of an individual's concepts . . . is sometimes dependent on his interaction with others" (185–86). In this phrasing, Burge's claim is certainly true, and should even be fairly uncontroversial. It would seem that the individuation of one's concepts is *always* dependent on one's interaction with others. Even if one believes that concepts are innate in their broad structures, one is likely to believe that they are specified and linked with at least some referents by way of social interaction. Elsewhere, however, Burge makes the much stronger claim that the individuation of an individual's concepts is sometimes dependent on the community, even when there is no relevant interaction (see Burge 1979). Imagine a real person who has

a wide range of correct beliefs about arthritis plus the incorrect belief that it can occur in the thigh. (It can only occur in joints.) Now imagine the very same person, identical in all physical, mental, and biographical details. But in his/her (counterfactual) world, 'arthritis' is used in such a way as to include a rheumatoid condition of the thigh. Let us call our (real world) notion 'arthritis1' and the counterfactual notion 'arthritis2'. As I understand Burge, he is claiming that we would attribute a slightly mistaken use of 'arthritis1' (not an accurate use of 'arthritis2') to the real person ('Jones1') and an accurate use of 'arthritis2' (not a slightly mistaken use of 'arthritis1') to the counterfactual person ('Jones2'). Thus the two concepts are individuated differently, despite the fact that Jones1 and Jones2 are identical in every way, including all aspects of history and physiology. This entire argument remains idiolectal, as Burge notes in the 1989 essay. Thus there is no conflict with the my idiolectalism. There is, however, a conflict with my stipulativism (and perhaps with my more specific views about the internal lexicon, to be discussed below). Burge no doubt describes accurately our propensities in this case. We assume that both Joneses have set out to use 'arthritis' in accordance with the way it is used by other people in the community. Thus we judge the use of each relative to the use of the relevant community. But I do not see how this has any substantive implications. We can stipulate our meaning for 'concept' so that it includes a social norm or so that it excludes such a norm. In the former case, a person's 'concepts' will indeed be 'individuated' by reference to the community. But in the latter case, they will not. And, in any event, all this is *posterior* to the stipulation.

2 In my view, Kripke's presentation substantially distorts Wittgenstein's position—for example, by ignoring writings such as *On Certainty* and lectures such as those reported by Rush Rhees (see Rhees 1984). Other readers (Goldfarb, Summerfield, and Wright, for example) have reached similar conclusions. Indeed, S. G. Shanker has maintained that "Kripke's version of this problem is the very antithesis of Wittgenstein's" (Shanker 1984, 429). The most extended and compelling case against Kripke's interpretation has been made by G. P. Baker and P. M. S. Hacker, in *Skepticism, Rules, and Language*—though their own interpretation is somewhat obscure, and their solution to the philosophical problems raised by Kripke seems beside the point. In any event, because of the problems of Kripke's interpretation of Wittgenstein, here and below I shall refer not to 'Wittgenstein's argument' but to 'Kripke/Wittgenstein's argument'.

3 For example, Paul Boghossian argues along similar lines that "According to [Kripke/Wittgenstein's] account, then, I will judge that Jones means addition by 'plus' only if Jones uses 'plus' enough times in the same way I am inclined to use it," but this means that "Kripke's communitarian conditions [or social rules] are parasitic on the solitary conditions [or idiolectal rules]" (Boghossian 1989, 522). On the other hand, Boghossian takes this to indicate that we need

some type of autonomist semantics. His argument here is that any individual can be wrong (he/she can be drunk and fail to add correctly) and thus misjudge other people. This is only a problem if we assume that individuals cannot be said to follow rules. Typically, we would say that these (idiolectal) rules are what determine the valid use of 'plus' and so forth, independent of individual errors. But Boghossian is not free to assume that such rule following is not possible. First of all, this is precisely the point at issue. Second, it would seem that Boghossian's account would also have to assume that we can follow rules in gaining access to the (autonomous) semantic 'facts'. Thus the assumption is both question begging and destructive of his own argument.

4 Certainly, the problem of numbers cannot be resolved by reference to a mathematical correlate of common intent. It may be resolvable, however, by reference to a mathematical correlate of what might be called 'semantics'—the meaning of a text according to common rules. Usually the semantics of a text are the same as some common responsive intent. But the complexity of a passage may be such as baffles people, so that they do not accurately follow their own rules. In this case, semantics and common intent—though both are abstractions from idiolect—would diverge. A parallel account of mathematics is facilitated if we, in addition, follow Benacerraf in reducing numbers to *numerals,* to bare sequence (see Benacerraf 1983a). In any event, this sort of account should be able to satisfy the adequacy criteria proposed by Benacerraf in "Mathematical Truth" (Benacerraf 1983b). Benacerraf's work has been an important influence on this study, including this chapter as a whole. In this case, his work helps indicate the redundancy of autonomous, abstract numbers and thus controverts what is for Katz the paradigmatic case of autonomy.

5 Actually, Kripke does not accept all relevant intuitions as data (as, for example, Haight has stressed). Rather, he rejects intuitions—in these cases termed "illusory 'gut feeling'" (1980, 75), "temptation to think" (139), a "feeling" that is "illusory" (153), and so on—when they do not fit his view. Hilary Putnam makes the same slippery use of intuition in "The Meaning of 'Meaning'"; compare, for example, his distinction between "preconceptions" and "clear intuitions" in the claim that "we have, if we shed preconceptions, pretty clear intuitions" (Putnam 1975, 271). But these concerns are not as central to Putnam's argument, and, in fact, he has since criticized this intuitive method—for example, in comments on Kripke's work made at the Twenty-seventh World Congress of Philosophy (Montreal, August 1983).

6 This and what follows is greatly simplified, though in ways unimportant for the argument. An introduction to transformational analysis may be found in most introductory linguistics textbooks—such as Jannedy, Poletto, and Weldon, 1994. A more thorough introduction to Chomsky's recent thinking may be found in Radford 1981, van Riemsdijk and Williams 1986, and Lasnik and Uriagereka 1988. Chomsky's own formulations may be found in Chomsky 1981,

Chomsky 1982b, and, in a less technical form, in Chomsky 1986 and Chomsky 1988a.

7 I do think, however, that Davidson takes his claims too far in insisting that we have "no shared grammar or rules." In fact, we have many rules—for example, the rule for forming plurals by adding [əz] after sibilants. English speakers don't, for example, insert [ik] after the first consonant to form the plural in such cases. Indeed, they don't even add [s].

8 Holland et al. emphasize the importance of aim to any inductive reasoning. As they explain, "Without denying the possibility that specific innate knowledge may guide induction for some organisms in some domains, our own approach will be to emphasize constraints that can be derived from the general nature of an information-processing system that pursues goals in a complex environment and receives feedback about its success in attaining its goals. . . . Our approach assumes that the central problem of induction is to specify processing constraints that will ensure that the inferences drawn by a cognitive system will tend to be plausible and relevant to the system's goals. Which inductions should be characterized as plausible can be determined only with reference to the current knowledge of the system. Induction is thus highly context dependent, being guided by prior knowledge activated in particular situations that confront the system as it seeks to achieve its goals" (4, 5). Communication is, obviously, one of the child's primary goals—probably *the* primary goal—in learning language. In consequence, it should have an equally prominent place in theories of language learning.

Geoffrey Sampson provides further criticisms of Chomsky's 'poverty of stimulus' argument concerning language acquisition. Most important, Sampson points out that "the argument from the rapidity of language acquisition seems wholly empty unless we are given some quantification of 'maximum rate at which things in general can be learned' and of 'degree of overall complexity of a natural language', allowing us to calculate that children could not complete the task of language-acquisition in the observed time if they had to start from scratch. . . . Putting the same point another way, this argument of Chomsky's dissolves as soon as one asks what particular period of time children would have to take to acquire their first language before Chomsky would be content to regard the non-nativist account of language-acquisition as plausible. Whether one thinks of first-language acquisition as a fast or a slow process has more to do, I suspect, with one's prior assumptions . . . than with any observable facts; I find it easy to see children as surprisingly slow at picking up their parents' language" (114). Sampson makes worthwhile criticisms of other of Chomsky's views also—for example, on the innateness of semantic 'primitives' and on several semantic and nonsemantic universals. I do not, however, find Sampson's positive views convincing—and I find his treatment of Chomsky's politics and his occasional political claims about Chomsky's linguistic work appalling.

9 In his Managua lectures (Chomsky 1988a), Chomsky discusses simplicity considerations and concludes that they are irrelevant to language acquisition. However, Chomsky takes relatively complex sentences—for instance, "Is the man, who is happy, at home?" (43)—and tries to imagine what would be the simplest grammatical analysis of such sentences *considered in isolation from any body of previously learned sentences.* But, again, a crucial aspect of simplicity, as I am using the term and as it operates in rational inference, is that it is *systemic.* By the time a child learns a sentence such as this, he/she has learned a large number of grammatical structures, and it is in relation to these, and not in isolation, that he/she would determine simplicity. In this way, Chomsky's entire analysis of and argument against explanation in terms of simplicity considerations is beside the point.

10 But for an excellent discussion of some less obviously communicatively based universals, see Comrie 1981; see also Sampson 1980. Sampson discusses the universal hierarchical structure of languages most extensively. I am not particularly convinced by his account, but the important thing for our purposes is that, as Sampson points out, human thought appears to be hierarchical quite generally—a point that, for example, Holland, et al., make clear. Thus there is no reason to see the universally hierarchical structure of language as innate or specific to language capacities.

11 Note that this concern applies only to 'representations', which is to say, mental objects or 'contents'. It does not apply to rules. Again, I agree completely with Chomsky that our linguistic competence is a matter of following rules and that these rules are not accessible to introspection. On the other hand, as already indicated, I do not view these rules primarily as strict algorithms but (most often) as something more like skills plus patterns of action plus various tacit sorts of rule of thumb. Note that all this is a standard part of intentional subjectivity and fits unproblematically into 'final causal' or 'folk psychological' accounts of action, which is to say accounts based on aims, beliefs or knowledge, and inferential principles, as we shall discuss in more detail in chapter 4.

3 LEGAL INTERPRETATION

1 Giving moral evaluation pride of place is, of course, a common approach to legal evaluation. Indeed, there is evidence that this was the attitude of the 'founding fathers' themselves—see Sherry 1987.

2 Fish's arguments are, in a sense, crude versions of the incommensurability discussed by Kuhn (unresolvable difference of opinion) and the indeterminacy claimed by Quine and, in other versions, by Goodman and Kripke/Wittgenstein (the potential defensibility of any thesis). Fish's general debt to Kuhn's writings (relativistically interpreted) is clear in a number of places. Other legal

theorists have drawn on these philosophers as well, predictably reaching conclusions about legal interpretation that are at odds with those presented in this chapter. For example, Fred Dallmayr takes Kuhnian incommensurability and (Kripkean/)Wittgensteinian indeterminacy as givens indicating that legal interpretation is not " 'scientific' . . . analysis" (Dallmayr 1992, 14), but rather the "hermeneutic" application of the past text to the present. Such application, Dallmayr tells us, is, in Gadamer's words, "tied to the meaning of the text" (17). But how this might be possible, given Dallmayr's presuppositions, is unclear. Having invoked incommensurability and skepticism in his argument against "scientific" approaches (irrelevantly conceived of in terms of 'value neutrality' [14]), Dallmayr seems to forget about both when it comes to hermeneutics. But, if incommensurability and skepticism are effective against a rigorous methodology of empirical investigation, simplicity, and so on, they are *a fortiori* effective against the more vaguely formulated and more intuitive (thus more cognitively biased) method of hermeneutics.

3 Some readers might expect in this context a response to the views of writers in the Critical Legal Studies (CLS) movement. I have not responded to these views for several reasons. First, a good deal of CLS is deconstructive in inspiration (see, for example, Tushnet 1984 and Hussan 1986). I have criticized deconstructive principles elsewhere (see chapter 2 of Hogan 1990a) and see no reason to criticize them again here. Second, I have very limited aims in the present chapter. I am setting out only to clarify the varieties of intent that are germane to legal interpretation and, secondarily, to offer a tentative hierarchization of these varieties. Thus I take no stand on most of the issues addressed by CLS, which are, then, irrelevant to the present chapter. Finally, when CLS writers do address interpretation per se, they seem to share with writers in other schools the lack of clarity about meaning and the lack of discrimination between different varieties of meaning that the present essay aims to address and, perhaps to some degree, dispel.

Consider by way of a brief illustration the "standard four-part critical method" of CLS as isolated by Mark Kelman:

> First, the Critics attempted to identify a contradiction in liberal legal thought. . . . Second, the Critics tried to demonstrate that each of the contradictions is utterly pervasive in legal controversy. . . . Third, Critics have attempted to show that mainstream thought invariably treats one term in each set of contradictory impulses as *privileged*. . . . Fourth, the Critics note that, closely examined, the 'privileged' impulses describe the program of a remarkably right-wing, quasilibertarian order. (Kelman 1987, 3–4)

Readers familiar with deconstruction will recognize this immediately as a fairly straightforward transposition of deconstructive method to law. Deconstructive analyses tend to have an a priori commitment to uncovering bipolar, hierarchized oppositions. This commitment derives from a belief that language is structured by bipolar oppositions that come to be hierarchized in the metaphysical systems pervading Western thought. Such oppositions are (in this view), however, mutually definitive and thus cannot ultimately be hierarchized. Indeed, their meaning cannot even be fixed, for, as part of an autonomous system of language in which every term is defined by its relation to other terms, all meaning is continuously ramifying throughout the entire system.

As I agree with deconstructionists that society and ideology involve oppressive hierarchies, and as I agree with the Critics that the legal system as a whole will tend to function in such a way as to preserve current hierarchies, I will leave this point aside. The first point at issue, then, is whether such hierarchization is necessarily manifest in bipolar oppositions, which are the defining structural unit of language and thus of more specific discursive structures (such as law). In fact, there is absolutely no reason to believe that this is the case. The a priori commitment to bipolar, linguistic oppositions derives from a Saussurean linguistic theory. Given our current understanding of language, this theory seems entirely inadequate. Obviously, many social oppositions are dual (male/female), but this has no consequences for the structure of language, meaning, or discourse and thus for the general principles of interpretation. The second and more important point at issue would then be the indeterministic dissemination of meaning throughout the system of autonomous language. But this I take to be implausible for reasons discussed in the preceding chapter.

Of course, CLS arguments may be valid independently of deconstruction. But, insofar as these arguments might pose a challenge to legal interpretation in the sense of the present chapter, this does not appear to be the case. Indeed, the problems with some of the central arguments of CLS become particularly clear in the context of the interpretive principles discussed above, both the general principles and those specific to legal interpretation. For example, when Critics find a certain contradiction pervasive within the legal system, or when (related to this) they find pervasive indeterminacy, they are often demonstrating only that two contradictory views are possible and that neither is *definitively* eliminated—that a decision is "not preordained by prior law" in Kress's phrase (Kress 1992, 200—see also Cornell 1992, 157). But, once again, this is inconsequential for reasons discussed in the preceding chapters (compare Graff 1982 on Levinson). The tacit assumption of this argument is that adjudication necessarily takes place without the benefit of simplicity criteria. But this is clearly false. Moreover, critics frequently find such contradictions or indeterminacies precisely at points where two or more distinct meanings are at issue—in other words, where the object of interpretation has not been stipulated and is, in consequence, multiple or vacillating.

This is not to say, of course, that writers in CLS do not raise important issues about the coherence of our legal system, as well as its ideological bias—they do. Nor is it to say that all apparent contradictions are resolvable by reference to simplicity considerations and varieties of meaning—they are not. Nor is it to say that there are no genuine contradictions or indeterminacies in the legal system—there are. It is to say, however, that, contrary to what some writers might think, there are no relevant problems of principle for interpretation (for example, there is no pervasive indeterminacy of the deconstructive sort). There are, rather, only the usual (sometimes irresolvable) problems of evidence, simplicity, and so on, along with ordinary (sometimes irresolvable) problems of conflicting values, human fallibility, local indeterminacy (compare Brest 1988, 74), and so on.

4 Occasionally, theorists have felt that there is more to meaning than the (somewhat muddled) trio of text, author, and purpose, though their formulations have usually been so vague as to be of little direct theoretical or practical value. For example, David Hoy recognizes that there are "different kinds of intention" that require clarification (Hoy 1992, 180), but he does not specify these himself. Steven Knapp and Walter Benn Michaels, in their reply to Hoy, do draw a version of "extensional intent" as defined above. For example, they speak of "the meaning of the word *vehicle*" in contrast with the "beliefs" required "to determine what objects would count as vehicles" (Knapp and Michaels 1992, 193). This allows them to go beyond earlier intentionalist accounts and argue (correctly) that "it make[s] sense to argue . . . that a court remains faithful to the authors' intentions even while going *against* the authors' beliefs" (193). This is certainly an important first step in articulating the varieties of meaning germane to legal interpretation. But even Knapp and Michaels do not go beyond this first step.

5 The interpretive conservatism advocated in this chapter may seem to conflict with the anarchist views set forth in the final chapter of *The Politics of Interpretation* (published much earlier, but written concurrently with the first draft of this manuscript). However, the same principles apply to an anarchist society as apply to any other society; the same factors determine the moral force and attendant judicial obligations of an anarchist legal system as determine those of any legal system. If the establishment of an anarchist society involves the establishment of laws—for example, laws guaranteeing very broad civil liberties, providing for an egalitarian economic order, and so on—it would, I think, be wrong for a court to undermine, through capricious interpretation, the freedoms and rights such laws were designed to guarantee. (For a discussion of issues surrounding anarchism and law, I refer interested readers to the essays collected in Holterman and van Maarseveen 1984.) In any case, this conservatism is, again, contingent upon the degree to which we judge the law superior to a state of nature, as discussed at the beginning of the chapter.

4 PSYCHOANALYTIC INTERPRETATION

1 However, see the interesting discussions of this issue by Kenneth Starr and Abner Mikva (Starr 1987 and Mikva 1987).

2 In undertaking such a revision of psychoanalytic theory, I have before me the models of Jacques Lacan and Roy Schafer (see Schafer 1976). Though my final causal principles are quite different from the linguistics of the former and the action language of the latter, their work convinced me of the need for such a revision and indicated to me, in general terms, the way it might proceed.

3 To fit the classical notion, sublimation would require in addition that the person in question rework the private fantasies surrounding the private substantial pleasure into another, public object, an object of public pleasure.

4 Actually, I am uncertain about this. It is possible—and is one standard view—that traumas are actually repressed only under circumstances where their recollection does not satisfy norms or otherwise comes into conflict with pleasures of fact. This is an important issue on which I have nothing worthwhile to say. Fortunately, nothing in the following pages rests on any assumption about this problem.

5 I should note that, although I speak of this as a 'lexicon', it could equally be conceived of as based on personal memory or empirical beliefs, rather than words. The point is that our memories, beliefs, etc., are structured or interrelated in specific ways. For example, when I think of one sort of thing, I am more likely to recall other related things, or to recall them more quickly, or to understand them more readily. I speak of this structure or network as a lexicon—and do so, in addition, in partially objectivist terms—simply as a convenience. It gives us a concrete model that allows us to think about the phenomena more easily. But it is more accurately thought of as a coordinated structure of subjective memories, beliefs, linguistic principles, and so on.

6 I leave aside here what may actually be the most common form of interpretation: by reference to a standardized set of correlations. This sort of interpretation involves the reduction of the analysand's utterance (action, dream) to a type, and the replacement of particular and individual inference with formulaic generalities. Sometimes these are crude (all long things are phalluses); sometimes they are not (all obsessions involve a disturbed relation to death). In my view, such stereotypic or formulaic interpretation is, at best, a stopgap; it is highly unreliable and should be used only when the analytic dialectic has degenerated to such a point that there are no other options—and even then its only function is to revivify that dialectic (compare Freud 1965, 388). Unfortunately, in actual practice it more often functions to stifle dialectic. A particularly horrifying example of the perversion of analysis through facile, stereotypic interpretation may be found in Grunbaum 1984, 212–13. Of course, it is always possible that epidemiological investigation will lead to significant generaliza-

tions. Empirically well-supported generalizations of this sort could then play a role, as tentative hypotheses, in psychoanalytic interpretation. Thus stereotypic/formulaic interpretation cannot be dismissed a priori in its entirety. Even under the best of circumstances, however, it would be only the starting point of interpretation, not the conclusion.

7 In light of the preceding discussion of simplicity, it is worth noting a few things about the similarities between Lakatos's view and my own. First of all, Lakatos's account is comparative, not absolute. Like the view of theory evaluation presented in chapter 1, Lakatos's "falsificationism" is not a matter of evaluating isolated theories but of comparing rival theories. It is also tentative rather than definitive—again, like the conception presented in chapter 1. Finally, in demanding that theoretical revisions increase overall empirical content, Lakatos demands, in effect, a form of simplicity. If a revised theory merely adds a principle or set of principles while maintaining the same range of explanation, then it has merely become more complex. I do have several disagreements with Lakatos, however. First, in my view, a theory advances if it is rendered simpler, even if no further empirical content is added. Second, even in cases where revision is spurred by an attempt to explain recalcitrant data, I would not be so insistent that the revision have empirical content beyond this recalcitrant data—that it "successfully anticipates novel facts" (187). Rather, I would adopt a looser principle of evaluating the ratio of principles and posits to data, relative to alternatives. Finally, I would not link any of this to "falsification" but would speak rather of theory adjudication and so on. (Moreover, because of the fallibility of all such adjudication, because of our broader cognitive fallibility, and because of the perversions of research resulting from political economy, I would advocate an anarchistic proliferation of theories of the sort advocated by Feyerabend.)

8 *Shlag* also relates to *beating* and is one ordinary way of referring to a *clap* of thunder, which may relate it to the compulsive counting mentioned in the previous session. Its significance probably derives from an incident that arises later in the analysis, where Ernst is beaten by (or is subjected to blows—"*Schlaegen*"—from) his father for biting his governess—an event that occurred around the time Camilla died (Freud 1982, 47). This punitive *Schlag*, which interferes in Ernst's sexual play with the governess, is no doubt a significant moment in the development of Ernst's oedipal antipathy toward his father. In this way, it fits perfectly with his wish that the (interfering) professor die of a *Shlag*. It is also another crucial moment in the development of Ernst's sense that Camilla's death resulted from his precocious, punishable sexuality.

9 On the other hand, it is important to point out that this situation is complicated by the fact that Ernst's mother has been interfering with the fulfillment of Ernst's desire, rather like Ernst's father or Gisela's grandmother, and thus is probably the object not only of an infantile desire but of a more current death

wish as well. This, however, does not appear to be the factor of the greatest etiological significance to the case as a whole.

5 LITERARY INTERPRETATION

1 Indeed, as would be expected, this privileging of literary association has been a crucial element of literary composition from earliest times. Thus, as Calvert Watkins points out, oral "formulaic poetry by its nature continually evokes associative chains" in a standardized literary fashion (Watkins 1982, 111).

2 By 'idiosyncracy' I merely mean a sort of associative oddity. It is not idiosyncratic to associate deep sorrow with the death of a close relative, even though different readers' memories of such sorrow will obviously concern different people. It is, however, idiosyncratic to associate, say, perfume counters with deep sorrow (if one's close relative happened to die at a perfume counter). Part of being a sahṛdaya (either as an author or as a reader) is being able to access or prime the nonidiosyncratic memories without accessing or priming the idiosyncratic ones, or while doing so more limitedly. Again, this may be conceived of in terms of lexical ordering, in terms of access followed by suppression, and so on.

3 Indeed, there are further connections of detail as well. For example, in *King Lear* three servants attend Cornwall at the time of Gloucester's blinding, and one of the three opposes the act. Similarly, in *King John,* several "executioners" (not "assistants [in blinding]") — presumably two or three — attend Hubert in his preparations. While none actively opposes the act — there is, after all, no act to oppose — one does express his distaste for the act (IV. i. 84–85). Interestingly, this is a motif found elsewhere in Shakespeare's works (for example, in *Richard III*) and in the work of his contemporaries (see, for example, Marlowe's *Massacre at Paris*).

4 Tiresias may be relevant here, for he too is blinded for a sort of sexual deviation. In both major versions of the myth, however, the blinding is the result of Tiresias's gaining a sort of sexual knowledge he should not have gained. Thus his blinding is, I think, related to a different complex of associations — possibly a complex involving the falls of Icarus, to whom Arthur compares himself in *The Troublesome Raigne* (1972, 27), and Bladud, father of Lear, two characters who also aspire beyond their station.

5 There are various reasons outside of connections with *King Lear* that indicate that Shakespeare was familiar with and influenced by this translation. For example, as Oedipus approaches the sea and the cliff from which he desires to throw himself, he says to Antigone, "Oh Stay me not I thee desire, behold, behold, I heare / My Fathers ghost to bidde me come apace, and not to feare" (1927, 102). Compare Horatio's and Hamlet's responses when Hamlet's father's ghost "beckons [Hamlet] to go away with it." Horatio tries to stop Hamlet,

worrying that the ghost might "tempt [him] toward the flood . . . Or to the dreadful summit of the cliff" (I. iv. 58ff.)—even making him act in "desperation" (75), which is to say, out of despair. Hamlet protests, "Hold off your hands . . ." (80), and so on.

6 A look at Ravisius Textor's often helpful *Officina* is useless in this context, as it is in connection with blinding. Under "Praecipitati," Textor provides the uninspiring list: Astyamactem, Manlius, Thessalus, Tarpeia, Lycas, Lycurgus, Aesop, and Nauplius. Similarly, under "Caeci, et Excaecati," he provides a wealth of insignificance, broken only by the obvious Tyresias and Oedipus; in the latter case, moreover, the reader is referred only to Ovid's *Invective Against the Ibis!*

7 This point could be explored further by considering the historico-political associations of the play. Indeed, the bulk of interpretive criticism written on the play, especially that of the last few years, has focused on such historical and political issues (see, for example, the essays in Curren-Aquino 1989). Much of this work could prove relevant to an extension of the present study. One particularly important set of associative and structural connections is that relating John's problem with Arthur to Elizabeth's problem with Mary. (For an illuminating treatment of the structural relation linking John with Elizabeth and Arthur with Mary, see Lily Bess Campbell 1947.) I have not discussed this as it does not have direct bearing on the particular issues of blinding and falling.

AFTERWORD

1 This is, of course, not to say that there are no exceptions. There are many. In literary theory, one of the most important is Edward Said. Anyone concerned with the relation between literature and real issues of justice and decency can only hope that his illness abates and that he is able to continue writing vigorous analyses for many years.

WORKS CITED

Abhinavagupta. 1968. *The Aesthetic Experience According to Abhinavagupta*. Translated and edited by Raniero Gnoli. 2nd ed. Varanasi, India: Chowkhamba Sanskrit Series.

———. 1990. "Locana." In *The Dhvanyāloka of Ānandavardhana with the Locana of Abhinavagupta*. Translated by Daniel Ingalls, Jeffrey Masson, and M. V. Patwardhan. Cambridge, Mass.: Harvard University Press.

Amaladass, Anand. 1984. *Philosophical Implications of Dhvani: Experience of Symbol Language in Indian Aesthetics*. Vienna: De Nobili Research Library.

Ānandavardhana. 1990. *The Dhvanyāloka of Ānandavardhana with the Locana of Abhinavagupta*, translated by Daniel Ingalls, Jeffrey Masson, and M. V. Patwardhan. Cambridge, Mass.: Harvard University Press.

Anderson, John R. 1983. *The Architecture of Cognition*. Cambridge, Mass.: Harvard University Press.

Anscombe, G. E. M. 1963. *Intention*. 2nd ed. Ithaca: Cornell University Press.

———. 1981. "On the Grammar of 'Enjoy'." In *Metaphysics and the Philosophy of Mind: Collected Philosophical Papers*. Vol. 2. Minneapolis: University of Minnesota Press.

Apollodorus Atheniensis. 1972. *Bibliothecae Libri Tres et Fragmenta*. New York: Georg Olms.

———. 1976. *Gods and Heroes of the Greeks: The "Library" of Apollodorus*. Translated by Michael Simpson. Amherst: University of Massachusetts Press.

Aristotle. 1927. "Peri Poietikes." In *Aristotle: The Poetics; "Longinus": On the Sublime; Demetrius: On Style*, edited by E. Capps, T. E. Page, and W. H. D. Rouse. London: William Heinemann.

———. 1984. "Topics." Translated by W. A. Pickard-Cambridge. In *The Complete Works of Aristotle*, edited by Jonathan Barnes. Vol. 1. Princeton: Princeton University Press.

Augustine. 1966. *Selected Sermons of St. Augustine*. Translated and edited by Quincy Howe. New York: Holt, Rinehart, and Winston.

Austin, John. 1962. *How To Do Things with Words*. Cambridge, Mass.: Harvard University Press.

———. 1971. "Performative-Constative." In *The Philosophy of Language,* edited by John Searle. Oxford: Oxford University Press.

Babbitt, Milton, 1972. "Past and Present Concepts of the Nature and Limits of Music." In *Perspectives on Contemporary Music Theory,* edited by Benjamin Boretz and Edward T. Cone. New York: W. W. Norton.

Baker, G. P., and P. M. S. Hacker. 1984. *Skepticism, Rules, and Language.* Oxford: Basil Blackwell.

Baker, Mark. 1985. "The Mirror Principle and Morphosyntactic Explanation." *Linguistic Inquiry* 16, no. 3: 373–415.

Baldwin, T. W. 1944. *William Shakspere's Small Latine and Lesse Greeke.* 2 vols. Urbana: University of Illinois.

Beardsley, Monroe C. 1987. "The Aesthetic Point of View." In *Philosophy Looks at the Arts: Contemporary Readings in Aesthetics,* edited by Joseph Margolis. 3rd ed. Philadelphia: Temple University Press.

Benacerraf, Paul. 1983a. "What Numbers Could Not Be." In *Philosophy of Mathematics: Selected Readings,* edited by Benacerraf and Hilary Putnam. Cambridge: Cambridge University Press.

———. 1983b. "Mathematical Truth." In *Philosophy of Mathematics: Selected Readings,* edited by Benacerraf and Hilary Putnam. Cambridge: Cambridge University Press.

Bennett, Tony. 1990. *Outside Literature.* New York: Routledge.

Bharata-Muni. 1967. *The Nāṭyaśāstra.* Translated and edited by Manomohan Ghosh. 2nd ed. Vol. 1. Calcutta: Manisha Granthalaya.

Bhaskar, Roy. 1989. *Reclaiming Reality: A Critical Introduction to Contemporary Philosophy.* New York: Verso.

Billman, D. 1983. "Inductive Learning of Syntactic Categories." Ph.D. diss., University of Michigan.

Blackburn, Simon. 1984. "The Individual Strikes Back." *Synthese* 58 (March): 281–302.

Block, Ned, ed. 1980–81. *Readings in the Philosophy of Psychology.* 2 vols. Cambridge, Mass.: Harvard University Press.

Bocchii, Achillis. 1979. *Symbolicarum Quaestionum de Universo Genere.* New York: Garland. Facsimile of Bologne, 1574.

Boghossian, Paul. 1989. "The Rule-Following Considerations." *Mind* 98 (October): 507–49.

Bordwell, David. 1989. *Making Meaning: Inference and Rhetoric in the Interpretation of Cinema.* Cambridge, Mass.: Harvard University Press.

Brand, Myles. 1984. *Intending and Acting: Toward a Naturalized Action Theory.* Cambridge, Mass.: MIT Press.

Bransford, J. D., and N. S. McCarrell. 1977. "A Sketch of a Cognitive Approach to Comprehension: Some Thoughts About Understanding What It Means to

Comprehend." In *Thinking: Readings in Cognitive Science,* edited by Philip N. Johnson-Laird and P. C. Wason. Cambridge: Cambridge University Press.

Brennan, William J., Jr. 1988. "The Constitution of the United States: Contemporary Ratification." In *Interpreting Law and Literature: A Hermeneutic Reader,* edited by Sanford Levinson and Steven Mailloux. Evanston: Northwestern University Press.

Brest, Paul. 1988. "The Misconceived Quest for the Original Understanding." In *Interpreting Law and Literature: A Hermeneutic Reader,* edited by Sanford Levinson and Steven Mailloux. Evanston: Northwestern University Press.

Brown, Gillian, and George Yule. 1983. *Discourse Analysis.* New York: Cambridge University Press.

Burge, Tyler. 1979. "Individualism and the Mental." In *Studies in Metaphysics,* edited by Peter French, Theodore Uehling, and Howard Wettstein. Midwest Studies in Philosophy, vol. 4. Minneapolis: University of Minnesota Press.

———. 1986. "Individualism and Psychology." *Philosophical Review* 95, no. 1: 3–45.

———. 1989. "Wherein Is Language Social?" In *Reflections on Chomsky,* edited by Alexander George. New York: Basil Blackwell.

Butcher, S. H. 1951. *Aristotle's Theory of Poetry and Fine Art with a Critical Text and Translation of "The Poetics."* 4th ed. New York: Dover.

Campbell, Lily B. 1947. *Shakespeare's 'Histories': Mirrors of Elizabethan Policy.* San Marino: Huntington Library.

Cantarino, Vicente, ed. and trans. 1975. *Arabic Poetics in the Golden Age: Selection of Texts Accompanied By a Preliminary Study.* Leiden: E. J. Brill.

Carter, William. 1986. "Mapping Semantic Paths: Is Essentialism Relevant?" In *Studies in Metaphysics,* edited by Peter French, Theodore Uehling, and Howard Wettstein. *Midwest Studies in Philosophy,* vol. 4. Minneapolis: University of Minnesota Press.

Chomsky, Noam. 1959. *"Verbal Behaviour."* Review of B. F. Skinner. *Language* 35, no. 1: 26–58.

———. 1972. *Language and Mind.* 2nd ed. New York: Harcourt Brace Jovanovich.

———. 1975. *Reflections on Language.* New York: Pantheon.

———. 1979. *Language and Responsibility.* Translated by John Viertel. New York: Pantheon.

———. 1980. *Rules and Representations.* New York: Columbia University Press.

———. 1981. *Lectures on Government and Binding.* Dordrecht, Neth.: Foris.

———. 1982a. *Noam Chomsky on the Generative Enterprise: A Discussion with Riny Huybregts and Henk van Riemsdijk.* Dordrecht, Neth.: Foris.

———. 1982b. *Some Concepts and Consequences of the Theory of Government and Binding.* Cambridge, Mass.: MIT Press.

———. 1984. *Modular Approaches to the Study of the Mind.* San Diego: San Diego State University Press.

————. 1986. *Knowledge of Language: Its Nature, Origin, and Use.* New York: Praeger.

————. 1988a. *Language and Problems of Knowledge: The Managua Lectures.* Cambridge, Mass.: MIT Press.

————. 1988b. *Language and Politics.* Edited by C. P. Otero. Montreal: Black Rose Books.

Comrie, Bernard. 1981. *Language Universals and Linguistic Typology: Syntax and Morphology.* Chicago: University of Chicago Press.

Cornell, Drucilla. 1992. "From the Lighthouse: The Promise of Redemption and the Possibility of Legal Interpretation." In *Legal Hermeneutics: History, Theory, and Practice,* edited by Gregory Leyh. Berkeley: University of California Press.

Croft, William. 1990. *Typology and Universals.* New York: Cambridge University Press.

Curren-Aquino, Deborah, ed. 1989. *King John: New Perspectives.* Newark: University of Delaware Press.

Dallmayr, Fred. 1992. "Hermeneutics and the Rule of Law." In *Legal Hermeneutics: History, Theory, and Practice,* edited by Gregory Leyh. Berkeley: University of California Press.

Davidson, Donald. 1984. "On the Very Idea of a Conceptual Scheme." In his *Inquiries into Truth and Interpretation.* Oxford: Oxford University Press.

————. 1986. "A Nice Derangement of Epitaphs." In *Philosophical Grounds of Rationality: Intentions, Categories, Ends,* edited by Richard Grandy and Richard Warner. Oxford: Oxford University Press.

de Man, Paul. 1983. *Blindness and Insight: Essays in the Rhetoric of Contemporary Criticism.* Minneapolis: University of Minnesota Press.

Derrida, Jacques. 1981. *Dissemination.* Translated by Barbara Johnson. Chicago: University of Chicago Press.

Dickie, George. 1989. "All Aesthetic Attitude Theories Fail: The Myth of the Aesthetic Attitude." In *Aesthetics: A Critical Anthology,* edited by Dickie, Richard Sclafani, and Ronald Roblin. 2nd ed. New York: St. Martin's Press.

Dimock, Edward C. 1967. Introduction to *In Praise of Krishna: Songs from the Bengali,* translated and edited by Edward C. Dimock, Jr., and Denise Levertov. Garden City, N.Y.: Doubleday.

Donnellan, Keith. 1972. "Proper Names and Identifying Descriptions." In *Semantics of Natural Language,* edited by Donald Davidson and Gilbert Harman. 2nd ed. Dordrecht, Neth.: Reidel.

Dufrenne, Mikel. 1979. "Artistic Creation." In his *Main Trends in Aesthetics and the Sciences of Art.* New York: Holmes and Meier.

Dummett, Michael. 1993. *The Seas of Language.* Oxford: Oxford University Press, 1993.

Dworkin, Ronald. 1978. *Taking Rights Seriously.* Cambridge, Mass.: Harvard University Press.

———. 1983a. "Law as Interpretation." In *The Politics of Interpretation,* edited by W. J. T. Mitchell. Chicago: University of Chicago Press.

———. 1983b. "My Reply to Stanley Fish (and Walter Benn Michaels): Please Don't Talk about Objectivity Any More." In *The Politics of Interpretation,* edited by W. J. T. Mitchell. Chicago: University of Chicago Press.

———. 1985. *A Matter of Principle.* Cambridge, Mass.: Harvard University Press.

Earman, John. 1993. "Carnap, Kuhn, and the Philosophy of Scientific Methodology." In *World Changes: Thomas Kuhn and the Nature of Science,* edited by Paul Horwich. Cambridge, Mass.: MIT Press.

Eco, Umberto. 1990. *The Limits of Interpretation.* Bloomington: Indiana University Press.

Eissler, Kurt. 1965. *Medical Orthodoxy and the Future of Psychoanalysis.* New York: International Universities Press.

Evans, Gareth and John McDowell, eds. 1976. *Truth and Meaning.* Oxford: Oxford University Press.

Faust, David. 1984. *The Limits of Scientific Reasoning.* Minneapolis: University of Minnesota Press.

Fausto-Sterling, Anne. 1985. *Myths of Gender: Biological Theories about Women and Men.* New York: Basic Books.

Feyerabend, Paul. 1978. *Against Method: Outline of an Anarchistic Theory of Knowledge.* London: Verso.

Fichte, J. G. 1982. *The Science of Knowledge.* Translated and edited by Peter Heath and John Lachs. New York: Cambridge University Press.

Fish, Stanley. 1980. *Is There a Text in This Class? The Authority of Interpretive Communities.* Cambridge, Mass.: Harvard University Press.

———. 1983. "Working on the Chain Gang: Interpretation in the Law and in Literary Criticism." In *The Politics of Interpretation,* edited by W. J. T. Mitchell. Chicago: University of Chicago Press.

———. 1985. "Anti-Professionalism" and "Resistance and Independence: A Reply to Gerald Graff." *New Literary History* 17, no. 1: 89–108; 119–27.

———. 1989. *Doing What Comes Naturally: Change, Rhetoric, and the Practice of Theory in Literary and Legal Studies.* Durham: Duke University Press.

Freud, Sigmund. 1941. *Zur Psychopathologie des Alltagslebens, Gesammelte Werke, Vierter Band.* Frankfurt: Fischer.

———. 1960. *Jokes and Their Relation to the Unconscious.* Translated and edited by James Strachey. New York: W. W. Norton.

———. 1963. *Therapy and Technique: Essays on Dream Interpretation, Hypnosis, Transference, Free Association, and Other Techniques of Psychoanalysis.* Edited by Philip Rieff. New York: Collier.

———. 1965. *The Interpretation of Dreams.* Translated and edited by James Strachey. New York: Avon Books.

———. 1974. *L'Homme aux rats: Journal d'une analyse*. Edited by Elza Ribeiro Hawelka. Paris: Presses Universitaires de France.

———. 1982. "Bemerkungen ueber einen Fall von Zwangsneurose." In *Zwei Fall-darstellungen*. Frankfurt: Fischer Taschenbuch.

Friedman, Kenneth. 1990. *Predictive Simplicity: Induction Exhum'd*. Oxford: Pergamon.

Friedmann, W. 1967. *Legal Theory*. New York: Columbia University Press.

Frye, Northrop. 1957. *Anatomy of Criticism*. Princeton: Princeton University Press.

———. 1990. "Lacan and the Full Word." In *Criticism and Lacan: Essays and Dialogue on Language, Structure, and the Unconscious*, edited by Patrick Colm Hogan and Lalita Pandit. Athens: University of Georgia Press.

Garman, Michael. 1990. *Psycholinguistics*. Cambridge: Cambridge University Press.

Geertz, Clifford. 1973. *The Interpretation of Cultures*. New York: Basic Books.

Gerow, Edwin. 1977. *Indian Poetics*. Wiesbaden: Otto Harrossowitz.

Goethe, Johann Wolfgang von. 1950. *Aus Meinem Leben Dichtung und Wahrheit*. *Goethes Poetische Werke*. Vol. 8. Stuttgart: J. G. Cotta'sche Buchhandlung.

Goldfarb, Warren. "Kripke on Wittgenstein on Rules." *Journal of Philosophy* 82, no. 9: 471–88.

Goodman, Nelson. 1971. "The Epistemological Argument." In *The Philosophy of Language*, edited by John Searle. Oxford: Oxford University Press.

———. 1978. "When Is Art?" In his *Ways of Worldmaking*. Indianapolis: Hackett.

———. 1983. *Fact, Fiction, and Forecast*. 4th ed. Cambridge, Mass.: Harvard University Press.

Gopnik, Alison. 1993. "How We Know Our Minds: The Illusion of First-Person Knowledge of Intentionality." In *Readings in Philosophy and Cognitive Science*, edited by Alvin Goldman. Cambridge, Mass.: MIT Press.

Gorman, David. 1993. "Davidson and Dummett on Language and Interpretation." In *Literary Theory after Davidson*, edited by Reed Way Dasenbrock. University Park: Pennsylvania State University Press.

Gorney, James. 1990. "Reflections on Impasse." In *Criticism and Lacan: Essays and Dialogue on Language, Structure, and the Unconscious*, edited by Patrick Colm Hogan and Lalita Pandit. Athens: University of Georgia Press.

Graff, Gerald. 1982. " 'Keep off the Grass', 'Drop Dead', and Other Indeterminacies: A Response to Sanford Levinson." *Texas Law Review* 60: 405–13.

Graff, Gerald, and Reginald Gibbons, eds. 1985. *Criticism in the University*. Evanston: Northwestern University Press.

Greimas, Algirdas Julien. 1990. *The Social Sciences: A Semiotic View*. Translated by Paul Perron and Frank H. Collins. Minneapolis: University of Minnesota Press.

Grice, Paul. 1989. *Studies in the Way of Words*. Cambridge, Mass.: Harvard University Press.

Grunbaum, Adolf. 1980. "Epistemological Liabilities of the Clinical Appraisal of Psychoanalytic Theory." *Nous* 14 (September): 307–85.

————. 1984. *The Foundations of Psychoanalysis: A Philosophical Critique*. Berkeley: University of California Press.

————. 1989. "Why Thematic Kinships between Events DO NOT Attest Their Causal Linkage." In *A Festschrift for Robert Butts*, edited by J. R. Brown and J. Mittlestrass. Boston: Reidel.

————. 1993. *Validation in the Clinical Theory of Psychoanalysis: A Study in the Philosophy of Psychoanalysis*. Madison, Conn.: International Universities Press.

Habermas, Jurgen. 1988. *On the Logic of the Social Sciences*. Translated by Shierry Weber Nicholsen and Jerry A. Stark. Cambridge, Mass.: MIT Press.

Hacking, Ian. 1993. "On Kripke's and Goodman's Uses of 'Grue'." *Philosophy* 68 (July): 269–95.

Haight, M. R. 1991. "Conditional Essences." *British Journal of Aesthetics* 31 (January): 48–57.

Halasz, Laszlo. 1991. "Emotional Effect and Reminding in Literary Processing." *Poetics* 20 (June): 247–72.

Happe, Peter, ed. 1975. *English Mystery Plays: A Selection*. London: Penguin.

Hauser, Arnold. 1957. *The Social History of Art*. Translated by Stanley Godman. Vol. 1, *Prehistoric, Ancient-Oriental, Greece and Rome, Middle Ages*; Vol. 4, *Naturalism, Impressionism, The Film Age*. New York: Vintage.

Heidegger, Martin. 1976. *Sein und Zeit*. Tübingen: Max Niemeyer.

Hartmann, Heinz. 1958. *Ego Psychology and the Problem of Adaptation*. Translated by David Rapaport. New York: International Universities Press.

Higgins, John, and Thomas Blenerhasset. 1946. *Parts Added to the Mirror for Magistrates* (1574, 1575, 1578, and 1587 editions). Edited by Lilly B. Campbell. Cambridge: Cambridge University Press.

Hirsch, E. D., Jr. 1976. *The Aims of Interpretation*. Chicago: University of Chicago Press.

————. 1988. "Counterfactuals in Interpretation." In *Interpreting Law and Literature: A Hermeneutic Reader*, edited by Sanford Levinson and Steven Mailloux. Evanston: Northwestern University Press.

Hobbs, Jerry. 1990. *Literature and Cognition*. Stanford: Center for the Study of Language and Information.

Hoffman, Paul. 1985. "Kripke on Private Language." *Philosophical Studies* 47 (January): 23–28.

Hogan, Patrick Colm. 1980. "Meaning and Hegel." *Southern Journal of Philosophy* 18, no. 1: 51–61.

————. 1990a. *The Politics of Interpretation: Ideology, Professionalism, and the Study of Literature*. New York: Oxford University Press.

————. 1990b. "Structure and Ambiguity in the Symbolic Order: Some Prolegomena to the Understanding and Criticism of Lacan." In *Criticism and Lacan: Essays and Dialogue on Language, Structure, and the Unconscious*, edited by Hogan and Lalita Pandit. Athens: University of Georgia Press.

———. 1993. "Teaching and Research as Economic Problems." *Education and Society* 11, no. 1: 15–25.

Holinshed, Raphael. 1965. *Chronicles of England, Scotland, and Ireland.* 2 vols. New York: AMS Press.

Holland, John, Keith Holyoak, Richard Nisbett, and Paul Thagard. 1986. *Induction: Processes of Inference, Learning, and Discovery.* Cambridge, Mass.: MIT Press.

Holland, Norman. 1968. *The Dynamics of Literary Response.* New York: Oxford University Press.

———. 1975. *Poems In Persons: An Introduction to the Psychoanalysis of Literature.* New York: W. W. Norton.

Holterman, Thom, and Henc van Maarseveen. 1984. *Law and Anarchism.* Montreal: Black Rose Books.

Horgan, Terence, and James Woodward. 1990. "Folk Psychology Is Here to Stay." In *Mind and Cognition: A Reader,* edited by William Lycan. Oxford: Basil Blackwell.

Hoy, David Couzens. 1992. "Intentions and the Law: Defending Hermeneutics." In *Legal Hermeneutics: History, Theory, and Practice,* edited by Gregory Leyh. Berkeley: University of California Press.

Hudson, R. A. 1980. *Sociolinguistics.* New York: Cambridge University Press.

Hussan, Christine A. Desan. 1986. "Note: Expanding the Legal Vocabulary: The Challenge Posed by Deconstruction and Defense of Law." *Yale Law Journal* 95 (April): 969–91.

Husserl, Edmund. 1973. *Cartesian Meditations: An Introduction to Phenomenology.* Translated by Dorion Cairns. The Hague: Martinus Nijhoff.

Hyginus. 1960. *The Myths of Hyginus.* Translated and edited by Mary Grand. Lawrence: University Press of Kansas.

Ingarden, Roman. 1973. *The Literary Work of Art: An Investigation on the Borderlines of Ontology, Logic, and Theory of Literature.* Translated by George G. Brabowicz. Evanston: Northwestern University Press.

Jackendoff, Ray. 1983. *Semantics and Cognition.* Cambridge, Mass.: MIT Press.

Jackson, Frank. 1990. "Epiphenomenal Qualia." In *Mind and Cognition: A Reader,* edited by William Lycan. Oxford: Basil Blackwell.

Jakobson, Roman. 1961. *Structure of Language and Its Mathematical Aspects.* Proceedings of the Symposia in Applied Mathematics, vol. 12. Providence: American Mathematical Society.

———. 1979. *Selected Writings.* Vol. 5, *On Verse, Its Masters and Explorers.* The Hague: Mouton.

Jannedy, Stefanie, Robert Poletto, and Tracey Weldon. 1994. *Language Files: Materials for an Introduction to Language and Linguistics.* Columbus: Ohio State University Press.

Jauss, Hans Robert. 1982. *Toward an Aesthetic of Reception.* Translated by Timothy Bahti. Minneapolis: University of Minnesota Press.

Johnson-Laird, Philip N. 1988. *The Computer and the Mind: An Introduction to Cognitive Science.* Cambridge, Mass.: Harvard University Press.

——. 1993. "The Mental Representation of the Meaning of Words." In *Readings in Philosophy and Cognitive Science,* edited by Alvin Goldman. Cambridge, Mass.: MIT Press.

Johnson-Laird, Philip N., and P. C. Wason, eds. 1977. *Thinking: Readings in Cognitive Science.* Cambridge: Cambridge University Press.

Jones, Emrys. 1977. *The Origins of Shakespeare.* Oxford: Clarendon Press.

Kant, Immanuel. 1956. *Critique of Practical Reason.* Translated by Lewis White Beck. Indianapolis: Bobbs-Merrill.

——. 1964. *Groundwork of the Metaphysic of Morals.* Translated by H. J. Paton. New York: Harper.

——. 1965. *The Metaphysical Elements of Justice.* Translated by John Ladd. New York: Bobbs-Merrill.

Katz, Jerrold. 1981. *Language and Other Abstract Objects.* Totowa, N.J.: Rowman and Littlefield.

——. 1988. "The Refutation of Indeterminacy." *Journal of Philosophy* 85, no. 5: 227–52.

Kelman, Mark. 1987. *A Guide to Critical Legal Studies.* Cambridge, Mass.: Harvard University Press.

Kenner, Hugh. 1987. *Dublin's Joyce.* New York: Columbia University Press.

Khan, M. Masud R. 1979. *Alienation in Perversions.* New York: International Universities Press.

Kiparsky, Paul. 1983. "Roman Jakobson and the Grammar of Poetry." In *A Tribute to Roman Jakobson: 1896–1982.* Berlin: Mouton.

——. 1987. "On Theory and Interpretation." In *The Linguistics of Writing: Arguments Between Language and Literature,* edited by Nigel Fabb, Derek Attridge, Alan Durant, and Colin MacCabe. New York: Methuen.

Knapp, Steven, and Walter Benn Michaels. 1992. "Intention, Identity, and the Constitution: A Response to David Hoy." In *Legal Hermeneutics: History, Theory, and Practice,* edited by Gregory Leyh. Berkeley: University of California Press.

Kress, Ken. 1992. "Legal Indeterminacy and Legitimacy." In *Legal Hermeneutics: History, Theory, and Practice,* edited by Gregory Leyh. Berkeley: University of California Press.

Kripke, Saul A. 1980. *Naming and Necessity.* Cambridge, Mass.: Harvard University Press.

——. 1982. *Wittgenstein on Rules and Private Language: An Elementary Exposition.* Cambridge, Mass.: Harvard University Press.

Krouse, F. Michael. 1949. *Milton's Samson and the Christian Tradition.* Princeton: Princeton University Press.

Kuhn, Thomas. 1970. *The Structure of Scientific Revolutions.* 2nd ed. Chicago: University of Chicago Press.

————. 1993. "Afterwords." In *World Changes: Thomas Kuhn and the Nature of Science,* edited by Paul Horwich. Cambridge, Mass.: MIT Press.

Lacan, Jacques. 1966. *Ecrits.* Paris: Editions du Seuil.

————. 1973. *Le séminaire, livre XI: Les quatre concepts fondamentaux de la psychanalyse.* Paris: Editions du Seuil.

————. 1975. *Le séminaire, livre I: Les écrits techniques de Freud.* Paris: Editions du Seuil.

————. 1978. *Le séminaire, livre II: Le moi dans la théorie de Freud et dans la technique de la psychanalyse.* Paris: Editions du Seuil.

Lakatos, Imre. 1965. "Falsification and the Methodology of Scientific Research Programmes." In *Criticism and the Growth of Knowledge,* edited by Imre Lakatos and Alan Musgrave. Cambridge, Mass.: Cambridge University Press.

Laplanche, J., and J.-B. Pontalis. 1973. *The Language of Psychoanalysis.* Translated by D. Nicholson-Smith. New York: W. W. Norton.

Larsen, Steen, Janos Laszlo, and Uffe Seilman. 1991. "Across Time and Place: Cultural-Historical Knowledge and Personal Experience in Appreciation of Literature." In *Empirical Studies of Literature,* edited by E. Ibsch, D. Schram, and G. Steen. Amsterdam: Rodopi.

Lasnik, Howard, and Juan Uriagereka. 1988. *A Course in GB Syntax: Lectures on Binding and Empty Categories.* Cambridge, Mass.: MIT Press.

Levi, Werner. 1979. *Contemporary International Law: A Concise Introduction.* Boulder, Colo.: Westview Press.

Levinson, Sanford, and Mailloux, Steven. 1988. "Introduction." In their *Interpreting Law and Literature: A Hermeneutic Reader.* Evanston: Northwestern University Press.

Lévi-Strauss, Claude. 1969a. *Elementary Structures of Kinship.* Translated by James Harle Bell, John Richard von Sturmer, and Rodney Needham; edited by Needham. Boston: Beacon Press.

————. 1969b. *Introduction to a Science of Mythology.* Vol. 1, *The Raw and the Cooked.* New York: Harper.

Lewis, David. 1969. *Convention.* Cambridge, Mass.: Harvard University Press.

Locke, John. 1992. *An Essay Concerning Human Understanding.* In *Critical Theory since Plato,* edited by Hazard Adams. Rev. ed. New York: Harcourt Brace Jovanovich.

Lukács, Georg. 1980. *Essays on Realism.* Translated by David Fernbach and edited by Rodney Livingstone. Cambridge, Mass.: MIT Press.

Lycan, William. 1990. "Introduction." In *Mind and Cognition: A Reader,* edited by Lycan. Oxford: Basil Blackwell.

Lyotard, Jean-François. 1979. "The Psychoanalytical Approach." In *Main Trends in Aesthetics and the Sciences of Art,* edited by Mikel Dufrenne. New York: Holmes and Meier.

Macherey, Pierre. 1970. *Pour une théorie de la production littéraire.* Paris: Maspero.

Mahoney, Michael. 1977. "Publication Prejudices: An Experimental Study of Confirmatory Bias in the Peer Review System." *Cognitive Therapy and Research* 1, no. 1: 29–39.

———. 1987. "Scientific Publication and Knowledge Politics." *Journal of Social Behavior and Personality* 2 (May): 165–76.

Mahony, Patrick J. 1986. *Freud and the Rat Man.* New Haven: Yale University Press.

Mammaṭa. 1970. *The Kāvyaprakāśa of Mammaṭa: First, Second, Third and Tenth Ullasas.* Edited and translated by A. B. Gajendragadkar. 3rd ed., revised by S. N. Gajendragadkar. Bombay: Popular Prakashan.

Maratsos, M. and A. Chalkley. 1980. "The Internal Language of Children's Syntax: The Ontogenesis and Representation of Syntactic Categories." In *Children's Language,* edited by K. E. Nelson. Vol. 2. New York: Gardner Press.

Matchett, William. 1966. Introduction and "The Sources of *The Life and Death of King John.*" In William Shakespeare, *The Life and Death of King John,* edited by Matchett. New York: Signet.

McCawley, James D. 1979. "On Interpreting the Theme of This Conference." In his *Adverbs, Vowels, and Other Objects of Wonder.* Chicago: University of Chicago Press.

McMullin, Ernan. 1993. "Rationality and Paradigm Change in Science." In *World Changes: Thomas Kuhn and the Nature of Science* edited by Paul Horwich. Cambridge, Mass.: MIT Press.

Meese, Edwin, III. 1988. "Address before the D.C. Chapter of the Federalist Society Lawyers Division." In *Interpreting Law and Literature: A Hermeneutic Reader,* edited by Sanford Levinson and Steven Mailloux. Evanston: Northwestern University Press.

Milton, John. 1957. *Paradise Lost.* In *John Milton: Complete Poems and Major Prose,* edited by Merritt Y. Hughes. Indianapolis: Odyssey Press.

Mikva, Abner. 1987. "A Reply to Judge Starr's Observations." *Duke Law Journal* 1987, no. 3: 380–86.

Mitchell, W. J. T., ed. 1983. *The Politics of Interpretation.* Chicago: University of Chicago Press.

Mothersill, Mary. 1984. *Beauty Restored.* Oxford: Oxford University Press.

Mulhall, Stephen. 1989. "No Smoke without Fire: The Meaning of Grue." *Philosophical Quarterly* 39 (April): 166–89.

Musgrave, Alan. 1980. "Kuhn's Second Thoughts." In *Paradigms and Revolutions: Appraisals and Applications of Thomas Kuhn's Philosophy of Science,* edited by Gary Gutting. Notre Dame: University of Notre Dame Press.

Nagel, Thomas. 1979. *Mortal Questions.* Cambridge: Cambridge University Press.

———. 1986. *The View from Nowhere.* Oxford: Oxford University Press.

Nisbett, R. E. and L. Ross. 1980. *Human Inference: Strategies and Shortcomings of Social Judgment.* Englewood Cliffs, N.J.: Prentice-Hall.

Nisbett, R. E., and T. D. Wilson. 1977. "Telling More Than We Can Know: Verbal Reports on Mental Processes." *Psychological Review* 84 (May): 231–59.

Ong, Walter J. 1982. *Orality and Literacy: The Technologizing of the Word.* New York: Methuen.

Osgood, Charles E., William H. May, and Murray S. Miron. 1975. *Cross-Cultural Universals of Affective Meaning.* Urbana: University of Illinois Press.

Pandit, Lalita. 1995. "A Sense of Detail and a Sense of Order: An Interview with Anita Desai." In *Literary India: Comparative Studies in Aesthetics, Colonialism, and Culture,* edited by Patrick Colm Hogan and Pandit. Albany: State University of New York Press.

Pausanias. 1931. *Description of Greece.* Translated by W. H. S. Jones. 6 vols. New York: G. P. Putnam's Sons.

Piaget, Jean. 1969. *The Language and Thought of the Child.* Translated by Marjorie Gabain. New York: World Publishing Co.

Piattelli-Palmarini, Massimo, ed. 1980. *Language and Learning: The Debate Between Jean Piaget and Noam Chomsky.* Cambridge, Mass.: Harvard University Press.

Plaks, Andrew. 1977. "Towards a Critical Theory of Chinese Narrative." In *Chinese Narrative: Critical and Theoretical Essays,* edited by Plaks. Princeton: Princeton University Press.

Pollard, David. 1978. "*Ch'i* in Chinese Literary Theory." In *Chinese Approaches to Literature from Confucius to Liang Ch'i-ch'ao,* edited by Adele Rickett. Princeton: Princeton University Press.

Popper, Karl. 1968. *The Logic of Scientific Discovery.* New York: Harper and Row.

Popper, Karl, and John Eccles. 1977. *The Self and Its Brain: An Argument for Interactionism.* New York: Springer International.

Pratt, Mary Louise. 1977. *Toward a Speech Act Theory of Literary Discourse.* Bloomington: Indiana University Press.

Putnam, Hilary. 1971. "The 'Innateness Hypothesis' and Explanatory Models in Linguistics." In *The Philosophy of Language,* edited by John Searle. Oxford: Oxford University Press.

———. 1975. *Mind, Language, and Reality.* Cambridge: Cambridge University Press.

———. 1978. *Meaning and the Moral Sciences.* Boston: Routledge and Kegan Paul.

———. 1980. "What Is Innate and Why: Comments on the Debate" and "Comments on Chomsky's and Fodor's Replies." In *Language and Learning: The Debate between Jean Piaget and Noam Chomsky,* edited by Massimo Piattelli-Palmarini. Cambridge, Mass.: Harvard University Press.

———. 1983a. "There Is At Least One *A Priori* Truth." In his *Realism and Reason.* Cambridge: Cambridge University Press.

———. 1983b. "Why There Isn't a Ready-made World." In his *Realism and Reason.* Cambridge: Cambridge University Press.

Quine, W. V. 1960. *Word and Object.* Cambridge, Mass.: MIT Press.

————. 1961. "Two Dogmas of Empiricism." In his *From a Logical Point of View: Nine Logico-Philosophical Essays.* Rev. ed. New York: Harper and Row.

————. 1969. *Ontological Relativity and Other Essays.* New York: Columbia University Press.

————. 1976a. "Carnap and Logical Truth." In his *The Ways of Paradox and Other Essays.* Cambridge, Mass.: Harvard University Press.

————. 1976b. "Truth By Convention." In his *The Ways of Paradox and Other Essays.* Cambridge, Mass.: Harvard University Press.

————. 1976c. "On Simple Theories of a Complex World." In his *The Ways of Paradox and Other Essays.* Cambridge, Mass.: Harvard University Press.

————. 1987. "Indeterminacy of Translation Again." *Journal of Philosophy* 84, no. 1: 5–10.

Radford, Andrew. 1981. *Transformational Syntax: A Student's Guide to Chomsky's Extended Standard Theory.* New York: Cambridge University Press.

Redish, Martin, and Karen Drizin. 1987. "Constitutional Federalism and Judicial Review: The Role of Textual Analysis." *New York University Law Review* 62, no. 1: 1–51.

Rhees, Rush. 1984. "The Language of Sense Data and Private Experience—II: Notes of Wittgenstein's Lectures, 1936." *Philosophical Investigations* 7 (April): 101–40.

Rickett, Adele. 1978. "Method and Intuition: The Poetic Theories of Huang T'ing-chien." In *Chinese Approaches to Literature from Confucius to Liang Ch'i-ch'ao*, edited by Rickett. Princeton: Princeton University Press.

Rorty, Richard. 1991. *Objectivity, Relativism, and Truth.* Philosophical Papers, vol. 1. Cambridge: Cambridge University Press.

Sampson, Geoffrey. 1980. *Making Sense.* Oxford: Oxford University Press.

Schafer, Roy. 1976. *A New Language for Psychoanalysis.* New Haven: Yale University Press.

————. 1983. *The Analytic Attitude.* London: Hogarth Press.

Schleiner, Winfried. 1985. "Justifying the Unjustifiable: The Dover Cliff Scene in *King Lear.*" *Shakespeare Quarterly* 36 (Autumn): 337–43.

Searle, John. 1969. *Speech Acts: An Essay in the Philosophy of Language.* Cambridge: Cambridge University Press.

————. 1979. *Expression and Meaning.* New York: Cambridge University Press.

————. 1983. *Intentionality: An Essay in the Philosophy of Mind.* New York: Cambridge University Press.

Selvon, Sam. 1985. *The Lonely Londoners.* Harlow, England: Longman.

Seneca. 1927. *His Tenne Tragedies Translated into English.* Edited by Thomas Newton; introduction by T. S. Eliot. Vol. 1. New York: Knopf. Reprint of 1581 edition.

Shakespeare, William. 1966. *The Life and Death of King John.* Edited by William Matchett. New York: Signet.

Shanker, S. G. 1984. "Skeptical Confusions about Rule-Following." *Mind* 93 (July): 423–29.

Sherry, Suzanna. 1987. "The Founders' Unwritten Constitution." *University of Chicago Law Review* 54, no. 4: 1127–77.

Shih, Chung-Wen. 1976. *The Golden Age of Chinese Drama: Yuan Tsa-chu.* Princeton: Princeton University Press.

Sidney, Philip. 1912. *The Countesse of Pembrokes Arcadia.* Edited by Albert Feuillerat. Cambridge: Cambridge University Press.

Smith, Barbara Herrnstein. 1988. *Contingencies of Value: Alternative Perspectives for Critical Theory.* Cambridge, Mass.: Harvard University Press.

Sober, Elliott. 1975. *Simplicity.* Oxford: Clarendon Press.

Spenser, Edmund. 1912. *Poetical Works.* Edited by J. C. Smith and E. De Selincourt. Oxford: Oxford University Press.

Staal, Frits. 1988. *Universals: Studies in Indian Logic and Linguistics.* Chicago: University of Chicago Press.

Starr, Kenneth. 1987. "Observations about the Use of Legislative History." *Duke Law Journal* 1987, no. 3: 371–79.

Statius, Publius Papinius. 1928. *Statius.* Translated by J. H. Moyley. 2 vols. New York: G. P. Putnam's Sons.

Strawson, Peter F. 1950. "On Referring." *Mind* 59 (July): 320–44.

———. 1970. *Meaning and Truth.* London: Oxford University Press.

———. 1971. "Intention and Convention in Speech Acts." In *The Philosophy of Language,* edited by John Searle. Oxford: Oxford University Press.

———. 1986. "Direct Singular Reference: Intended Reference and Actual Reference." In *Philosophie et Culture: Actes du XVIIe Congrès Mondial de Philosophie, Montréal 1983,* edited by Venant Cauchy. Montreal: Editions du Beffroi, Editions Montmorency.

Stump, Gregory T. 1988. "Nonlocal Spirantization in Breton." *Journal of Linguistics* (September): 457–81.

Suderman, Hermann. 1930. "Geschwister. Zwei Novellen." *Romane und Novellen.* Stuttgart and Berlin: J. G. Cotta'sche.

Summerfield, Donna. 1990. "Philosophical Investigations 201: A Wittgensteinian Reply to Kripke." *Journal of the History of Philosophy* 28 (July): 417–38.

Suppes, Patrick. 1986. "The Primacy of Utterer's Meaning." In *Philosophical Grounds of Rationality: Intentions, Categories, Ends,* edited by Richard Grandy and Richard Warner. Oxford: Oxford University Press.

Textor, Johannes Ravisius. 1560. *Officina.* 2 vols. Lugduni: Sebasianum de Honoratis.

Thagard, Paul. 1988. *Computational Philosophy of Science.* Cambridge, Mass.: MIT Press.

———. 1992. *Conceptual Revolutions.* Princeton: Princeton University Press.

The Troublesome Raigne of King John. 1972. In *Miscellaneous Pieces of Antient English Poesie,* edited by John Bowle. New York: Garland.

The True Chronicle History of King Leir and his Three Daughters. 1973. In *The Tragedy of King Lear,* edited by E. A. Horsman. Indianapolis: Bobbs-Merrill, 1973.

Tompkins, Jane, ed. 1980. *Reader-Response Criticism: From Formalism to Post-Structuralism.* Baltimore: Johns Hopkins University Press.

Tushnet, Mark. 1984. "Critical Legal Studies and Constitutional Law: An Essay in Deconstruction." *Stanford Law Review* 36 (January): 623–47.

van Riemsdijk, Henk, and Williams, Edwin. 1986. *Introduction to the Theory of Grammar.* Cambridge, Mass.: MIT Press.

Vygotsky, Lev Semenovich. 1962. *Thought and Language.* Translated by E. Hanfmann and G. Vakar. Cambridge, Mass.: MIT Press.

Wang, John Ching-yu. 1972. *Chin Sheng-t'an.* New York: Twayne.

———. 1978. "The Chih-yen-chai Commentary and the *Dream of the Red Chamber:* A Literary Study." In *Chinese Approaches to Literature from Confucius to Liang Ch'i-ch'ao,* edited by Adele Rickett. Princeton: Princeton University Press.

Watkins, Calvert. 1982. "Aspects of Indo-European Poetics." In *The Indo-Europeans in the Fourth and Third Millennia,* edited by Edgar Polome. Ann Arbor: Karoma Publishers.

White, Patrick. 1976. *A Fringe of Leaves.* New York: Viking Press.

Wilson, Deirdre, and Dan Sperber. 1986. "On Defining Relevance." In *Philosophical Grounds of Rationality: Intentions, Categories, Ends,* edited by Richard Grandy and Richard Warner. Oxford: Oxford University Press.

Wittgenstein, Ludwig. 1958. *Philosophical Investigations.* Translated by G. E. M. Anscombe. 3rd ed. New York: Macmillan.

———. 1961. *Tractatus Logico-Philosophicus.* Translated by D. F. Pears and B. F. McGuinness. London: Routledge and Kegan Paul.

———. 1967. *Zettel.* Translated by G. E. M. Anscombe; edited by Anscombe and G. H. von Wright. Oxford: Basil Blackwell.

———. 1969. *On Certainty.* Translated by Denis Paul and G. E. M. Anscombe; edited by Anscombe and G. H. von Wright. New York: Harper and Row.

Wollheim, Richard. 1980. *Art and Its Objects.* 2nd ed. Cambridge: Cambridge University Press.

Woolf, Virginia. 1953. *Mrs. Dalloway.* New York: Harcourt Brace Jovanovich.

———. 1955. *To the Lighthouse.* New York: Harcourt Brace Jovanovich.

Wright, Crispin. 1984. "Kripke's Account of the Argument Against Private Language." *Journal of Philosophy* 81 (December): 759–78.

INDEX

Abhinavagupta, 7, 168–70, 172
Abraham, 183, 187–89
Adam, 39, 64
Adams, John, 146
Adler, Gisela, 152, 153, 155–58, 161, 207 (n. 9)
Aesthetical attitude, 7, 164–69, 171, 172, 174, 176–79
Aesthetical intent, 7–8, 12, 92, 163, 164, 169, 170, 172–74, 176–80, 183–85
Aim (law), 110, 113
Allusion, 175–77, 187
Amaladass, Anand, 164, 169, 171, 174, 176
Ambiguity. *See* Constitutive ambiguity
Amphitryon (Plautus), 183
Analyticity of meaning, 36–37, 59–60, 198 (n. 6)
Ānandavardhana, 7, 164, 171, 172, 174, 175
Anarchism: and law, 205 (n. 5); and scientific research, 207 (n. 7)
Andersen, James, x
Anderson, John R., 81
Anscombe, G. E. M., x, 7, 130
Antigone, 183, 191, 208
Apollodorus Atheniensis, 191
Apollon, Willy, 142
Arcadia (Sidney), 191
Aristotle, 30, 63, 69, 129, 164, 167, 173, 190

Arthur, Duke of Brittany (*King John*), 180–84, 186–89, 191–93, 208 (n. 4), 209 (n. 7)
Assertability conditions, 51–52
Assimilation, in psychoanalysis, 133, 135, 137–39
Association, in literature, 163, 164, 167, 169–79, 183, 185–93. See also *Dhvani*
Association, in psychoanalysis, 129, 137–43, 147, 153, 162
Ātman, 168
Augustine of Hippo, 188
Austin, John, 86
Autonomism. *See* Linguistic autonomism

Babbitt, Milton, 13
Baker, G. P., 52, 199 (n. 2)
Baker, Mark, 84–86
Baldwin, T. W., 185
Bauer, Thomas, x
Beardsley, Monroe C., 167
Behaviorism, 24, 25, 35
Benacerraf, Paul, 200 (n. 4)
Bennett, Tony, 179, 180
Bharata-Muni, 169, 172
Bhaskar, Roy, 30, 31
Bible, 187, 188
Billman, D., 81
Blackburn, Simon, 52
Blackmun, Harry, 117, 119, 121